THE COMPLETE IDIOT'S GUIDE® TO

Songwriting

Second Edition

by Joel Hirschhorn

ALPHA

A member of Penguin Group (USA) Inc.

To Jennifer, my greatest inspiration, the first woman to dive to the Titanic *and the first woman I've ever known who is all things to me—friend, artistic soulmate, and support system— everything a songwriter needs to bring out the music inside of him.*

Copyright © 2004 by Joel Hirschhorn

International Standard Book Number: 1-59257-211-1
Library of Congress Catalog Card Number: 2004100487

06 05 04   8 7 6 5 4 3 2 1

Interpretation of the printing code: The rightmost number of the first series of numbers is the year of the book's printing; the rightmost number of the second series of numbers is the number of the book's printing. For example, a printing code of 04-1 shows that the first printing occurred in 2004.

Printed in the United States of America

Most Alpha books are available at special quantity discounts for bulk purchases for sales promotions, premiums, fund-raising, or educational use. Special books, or book excerpts, can also be created to fit specific needs.

For details, write: Special Markets, Alpha Books, 375 Hudson Street, New York, NY 10014.

Publisher: *Marie Butler-Knight*
Product Manager: *Phil Kitchel*
Senior Managing Editor: *Jennifer Chisholm*
Senior Acquisitions Editor: *Renee Wilmeth*
Development Editor: *Jennifer Moore*
Production Editor: *Megan Douglass*
Copy Editor: *Ross Patty*
Illustrator: *Richard King*
Cover/Book Designer: *Trina Wurst*
Indexer: *Brad Herriman*
Layout/Proofreading: *John Etchison, Ayanna Lacey*

Contents at a Glance

Appendixes

Contents

Foreword

The majority of books about songwriting are written by individuals who have never had a hit. Contrast that with Joel Hirschhorn, who has won two Oscars (four nominations), five BMI Awards, a People's Choice Award, and four Angel Awards. He is also a two-time Tony nominee for Best Broadway musical score and the recipient of four Golden Globe nominations. Joel is the only composer/lyricist I know who has triumphed in every medium: pop, R&B, country, theater, and movie musicals—and he has sold more than 93 million records!

Joel and I met under the most auspicious of circumstances. He co-wrote two Oscar-winning songs, "The Morning After" from *The Poseidon Adventure* and "We May Never Love Like This Again" from *The Towering Inferno*. Both became million sellers worldwide and launched my career as a singer when I recorded them.

Aside from being a singer and an actor, one of my greatest loves is songwriting. I've recorded and performed many of my compositions in regional children's theater and concert halls, on television around the world, and with symphony orchestras, including the National Symphony and the Hartford Symphony Orchestra.

As a composer and a singer, I so deeply appreciate Joel's clear, practical approach to the composing craft. When he talks about "hooks," it's because he learned through trial and error (in the form of publishers, artists, and producers) that a song without a hook will be a song without a chart position. When he stresses the importance of ideas, titles, visual action, and structure, it's because he learned firsthand that including those elements almost always guaranteed acceptance.

His chapters on rewriting and demo production are valuable lessons in how to polish a song and show it to its best advantage. The advice Joel gives on casting and promoting your material offers indispensable shortcuts to success for the novice as well as the seasoned songwriter. You'll also see "what works" for Diane Warren, Stephen Sondheim, Billy Joel, Marvin Hamlisch, and other classic songwriters such as Johnny Mercer, Richard Rodgers, Oscar Hammerstein, Jule Styne, and Sammy Cahn.

I've always called "The Morning After" the "generic hope anthem" because it was generally specific for the movie, but also specifically general enough for the public to embrace it outside of the film and apply it to their own lives. Some 28 years later, I still receive letters from people telling me how "The Morning After" has changed or saved their lives or has seen them through difficult times with its life-affirming message, and that kind of reaction is the true test of a timeless song.

Any person who has had recording hits by such diverse artists as Elvis Presley, Sheena Easton, Julian Lennon, Taj Mahal, Charlie Rich, Roy Orbison, Charles Aznavour, and yours truly has insights that no other book writer on contemporary songwriting can duplicate.

If you want a career in composing or lyric writing, one that covers every conceivable area, you will find that in this gracious and insightful book; Joel Hirschhorn has dozens and dozens of great ideas, and our creative road is easier to travel for his sharing them with us. Thank you, Joel!

Maureen McGovern
Los Angeles
December 2000

Maureen McGovern's 28-year career spans recordings, concerts, theater, films, television, and radio. Her children's musical, *The Bengal Tiger's Ball*, had its East Coast premiere in 1999; Maureen wrote the music, co-created, and starred in the show. Her films include *Airplane, Airplane II: The Sequel, The Towering Inferno, The Cure for Boredom*, and the voice of Rachel in DreamWorks' animated video/DVD *Joseph: King of Dreams!* Her recording career began with being nominated for a Grammy for the Oscar-winning gold record "The Morning After," from *The Poseidon Adventure*, followed by the Oscar-winning gold record "We May Never Love Like This Again" from *The Towering Inferno*. Maureen made history in 1975 as the first singer to record two Oscar-nominated songs in the same year, "We May Never Love Like This Again" and "Wherever Love Takes Me" from *Gold*.

Introduction

When I first began writing songs, Manhattan's Brill Building was the magnet that drew every hungry, starry-eyed songwriter. Music publishers waited in their dark, tiny offices while eager hopefuls like me knocked on their doors, ventured timidly inside, and said, "I've got a song. I think it's a hit."

In those days, kids off the street could wander in and be assured of an audience. The first person to hear my masterpiece, "I'm Going to Peggy's Party," was named Sal Giancarlo. He was six feet four and 300 pounds and resembled a wrestler more than a man of musical taste. The needle went on the vinyl, and he listened, legs sprawled over his desk. After three or four bars, he abruptly yanked off the needle and said, "Buddy, this song doesn't have enough fire. Passion. And remember," he continued, delivering the worst possible advice any newcomer could receive, "craft doesn't matter in pop music. You have to feel it, and it'll come out right."

Minutes later, I was out on the street. My bleak mood wasn't helped by a sudden, drenching rain that soaked my sheet music. There's nothing more depressing than feeling like an 18-year-old has-been, and I walked down Broadway, replaying his words.

More than 30 years later, I now realize that Mr. Giancarlo was half right: Passion matters intensely. But passion without craft is a shortcut to oblivion. Even the successful songwriters who can't articulate all their composing methods have an instinctive understanding of certain rules. When a writer has no grasp of structure, his or her songs wander aimlessly. The music doesn't build, the rhythms are static, and the rhymes are clichéd.

This talk of craft isn't meant to exclude emotion: Without it, songwriting is meaningless. But no architect would build a house, however beautiful, without a foundation. This book will teach you how to build that foundation and incorporate all the necessary elements so that your songs will be recorded and reach an international audience.

As a two-time Oscar winner and composer/lyricist of songs that have sold more than 93 million copies, I've been fortunate. En route to those achievements, however, I fell into every trap and made every mistake. My goal is to provide you with the knowledge you need to avoid most of the pitfalls.

This book deals with the vital need for repetition, the ingredients required for a hit hook, and the importance of a colorful title. I also talk about the elements that make a melody unforgettable and analyze chord progressions to illustrate which ones draw the strongest response.

Through examination of various rhythms, you'll see which ones stimulate listener excitement. By studying lyrics from all genres (pop, country, Latin, R&B, hip-hop, Christian, musicals, and motion pictures), you'll become aware of why certain words touch the heart and stir the senses. After I cover basic rules for hit melodies, lyrics, and rhythms, you'll learn how to cut the kind of demo that excites producers and artists.

Finally, this book will teach you how to sell the hit song you've just written. The outlets for selling your material are more numerous than ever, but you have to know who to approach and how. Let me show you what those rules are and spell out the steps of the game, so you can play it and crash the Top 10.

The late Curtis Mayfield, legendary lead singer of the Impressions and writer of such classics as "Amen," "Keep on Pushing," and "It's All Right," once told me, "People listen to songs on the radio, then do the opposite. The rules are there—why do so few composers bother to learn them?"

The first thing this book asks you to do is absorb every influence around you and be willing to learn your craft. Writing hits is amazingly easy if you keep an open mind. You may have talent, but in this book, you'll find the tools for success that all major songwriters use.

How to Use This Book

This book is divided into five parts:

Part 1, "Topics, Titles, and Lyrics," deals with the many ways you can support yourself in musical fields while working to get your first break. It examines the issue of formal training and how to educate yourself musically even if you've never had a lesson. You will learn about the most important element of successful songwriting: a great idea! The best writers don't just wait for ideas to magically show up; they have numerous ways to locate them, and you'll find out what these ways are in this part.

You'll learn the best ways to find lyric ideas and dynamite titles, and to think in visual terms. We live in a visual age, and you'll discover the way to sharpen your sense of sight, smell, hearing, taste, and touch. I cover all kinds of rhyme, showing which rhyme schemes are used most often in hit songs.

Part 2, "It's All About the Music," explains the importance of repetition, and the necessity for catchy, memorable hooks. It goes over the basic rhythmic grooves that producers and artists look for. Once you get the hang of writing a hit hook, you're home free, and this part will show you how to do it.

I also analyze basic rhythmic grooves, the kind that appear in every kind of record, whether it be pop, country, or R&B.

Part 3, "Working with Genres," homes in on the elements that make great country, R&B, Latin, Christian, and hip-hop tunes. I also go into detail about writing and selling commercials and children's music. As a two-time Best Score Tony nominee for Best Broadway musical (*Copperfield* and *Seven Brides for Seven Brothers*) and two-time Oscar nominee for best movie musical (*Pete's Dragon*), I lived through the process of creating shows from the ground up. I also had the benefit of a brilliant mentor, Irwin Kostal (who scored *The Sound of Music, Mary Poppins,* and *West Side Story* for films). The information that you'll find here on movie and theater musicals explains everything you need to know about writing a show and getting it produced. You'll also learn how to write the kind of motion picture song that works within the film and has the ingredients to become a hit outside of it.

Part 4, "The Business of Songwriting," moves beyond writing into the commercially crucial phase: selling your song. I discuss the best and quickest ways of finding a top agent, manager, and publisher.

I also talk about the secrets of cutting a demo that matches any record on the air for quality, a demo so realized and exciting that artists and producers can't resist it. As a songwriter today, it pays to think of yourself as a producer, and the chapter on record production will help you to build and polish your producing skills, whether you work in a rented studio or your own home setup.

Part 5, "Finishing Touches," educates you about protecting your material. Royalties are a songwriter's lifeblood, and such organizations as BMI, ASCAP, SESAC, and the Songwriter's Guild of America exist to help you hold on to the money you earn and negotiate the best contracts.

This section also deals with collaborators—how to find them and how to make them work successfully. Collaboration can be incredibly satisfying, but only if both of you have similar creative and emotional styles. As a veteran of a 25-year partnership, I've experienced all the ins and outs of daily partnership. I know the challenges, but nothing is more rewarding when you're both on the same wavelength and hits start flowing.

I also discuss the miraculous new ways the Internet can aid your career, as an invaluable research tool and as a link to other writers, producers, and artists. I also look at the dynamics of popular music today and why opportunities for songwriters will continue to increase as traditional genre lines break down and recombine.

Finally, this book provides you with a glossary of key musical terms; a list of helpful websites; the names of influential publishers, organizations, and trade papers; and a guide to songwriting contests and competitions you can enter.

Extras

In addition to the information in the chapters and appendixes, the sidebars throughout the book contain fascinating quotes from songwriters and others in the music business, cautionary tales, helpful advice, and translations of terms you may not be familiar with. Here's what to look for:

Hirschhorn's Hints

These tips make the path to composing, producing, and selling songs easier.

Lyrical Lingo

These basic terms will equip you for dealing with the professional songwriting world.

Backstage Banter

Read these sidebars for colorful, informative quotes and stories about your favorite performers and songwriters.

Trouble Clef

You can avoid 95 percent of the pitfalls if you're aware of what they are. These sidebars give you every warning you need to know.

Acknowledgments

My deepest thanks to Renee Wilmeth and Jennifer Moore for their guidance, friendship, and enormous skill in helping me put together this manuscript. I'd also like to express gratitude to Marvin Hamlisch, Maureen McGovern, Peter Bart, Phil Gallo, Jerry Herman, Roger LaRocque, Steve Schalchlin, Russ Regan, Frances Preston, Del Bryant, Paige Sober, Michael Kerker, Rodney Mencia, Madeleine and Richard Desjardins, Evelyn Hirschhorn, Kevin Carter, Brent Carter, Derek Carter Jr., Aaron Meza, Emily Carter, Doreen Ringer Ross, Dory Dangoor, Tony and Ellyn Garofalo, Paul Williams, and Carole Bayer Sager.

Special Thanks to the Technical Reviewer

The Complete Idiot's Guide to Songwriting, Second Edition, was reviewed by an expert who double-checked the accuracy of what you'll learn here, to help us ensure that this book gives you everything you need to know about writing quality songs. Special thanks are extended to Steve Knopper.

Trademarks

All terms mentioned in this book that are known to be or are suspected of being trademarks or service marks have been appropriately capitalized. Alpha Books and Penguin Group (USA) Inc. cannot attest to the accuracy of this information. Use of a term in this book should not be regarded as affecting the validity of any trademark or service mark.

Part 1

Topics, Titles, and Lyrics

If you love music and you're determined to succeed as a songwriter, you have the potential to do it, even if you have no musical training. The first and most important step is to learn everything you can about songwriting and what makes a song a hit. Part 1 begins with ways to go about getting this education by finding work that can finance some musical training while also increasing your knowledge of the music business.

I also cover the basic points of lyric writing—how to find exciting ideas, think visually, create characters, hit all the main emotional points that people care about, and develop the skill to become an outstanding story-teller. Finally, I show you how to analyze hit songs and song titles to see what works and why.

Making Money While You Write and Learn

In This Chapter

- ◆ How training helps
- ◆ Ways to learn while you earn
- ◆ Staying focused on the positive
- ◆ Preserving what you write

I remember my mother standing over me, urging me to practice the Beethoven piece my teacher had assigned me for that week. I was bored and rebellious, and finally I shouted, "I want to be a songwriter. How can studying Beethoven help?" She shrugged her shoulders and said, "How can it hurt?"

Years later, I'm grateful for my mother's advice. Admittedly, formal knowledge of music isn't necessary to become a good songwriter. You might be able to write for yourself, for your band, or for other artists without a single lesson of any kind. But a musical background can make songwriting success easier.

Looking at the Hit-Makers

Songwriters can be trained by teachers or be entirely self-taught. The question you must ask yourself is this: If you want to make a career of songwriting, how much training do you need? Let's look at some different types of writers for an overview.

These songwriters studied music from the time they were young:

♦ Sheryl Crow received a degree in classical music from the University of Missouri and taught music at a St. Louis elementary school.

♦ Legendary blues guitarist Bo Diddley, major influence on such giants as Elvis Presley, the Rolling Stones, and the Clash, studied violin as a child at the Ebenezer Baptist Church in Mississippi.

♦ Ray Charles, singer and pianist known for such hits as "Crying Time" and "Hallelujah, I Love Her So," learned classical piano at St. Augustine's School for the Deaf and Blind in Orlando.

♦ Marvin Gaye, late Motown phenomenon identified with "Sexual Healing" and "Ain't No Mountain High Enough," was taught piano and drums at an early age.

♦ Folksinger Jewel attended Interlochen Fine Arts Academy in Michigan.

♦ Quincy Jones, who scored the Oscar-nominated Steven Spielberg film *The Color Purple*, was a master on trumpet by age 13. At 17, he won a scholarship to the Berklee College of Music in Boston. John Mayer also studied briefly at the Berklee College of Music (other Berklee graduates include Melissa Etheridge, Aimee Mann, and Paula Cole).

♦ Janis Ian, writer of the groundbreaking "Society's Child," started her classical training at the tender age of 2, and Billy Joel began piano lessons at 4 and continued them until he was 14.

Hirschhorn's Hints

More important than training and hard work is to believe in yourself and never give up. Martika, who wrote and recorded the number-one hit "Toy Soldiers," was two years old when she begged to go to dance and ballet class. At age 11, she was combing the telephone directory for agents, and by 12, she landed a role in the film version of *Annie*. More recent hyper-ambitious young pop stars include Britney Spears, Christina Aguilera, and Justin Timberlake, stars of *The New Mickey Mouse Club* in the late '90s before becoming huge.

On the other hand, many successful songwriters took a different road:

- Pete Townshend of The Who admits to being a self-taught guitarist, motivated by his desire to "get girls."

- Felice Bryant, who had numerous country hits with her husband Boudleaux Bryant, couldn't play an instrument or read music. She sang all her songs into a tape recorder or to her husband/collaborator, who then wrote them down.

- The late Barry White, whose melodies were a recurring plot device on the hit series *Ally McBeal*, claimed he had a "fantastic rhythm ability" although he never had music lessons.

- In 1994 liner notes, Johnny Cash wrote: "It doesn't matter to me that I only know three or four chords .... All that matters is that the guitar and I are one. I have to feel that the sound of the instrument comes out of me with the song, from inside, from the gut."

Hirschhorn's Hints

It's never too late to learn music. Jerry Herman, composer of *Mame*, *Hello, Dolly!*, and *La Cage Aux Folles*, disliked his piano teacher and gave up lessons. It wasn't until after he wrote his first Broadway hit, *Milk and Honey*, that he decided to learn how to read and write music.

- U2 bass player Adam Clayton was entirely self-taught until 1998, when he decided to take lessons and expand his skill.

Is There Success Without Counterpoint?

You don't have to be a walking textbook on theory, harmony, and *counterpoint* to be a successful songwriter; any amount of musical training you pick up will help. Carol Hall, composer/lyricist of *The Best Little Whorehouse in Texas*, was told by her college music instructor that she would never be able to write a Broadway musical because she didn't do her work in counterpoint. Carol later said, with satisfaction, "I went to New York and had a big Broadway hit without counterpoint."

Lyrical Lingo

Counterpoint is note against note. This type of polyphonic music—consisting of two or more independent melodic lines or voices—weaves the various musical lines against each other in a seamless pattern.

Producer/songwriter Chris Barbosa followed the success of his first hit song with music lessons and admits that they helped him to write faster. But he also feels, as do many other instinctive writers, that too many rules can get in the way of creativity. When that happens, he ignores them and composes with spontaneous feeling.

As three time Oscar-winning songwriter and *Chorus Line* composer Marvin Hamlisch says, talent can't be taught. Still, geniuses such as former Beatle Paul McCartney, who have all the talent in the world, have expressed regret that they didn't receive more formal training. (McCartney is the only Beatle who learned to read music.)

Hirschhorn's Hints _____

Whether you're formally trained or not, persistence and believing in your product are essential. As Diane Warren, composer of more than 80 hit songs and the songwriting voice behind Mary J. Blige, Aerosmith, and LeAnn Rimes puts it, "Don't give up if you believe in your heart that you're meant to be a songwriter." Diane admits that she knocked on doors, ran after people trying to give them tapes, and even followed people down the street in her car.

Prestige vs. Poverty

Some songwriters are able to enroll in a conservatory and gain their education at a prestigious music academy. Burt Bacharach, who collaborated with lyricist Hal David on 120 hits, co-wrote songs with Elvis Costello, and appeared in the Austin Powers movies, was one of these fortunate few. He took piano lessons in elementary school; studied at McGill University in Montreal, Canada; and acquired his training in the classics from such distinguished teachers as Darius Milhaud, Boguslav Martinu, and Henry Cowell.

Most aspiring songwriters lack Bacharach's advantages. They have to struggle for recognition without financial aid and cope with parental objections to "such an insecure business." Starting out, composers can't spend 24 hours a day expressing themselves creatively; they can write in their spare time or take gigs at night, but they also have to earn extra money to eat and pay the rent. But just because you need to work doesn't mean your musical education has to stop. Working with music in any capacity will teach you about the craft and business of songwriting.

Don't Delay Your Dreams

I once had a girlfriend who said, "You'll never make it in this business. It's too hard. If you love me, you'll give it up and find a better job." Her mother supported this bleak view. The message was "Stop in the Name of Love." Fortunately, I found the strength to tune it out. Sweet satisfaction came when I won my first Oscar, and my former girlfriend called to congratulate me.

The trick is to not panic and latch on to a tedious but necessary job from which you might never escape. If your job seems like a dead end, remind yourself that it's *only temporary*. You can't become so tired and discouraged by hours invested in uncreative pursuits that you drop out, vowing to get back to songwriting "eventually." Eventually never comes. The only defense against this thinking is blind, persistent tenacity and a reminder to yourself, no matter how much tension you feel, to keep writing!

> **Backstage Banter**
>
> Arnold Lanni, writer of the number-one song "When I'm with You" for Sheriff, shocked his Italian family when he announced in 1979 he was dropping out of York University in Toronto to join a rock-and-roll band. Parents, friends, and lovers (well-meaning and otherwise) often tell writers to give up their dreams. Ignore them; keep your eye trained on your goal and go for it!

From the Harbor Club to Elvis

A person with a solid background in music has dozens of exciting employment options to embrace. When I realized that Elvis wasn't going to record my songs immediately, I decided to take a gig in a nightclub. It was far from paradise. I lived in Manhattan, and the joint that hired me, the Harbor Club in Staten Island, could be reached only by driving to a ferry and then driving another hour from the dock. The Harbor Club was dingy and run-down and featured an over-the-hill stripper named Desiree.

My responsibility was to play easy listening pop, like "This Guy's in Love with You," or soft R&B, like Otis Redding's "Sittin' on the Dock of the Bay," until four in the morning. It wasn't the setting my mother had envisioned for me. I was groomed from earliest childhood to be a concert pianist, and my parents never considered the possibility that I would be playing Aretha Franklin's "(You Make Me Feel Like) A Natural Woman" for an overweight stripper and three drunks. Nevertheless, I was a skilled pianist, thanks to having studied my craft and attending Manhattan's High School of Performing Arts.

The Harbor Club allowed me to pay my bills and, with careful money management, eat cheeseburgers and tuna salads at a local dive called The Pink Cloud. I was able to write songs and survive until my hit record, "Your Time Hasn't Come Yet, Baby" by Elvis Presley, made it possible for me to compose all day and get some sleep at night.

Make It Big Through a Local Gig

You can be formally trained like Burt Bacharach or self-taught like Pete Townshend, but if you can perform—and particularly if you can perform your own material—you'll eventually be noticed by someone who can advance your career.

Where you play or how much you're being paid isn't the most important thing. The head of Columbia Records might just possibly be a guest at a bar mitzvah you've been hired for. If you're playing at a wedding, you might find out that a singing star is a cousin of the bride or groom. The point is to get out there and gain exposure!

Accompany Your Way to Success

If you're a pianist, you can become an accompanist for shows. Marvin Hamlisch was the dance arranger for *Funny Girl*. The job gave him a chance to strike up a lifelong friendship and working association with Barbra Streisand. Just as important, he worked with dancers and got to know them. Hamlisch makes light of it by saying that this experience made him "perverted every time he sees a leotard." What the experience did, even more powerfully, was give him an understanding of how dancers talked, danced, sang, and *thought*. When he wrote *A Chorus Line*, he had that wealth of understanding and experience behind him. Dance arranging was the first step toward the Tony Award and Pulitzer Prize he won for that groundbreaking show.

John Kander, composer of *Cabaret* and *Chicago*, recalls that he started playing piano at age four. When he moved to New York from Kansas City, everything he did to support himself was music-related. As John puts it, "The jobs I had were either accompanying, or coaching, or arranging; or later on, in summer stock, [I worked as a] choral director and a director. I don't think I skipped any stops."

The music industry is full of examples of talented people who started out in the background before moving into the limelight: Marty Stuart was in Johnny Cash's band for years before becoming a solo star. Sheryl Crow sang in Michael Jackson's touring bands in the '80s. Jimi Hendrix backed Little Richard and the Isley Brothers before making it big. Jennifer Lopez was a "Fly Girl" dancer on the early '90s Fox show *In Living Color*. The Eagles were the backup band for Linda Ronstadt.

Play Sessions

Guitar players who read proficiently and have a creative grasp of country, blues, and rock have a good shot at being noticed and hired for record sessions. The same is true if you're a percussionist. In addition to overall skill on every type of percussion instrument, sight-reading counts for a lot in session playing. If you're an excellent player but a poor reader, you can easily remedy that with practice. Playing by ear is something you're born with; reading is a skill any student can master. Give it an hour a day, and within a few months you'll be astonished at what an outstanding reader you've become.

Join an Orchestra

Not everything is rock. If you played oboe or flute in a high school or college orchestra, you might be good enough to play on motion picture dates or orchestral record sessions, or become, like Dan Lipton, a pit pianist for such shows as *The Full Monty*. Did you study violin, viola, or cello? Even if you're a little rusty, you might be able, with practice, to polish your technique and do orchestra work.

Grab Every Opportunity

Sometimes, even with formal training, you're not specifically trained for a particular job when it comes along. If at all possible, if the offer comes, say yes anyway. Seize the opportunity and know when it's a break. You must recognize that a given situation is important. Take a shot. It's true the gig may not work out, but think how great you'll feel if it does.

Put Your Musical Knowledge to Work

When I started working, I had two choices: become a typist at a law firm or work as a typist at a music publisher's office for half the money! I took the job with the lower salary because the office was in New York's Brill Building, home of countless music publishers. While I was typing letters, I watched songwriters as they came up and presented their material. I studied how my boss took these songs and promoted them to different artists. I went to the studio with him and observed how he made demos and worked with demo singers and musicians.

My musical background came in handy at that time, because he wanted me to write neat, correct lead sheets of songs he had in his musical catalogue. Between the typing (always a valuable skill) and song arrangements I supplied, I was in the right position to interest him in one of my songs: "I'll Get You (If I Only Play Hard to Get)," by Jay Bentley and the Jet Set. It didn't set the world on fire, but it gave me the impetus to go on.

As this experience shows, you don't have to be a performer to work in the music field. You can use whatever skills you have to help you move that much closer to your goal of being a songwriter.

Teach Me Tonight

If you're a pianist or guitarist, you can find a host of eager pupils. The best aspect of teaching is that it can be organized to give you mobility. You have no boss to answer to, so you can allow yourself enough time to write songs.

> **Backstage Banter**
>
> A young and rising songwriter named Neil Dorval found a creative way to earn money and continue his songwriting career. He became a music therapist, working in hospitals and motivating mentally troubled individuals with a combination of therapy and music. This growing field offers valuable insight into human emotions.

Spin Some Tunes

Being a deejay sharpens your instinct for what's current and what people respond to most enthusiastically. Chris Barbosa started out as a deejay spinning records at clubs and parties. With the money he earned, Chris bought a drum machine, a Roland Bass Line, and later a synthesizer. This new technology brought forth a tune, "Let the Music Play," which went to the top of the charts.

Let the Music Keep You Going

Sometimes finding work in the music world seems impossible. Kris Kristofferson was a janitor at a Nashville studio, and no one paid much attention to him at first. But he internalized everything he saw, and this education led to "Sunday Mornin' Comin' Down," "Me and Bobby McGee," and "Help Me Make It Through the Night."

Country legend Tammy Wynette ("Stand by Your Man") toiled in a shoe factory, a hair salon, a doctor's office, and the cotton fields. Allan Rich, who composed "I Don't Have the Heart" for James Ingram, waited tables in Beverly Hills and sold shoes in Venice Beach. Mariah Carey also waited tables and checked coats, but said, "The music kept me going." Jon Bon Jovi swept floors at New York City's Power Station studio before they'd let him record in the 1980s. And Courtney Love was a stripper!

Don't Let Your Great Ideas Get Away

No matter what level of music training you have, or whether you work in the music industry or the insurance industry, if you want to be a songwriter, you have to start writing songs. Don't panic—in the following chapters I'll provide you with the tools you need to get started, beginning with analyzing hit songs to show you what works and, just as important, what doesn't. Before you turn to the next chapter, though, you need to make sure that you have the right supplies handy to preserve your ideas. You don't want to have to start a hysterical search for paper and pencil if a great idea comes to you.

Always have the following within easy reach:

Writing paper

A package of eight-stave music paper

Some sharpened #2 pencils

Cassette recorder

Two or three 120-minute audiocassettes

Dictionary

Rhyming dictionary

Thesaurus

 Hirschhorn's Hints

If you play an instrument, chances are you know basic chords. Some composers scribble down music without using the piano or guitar, but it's perfectly fine to sit at a keyboard and peck away before making note of the tunes you hear. You'll be amazed, as you write out your ideas, how quickly you become proficient at it. The added bonus is that writing down melodies and chords stimulates your mind and gives you a flock of fresh ideas. You see what you have and are tempted to embellish on it.

Whether you're writing music down or just noodling idly, turn on the cassette recorder and let it play. I can't tell you how many times I've just been playing piano for relaxation and a great idea has popped into my head, prompting hasty, frantic efforts to turn the recorder on before the idea disappeared. Consider every second you spend at your instrument composing time. If you wear out a few batteries by letting it run, so be it.

The best tunes and concepts may sneak up unexpectedly. Spontaneous ideas don't stick unless you catch them—either on paper or on cassette—the second they occur to you.

The Least You Need to Know

- Musical training is helpful, but many composers have written great songs without it.

- Don't let anyone or anything stop you from pursuing your dreams.

- Perform your music at clubs, weddings, bar mitzvahs, industrial shows—wherever industry people might hear your material.

- Investigate off-beat avenues such as teaching music or being a deejay to keep you going while you write.

- Have on hand the supplies you need to keep track of your ideas.

Chapter 2

Developing Ideas for Songs

In This Chapter

- Studying people around you for inspiration
- Looking to media sources for hit material
- Titling your songs
- Creating a four-minute "screenplay" song
- Hypnotizing yourself into hit-writing

Ideas are the support system of a song. Without them, lyrics, tunes, and arrangements mean nothing. Before you begin thinking about embellishments, make sure you have a basic concept that excites you and justifies all the hard work.

There's a saying in the motion-picture business, "A great score won't save a poor film." But a wonderful idea, even imperfectly executed, usually shines through. Ideas are everything in songwriting. The tips in this chapter will help you generate them.

How to Get Started

Composers and lyricists all have the same emotional reaction when they start writing a song: uneasiness, insecurity, and even terror. If you experience these feelings when you're trying to write, don't panic. If you feel the need to walk around the house, water the flowers, wash dishes, or hang a picture, do it! With each passing minute, your subconscious is gathering the courage to start creating. Eventually, you'll find yourself in front of a piano, a guitar, or a computer.

Backstage Banter
Billy Joel on the writer's block experience: "The thing you don't have control of is writing. You have to pull it out of yourself. You pace the room with something like the dry heaves, having no control over the muse, horrified that it won't come. All that's out there with you is the piano, this big black beast with 88 teeth." —From *The Billboard Book of Number One Hits*, by Fred Bronson (Billboard Books, 1992)

Once there, tell yourself that it doesn't matter what you write. Suspend all judgment. Don't immediately start evaluating your work. Just jump in and get started. If the chords are ordinary and the lyrics are hackneyed, ignore it. Keep moving, and your sluggish creative engine will rumble into gear.

Dig Deeper

Once you've started writing, the next step is to find ideas that strike you as special. These ideas generally surface with increased focus and concentration, but not always. Sometimes you're just not satisfied, no matter how much effort you put into the song. Before indulging in self-flagellation (a typical response from writers), remember that there are numerous ways you can stimulate the brain and dig out worthwhile ideas.

Keep Your Eye on the Idea

When you have your story and you sit down to begin the lyric, it's easy to lose sight of the main idea and wander off in a dozen directions. Try writing a synopsis of the idea at the top of the page and keep referring back to it. If your song includes characters, write down every detail about them: how they dress, the cars they drive, their career aspirations. Keep yourself rooted in the main premise by putting reminders of what appears on every page.

> **Backstage Banter**
>
> The prolific songwriter Diane Warren had a friend who confided that her ex-husband still hoped for reconciliation, even though she had met someone else she wanted to marry. Diane's friend had to tell her ex that the relationship was beyond salvaging. Diane recognized that this situation would make a great song and told her friend, "I hope you're not too mad at me, but I used your life." That spark became the number-one hit "Look Away" by Chicago.
>
> —From *The Billboard Book of Number One Hits,* by Fred Bronson

Satisfy Yourself

Country great Tom T. Hall warns against writing to please others rather than creating what you personally want to write. "My blocks come when producers, publishers, agents, managers, people are on my back," he says. Don't become too concerned with the expectations of others, or your inner idea mechanism will get jammed.

Inspiring Characters

Successful songs always feature characters and conflicts that are familiar and universal. It's easy to identify with Jennifer Lopez's "Jenny from the Block," in which the main character gets rich. Similarly, many kids today can imagine themselves as the protagonist in Pink's "Goin' to California," a fantasy about moving from the streets of Philly to a promised land.

These characters convey the hopes and dreams of millions. Such aspirations are all around you, and all you need to do is develop your powers of observation. Study people you've never noticed before or those you've taken for granted. Once you've begun to look closely at the people around you, make it a daily habit.

The trick is to allow your imagination complete freedom. You're a hundred different people inside. Think of yourself as an actor, prepared at any moment to assume roles much different than your daily personality. The basic emotions exist in everyone, no matter how different they appear.

The People on the Street

All people are colorful and unique. Go to a club, and you'll encounter Bowling For Soup's "Girl All the Bad Guys Want." Soundgarden's "Girl U Want," Kid Rock's "Cowboy" and Toby Keith's "Whiskey Girl" are constantly passing by, encircling you at concerts, in the schoolyard, or on city blocks and beaches.

Suppose you have a neighbor who always wears custom-made suits. Yet one day you see him in a short-sleeve shirt and notice that he has tattoos. Or you've noticed an elderly woman who wears her hair loose and flowing, like a young girl. These clues define character. The conservatively dressed neighbor whom you know to be an accountant might once have been a gang member. The elderly woman might live in the past and wish she was still in college.

Hirschhorn's Hints

Janet Jackson claims, "My mother always said that ever since she could remember, I've been concerned with other people before myself." You'll be a much better writer and observer if you get off the subject of yourself and focus on the needs and feelings of others.

—From *The Billboard Book of Number One Hits,* by Fred Bronson

Trouble Clef

Some songwriters, particularly new ones, are afraid to write what they feel because it might touch upon other people's lives. Don't censor yourself. My first hit was called "Why Can't You Bring Me Home?" by Jay and the Americans, and it dealt with a girlfriend who wouldn't bring me to her house because she was ashamed of her family. She didn't resent the truthful lyrics, and the song got my career going.

Some people want to be kind even if they act tough. Some seem shy, but are boiling with aggression inside. Some are wildly sexual even though they present a bland, passionless front. Your job is to find out the real personality and write about it with depth and compassion. Ask yourself: Is the tough person disguising the pain of a childhood trauma? Is the shy person terrified of expressing his or her true emotions because he might be violent?

You can be a lyricist who reaches millions if you break through that first, superficial layer and uncover hidden truths. Just remember: Don't take any person or situation at face value.

Loved Ones

That "hit" character might be someone close to you. Emilio Estefan Jr., Gloria Estefan's producer and husband, was inspired to write "Coming Out of the Dark" after his wife nearly died in a bus accident. He wanted to capture the pain and heartbreak of her long rehabilitation and poured all his feelings into a song that portrayed her struggle.

Your Own Life

Sometimes the person you want to study is yourself. Maybe a relationship has gone sour, or the one you love doesn't return your feelings. We've all felt like Justin Timberlake's rejected lover in "Cry Me a River," telling his ex-girlfriend to cry as punishment for the heartache she caused him.

Universal Themes

Successful songs tap into the emotions that everyone feels. If you're feeling depressed, suffering a loss, being betrayed, ending a relationship, falling in love, feeling grateful to your parents, longing for the carefree days of youth, or wanting to ask forgiveness, there's a song for you. Thinking about these themes in terms of the characters you've observed is a good way to generate ideas for songs that everyone can relate to.

The Blues

When you're feeling depressed, you can do three things: give in to the despair, try to ignore it, or write about it. Using your heartache creatively will get you over the rough spots. John Lennon admitted that he didn't write the song "Help" just to fulfill a movie assignment. He was expressing desperation because, "It was my fat Elvis period. I was depressed and crying out for help."

Personal Loss

Personal tragedy, such as the loss of a friend, a spouse, a parent, or a child, can trigger a great song. B. A. Robertson, in collaboration with Mike Rutherford of Mike and the Mechanics, wrote "The Living Years," a haunting story of a son who loses his father before ever being able to express his love. Robertson's father died immediately after the first verse was written. Rutherford's dad also passed away that same year.

Eric Clapton's "Tears in Heaven" centered on the heartbreak of losing a child. Clapton himself experienced this tragedy when his son, Conor, fell from a window the maid had left open. Millions of parents could identify with Clapton's grief.

Playing Around

One painful but timeless theme is faithlessness. Some striking examples of cheating and its consequences include Dido's "All You Want," Brooks and Dunn's "Cheating On the Blues," and Alan Jackson's "Who's Cheating Who."

Breaking Up

Divorce is another increasingly relevant topic in today's society. Cher took on the subject when she informed her family, "You'd Better Sit Down, Kids," and "D-I-V-O-R-C-E," sung by Tammy Wynette, dealt with a young mother spelling out the D word so her children wouldn't understand what she was going through. Pink's "Family Portrait" ("Daddy don't leave") is a touching take on the tragedy of separation.

Sexual Obsession

Who hasn't been so overwhelmed by consuming attraction that they could hardly think straight? Write down these feelings, the way Billy Joel did in "Shameless." The song scored with Joel and then became a hit for Garth Brooks. Undying devotion has always been a staple of songs in every genre. Other examples are Faith Hill's "Breathe," Marc Anthony's "You Sang to Me," Shania Twain's "From This Moment On," and Beyoncé's "Crazy In Love."

> **Backstage Banter**
>
> Writing about intense, eternal love has been one of the secrets behind Diane Warren's success. She has had dozens of Top 10 records, and 300 artists have recorded her tunes.

Traveling Back in Time

Nostalgia always touches the heart, from "The Way We Were" to "Yesterday." Close your eyes and let your mind float back, or as a Diane Warren title wistfully expresses it, "If I Could Turn Back Time." All sorts of memories will bubble up from your subconscious, and you'll be deluged with first-rate song ideas.

> **Hirschhorn's Hints**
>
> Save everything you write. File it away for future use. Rejects re-examined at a later date have resulted in hits for numerous composers.

Forgiveness

A common theme in pop music is a request for forgiveness. Songs mining this territory include Nirvana's "All Apologies," OutKast's "Ms. Jackson," and R.E.M.'s "Sorry." Perhaps this approach is so successful because so many people who are hurt long for an apology, and so many others have difficulty offering one. You as a songwriter can speak for them.

Mining the Media

Television, books, movies, newspapers, and magazines are rich avenues for ideas. Songwriting is synonymous with emotion, and the ongoing conflicts portrayed in the media provide countless sagas of love, hate, fear, rivalry, and rebellion.

Don't forget the wealth of input available online. The Internet combines information from every possible source: news, movies, stage, music, and biography. Let this electronic library fill your mind with ideas, titles, and tunes.

Chance Encounters Lead to Hits

The late Johnny Cash went to see a film called *Inside the Walls of Folsom Prison* to kill time before catching a plane and found himself captivated by the picture's main character, a convict. During the flight, he wrote lyrics and then composed the melody for the composition that subsequently became a number-one country smash, "Folsom Prison Blues."

Even something as simple as a chance remark might stimulate creativity. Stephen Stills was attending a party when he overheard another guest, Billy Preston, say, "Love the one you're with." His ear latched on to that provocative phrase, and he asked Preston if he could pinch the line. Preston consented, and "Love the One You're With" became the title for a big hit.

> **Hirschhorn's Hints**
>
> Using an overheard comment creatively worked for Stephen Stills, but if you try it, always make sure—particularly if the line came from a fellow songwriter—that you have full permission to use it so you won't be surprised with a lawsuit later on.

Independent Women

When you're selecting ideas, try to tap into current attitudes. For example, women used to be seen as sweet and demure. Then in the 1970s, Helen Reddy screamed, "I am woman, hear me roar." Donna Summer gave men a lecture with "Enough Is Enough." Today, Cher clenches her fists and shouts, "I'm strong enough to live without you," adding "There's no more to say, so save your breath" and Shania Twain brushes aside a show-off boyfriend with "That Don't Impress Me Much." Christina Aguilera's "Fighter" says it all in the title, and Destiny's Child's "Survivor" is a compelling entry in the independent-woman vein.

Simple Starting Points

If no character intrigues you or offers any inspiration, the grand song themes leave you cold, and the media is not inspiring you, start with something small, such as an interesting image, phrase, or title. The following sections provide examples of how to turn these small elements into big hits.

Loving an Angel

The word "angel" is a staple of rock lyric writing. Some strong examples: Monica's "Angel of Mine," R. Kelly and Celine Dion's "I'm Your Angel," Sarah McLachlan's "Angel," and Lucinda Williams's "Drunken Angel."

What's in a Name?

Using names, male and female, has often been a key to coming up with good material. Think of how many name-based hits you've heard: "Barbara Ann," "Delilah," "Maybellene," "Gloria," "Jean," "Mrs. Robinson," and "Michelle." Public Announcement sings "Mamacita" and the Dixie Chicks score with "Goodbye Earl."

There aren't as many songs on the male front, but we still have "Tommy," "Daniel," "Big Bad John," "Hey, Jude," "Jesse," and "Stan."

Location, Location, Location

Chances are you've done some traveling. Even if you haven't, you know the neighborhood where you grew up, nearby cities, a mountain resort where you spent the summer. Use those backgrounds for a story. You've seen the area, so you can depict the details realistically. Places provide a wonderful framework for hits: Joe Ely's "Dallas," Lyle Lovett's "That's Right (You're Not from Texas)," Ryan Adams's "New York, New York," Chuck Berry's "Memphis, Tennessee," X's "Los Angeles," Phantom Planet's "California," and the Clash's "London's Burning."

Writers sometimes make the mistake of thinking that song settings have to be exotic and far removed from everyday reality in order to make an impact. They can be, as "Xanadu," "Montego Bay," and "Jamaica Farewell" testify. But Dolly Parton made life in an office entertaining and colorful with her buoyant "9 to 5." "Five O'Clock World" did the same thing, as did "Take a Letter, Maria," and David Allan Coe went for the jugular with "Take This Job and Shove It."

The Songwriter's Paintbrush

Colors are the key to many hit songs, such as "Nights in White Satin," "Blue Suede Shoes," "Purple Rain," "Red, Red Wine," "Crystal Blue Persuasion," "Yellow Submarine," "Paint It Black," and "Brown-Eyed Girl." Other songs effectively utilizing colors include LeAnn Rimes's "Blue," and Coldplay's "Yellow."

A great way to sharpen your sense of color is to become interested in art. Look at paintings, either in a museum or in a catalogue of color reproductions. Study the cinematography in a movie rather than just immersing yourself in the plot.

> **Backstage Banter**
>
> Birds figure in 24 of the Top 100 rock songs of all time. Dogs are the second-most mentioned animal (11 times), and cats come in a close third (9).

Animal Imagery

Did you enjoy visiting the zoo as a child? Do you have pets? Do you have an affinity for nature? Draw upon those feelings; these hit songs did: "Who Let the Dogs Out?" "When Doves Cry," "The Lion Sleeps Tonight," and "Muskrat Love."

Good Days and Bad Days

How often do we say we hate Mondays, because we have to go back to work? Do you love Fridays, because the weekend is coming up? Do you dread Saturday nights because you don't have a date? Do you resent Sundays, because the weekend is almost over? Take advantage of our attitudes toward the seven days of the week. Hit songs do it all the time: "Monday, Monday," "Ruby Tuesday," "Wednesday," "Just Another Manic Monday," and my Top Ten hit with Al Kasha, "Will You Be Staying After Sunday?"

Questions

Questions make good rock lyrics: "Where My Girls At?" (702), "What's It Gonna Be?" (Busta Rhymes), "What's Going On" (Marvin Gaye), "Why Can't I?" (Liz Phair), Who Wouldn't Wanna Be Me?" (Keith Urban), "Where Is the Love" (Black Eyed Peas), and "Are You Happy Now?" (Michelle Branch). A skilled writer can then answer the question in a way that satisfies the listener.

> **Hirschhorn's Hints**
>
> Titles are more than subjects. They also allow you to bend the language cleverly. "Hurts So Bad" became "Hurt So Good." "We've Got to Stop Meeting Like This" was turned into "We've Got to Start Meeting Like This."

Holiday Songs

If you have a great idea for a Christmas tune, go for it, but keep in mind that it's even more difficult to get seasonal songs recorded. If you write one, circulate it early in the year, because Christmas music is usually chosen and slated for albums by late summer or early fall.

The advantage of a Christmas cut is its longevity. If a yuletide number catches on, it often turns into a perennial, such as "Silver Bells," "The Christmas Song," or "White Christmas," which is one of the biggest-selling singles in history. The majority of Christmas songs may attain success without achieving immortality (such as Run-DMC's "Christmas in Hollis"), but those that evolve into standards become a permanent source of income. Christmas standards are re-recorded over and over again, as exemplifed by Bruce Springsteen's "Santa Claus Is Comin' to Town." The payoff is high if you hit, so it's worth the gamble.

The Four-Minute Screenplay

Do you have the storytelling gift? If you do, you're way ahead of your competitors. Absorbing stories are always in demand, and most writers lack the talent to create them. If you suspect that your talent lies in story songs—miniature "movies" set to music—give them your full concentration. I guarantee that the effort will pay off.

Examples of story songs include Don McLean's "American Pie," Bobbie Gentry's "Ode to Billie Joe," Richard Buckner's "22," Loudon Wainwright III's "The Man Who Couldn't Cry," and Public Enemy's "Get the **** Outta Dodge." A life-altering event can also be used for a dramatic story, whether it's a wedding ("Wedding Bell Blues") or a funeral ("Green, Green Grass of Home" and "He Stopped Loving Her Today").

Hirschhorn's Hints

If you blend inner motivation and outward observation, I promise you'll never again say, "I can't find any ideas." The problem will become, "I have too many ideas. Which ones will I use, and which will I discard?"

When you have the story clearly etched in your mind, with a beginning, middle, and end, the song will flow. To facilitate this process, you may want to work backward by devising the end first and then moving in reverse to the beginning.

Priming the Idea Pump

The process of developing ideas can be urged on even more quickly with a method I employ: Close your eyes and say to yourself, "I have dozens of great ideas." Do this over and over again, particularly before you drop off to sleep. To heighten the effect, say it into a tape recorder, put on earphones, and listen to your own voice repeating the thought, "I have dozens of great ideas." Within two or three days, your mind will be bursting with fresh ideas and concepts.

Just coming up with ideas isn't enough, though. You have to trust them and act on them and not let insecurity prevent you from completing them. You can conquer the fears that limit your creativity in these ways:

- Don't put songs aside in the middle because you're afraid of criticism.

- Don't rewrite too much; you may lose the special quality the idea started with.

- Don't automatically put ideas aside because someone you tell about them isn't enthusiastic about the premise.

- Don't drop an idea because you get the feeling that ideas by other writers are superior.

Travel the Highway to Hits

Good songwriters are observant. Be a student of all you see around you. All too often, we retreat into our private worlds, rarely gazing outward at the parade of events moving around us. Developing an intense fascination for this parade will guarantee the arrival of powerhouse ideas.

The Least You Need to Know

- Ideas are the support system of your song.

- Don't let pre-work jitters intimidate you.

- Use the tragedies and triumphs in your own life as inspiration for songs.

- Tackle emotional topics such as divorce, sexual betrayal, the loss of a child, or tragic love.

- Explore universal themes such as love and religion, and use names, places, animals, colors, and anything that engages you for ideas.

- Keep your ideas flowing. Trust them and act on them.

- Study everybody around you as character material.

Chapter **3**

Making Your Titles Meaningful

In This Chapter

- ◆ The elements of a hit title
- ◆ Conveying your songs' characters, plots, and themes
- ◆ Using words with universal appeal

Titles are so important that many composers can't even begin to write a song without one. Titles suggest a story, convey a mood, and establish a flavor. Good titles capture the essence of the entire song in just a few words.

Most of all, intriguing titles attract people. It's no different with songs than with books or movies. When you have a choice between "I'm in Love" and "Let's Get It On," which one would draw your interest right away? The suggestions in this chapter apply equally to pop, R&B, rap, country, and every other genre.

Titles That Tell the Story

An ideal song title announces the entire plot. Many songs have generic titles, and they can be made to work, but your job is half done if the

Lyrical Lingo

A **protagonist** is the main character, the one whose actions move the story forward.

title reveals your overall concept right away. Most effective ones tell you if the *protagonist* is happy, angry, or frustrated. Some examples: "Can't Stop, Won't Stop" (Young Gunz), "Lovin' You All Night" (Patty Loveless), and "I Want You" (Thalia, featuring Little Joe).

Simple and Straightforward

In *In Your Own Words*, Bruce Pollock quotes Frank Zappa as saying, perhaps somewhat cynically and pejoratively, "Basically what people want to hear is: I love you, you love me, the leaves turn brown, they fell off the trees, the wind is blowing, it got cold, you went away, my heart broke, you came back, and my heart was okay." Even though Zappa might have been oozing with sarcasm, such a straightforward approach has lead to success for hundreds of songwriters.

John Lennon and Paul McCartney's "I Want to Hold Your Hand" sets an easy, obvious direction. The music and rhythm may vary, the words may be simple or sophisticated, but the emotion is clear and direct. The song is not going to be dark and convoluted; it's an open, happy expression of affection.

"I Don't Wanna Miss a Thing," Aerosmith's recording of a Diane Warren song, is another title that writes itself, as is Van Morrison's "Have I Told You Lately?" Others in this straightforward category include the following:

"Can You Feel the Love Tonight" by Elton John (E. John and T. Rice)

"Let Me Let Go" by Faith Hill (D. Morgan and S. Diamond)

"Please Remember Me" by Tim McGraw (W. Jennings and R. Crowell)

"I Wanna Love You Forever" by Jessica Simpson (L. Biancaniello and S. Watters)

Hirschhorn's Hints

Keep a title book and carry it with you so you can jot down provocative ideas or phrases whenever one strikes you. Terry Lewis, writer of Janet Jackson's hit "Escapade," always checks his book of titles to find something appropriate. Anytime he hears a phrase or a saying, he writes it down as a potential song title.

Title Characters

Producers and artists love titles that sketch a character. Jim Croce introduced us to "Big Bad Leroy Brown," who's "meaner than a junkyard dog," and the personality was so vivid that it became Croce's first number-one single. Mick Jagger and Keith Richards sang a loving tribute to "Angie," and Simon and Garfunkel portrayed the cheating "Mrs. Robinson."

The Everly Brothers told the story of "Cathy's Clown," and "Lucy in the Sky with Diamonds" was about the hallucinatory sweetheart (LSD) devised by John Lennon and Paul McCartney. Pras Michael told us about a "Ghetto Superstar (That Is What You Are)," and ABBA sang about a "Dancing Queen." Others include "Uncle John from Jamaica" (The Vengaboys), "Summer Girls" (LFO), "Donna Everywhere" (Too Much Joy), "Winona" (Matthew Sweet), "Miss Independent" (Kelly Clarkson), "Barbie Girl" (Aqua), and "Hey Julie" (Fountains of Wayne).

Good character studies can have lasting appeal for different generations, such as Don Henley's "The Boys of Summer," a hit in 1985 and 2003. The character could be someone we all know, like Madonna's sanctimonious father in "Papa Don't Preach," OutKast's stern mom in "Ms. Jackson," the abused mother in Martina McBride's "Independence Day," and the protagonist in Wheatus's "Teenage Dirtbag."

> **Backstage Banter**
>
> You never know what kind of competitors you'll be faced with as a writer. My first Oscar-winning song, "The Morning After," was pitted against "Ben," Michael Jackson's song about a rat. My second, "We May Never Love Like This Again," faced opposition from a love song to a dog, "Benji."

Titles That Set the Tone

The common denominator that unites all good titles is exaggeration. Titles, like motion pictures, are not accurate reflections of life, but distorted, heightened exaggerations of it. Songs have three or four minutes to do what a movie does in two hours. "Boom" by Trinket compares his love interest to powerful weapons, with quotes like "she annihilates me." Unless your title is strong, unless it explodes with violent, raw emotion and raises that emotion to fever pitch, few listeners will become engrossed in what you have to say.

> **Backstage Banter**
>
> Songs that portray an era and voice protest have to begin with passion. Billy Joel's "We Didn't Start the Fire" hit us with Harry Truman, Doris Day, Red China, and Johnnie Ray, all in the first line. Rarely have four images been so unrelated, yet they paint an unforgettable picture and draw you into the spell of Joel's vision.

Built-In Drama

Titles don't always lay out the plot in detail, but the best of them set an intriguing mood, provoke curiosity, and contain built-in drama.

We don't, for instance, know where Youngblood Z (featuring Little John) is going with "Damn," but we know it won't be boring. Same goes for "Headstrong" (Trapt), "Addicted" (Simple Plan), "She Only Smokes When She Drinks" (Joe Nichols), and "Tough Little Boys" (Gary Allan).

The following are examples of titles that signal a fascinating, dramatic tale:

"Maneater" by Hall and Oates (D. Hall, J. Oates, and S. Allen)

"Gangsta's Paradise" by Coolio featuring L.V. (A. Ivey Jr., L. Sanders, and D. Rasheed)

"Wind Beneath My Wings" by Bette Midler (L. Henley and J. Silbar)

"My Vietnam" by Pink (Pink and L. Perry)

"Lithium" by Nirvana (K. Cobain)

"High Water Everywhere (for Charley Patton)" by Bob Dylan (B. Dylan).

The Message in the Music

Titles aimed at changing society reached a peak in the 1960s with Bob Dylan, but some composers are always eager to influence the masses and improve world conditions. If you're politically conscious, the following examples should inspire you:

"Self Evident" by Ani DiFranco (A. DiFranco)

"F--- Tha Police" by N.W.A. (M.C. Ren/Ice Cube)

"Courtesy of the Red, White and Blue" by Toby Keith (T. Keith)

"Bu$hleaguer" by Pearl Jam (E. Vedder)

Pleading, Hoping, Begging

In pop songs, lovers beg, fall to their knees, and cry out in despair. Michael Bolton asked, "How Am I Supposed to Live Without You?" Rick Astley vowed, "Never Gonna Give You Up." Little Anthony sobbed, "Take Me Back." These titles also beg you to listen:

"Don't Be Cruel" by Elvis Presley (O. Blackwell, E. Presley, J. Leiber, and M. Stoller)

"Don't Let Me Get Me" by Pink (Pink and D. Austin)

"(Don't You) Forget About Me" by Simple Minds

"Don't Cry" by Guns N' Roses (A. Rose and I. Stradlin)

"Don't Let Me Be the Last to Know" by Britney Spears (Lange/Scott/Twain)

Hot-Blooded

Purely sexual titles automatically command attention from publishers, producers, and artists. Robert Palmer's "Addicted to Love" falls into that group, as do the following:

"Hot Stuff" by Donna Summer (P. Bellotte, H. Faltermeyer, and K. Forsey)

"Kiss You All Over" by Exile (M. Chapman and N. Chinn)

"D'ya Think I'm Sexy?" by Rod Stewart (R. Stewart and C. Appice)

"Hold Me, Thrill Me, Kiss Me, Kill Me" by U2 (A. Clayton, D. Evans, P. Lawson, and L. Mullen)

"Magic Stick" by Lil' Kim

"Doin' It" by LL Cool J (G. Jones, J. Todd Smith, and R. Smith)

"Get Ur Freak On" by Missy Elliott

Hot blood also courses through angry titles, many of which have risen to the top. "I Will Survive" is a cry of rage and a declaration of independence that has just as much relevance to this generation as it did when it made the Top 5 in March of 1979. Aretha Franklin demanded "Respect." Jennifer Holliday blended hysteria and vulnerability when she cried out, "And I Am Telling You I'm Not Going," the standout song in the Broadway musical *Dreamgirls*. Eminem's "Kill You," Public Enemy's "Fight the Power!", Limp Bizkit's "Break Stuff!", and Metallica's "Frantic!" also pack angry, hot-blooded emotion.

Frank Sinatra let the world know that he did it "My Way." James Brown made his position clear with "Say It Loud, I'm Black and I'm Proud," and Paul McCartney told us "I've Had Enough."

For All the Victims of the World

Powerful emotion in song isn't only direct, confrontational, and angry. It can also take the form of masochistic, long-suffering, pathetic cries from victims of love: "Rape Me," by Nirvana, "Changed the Locks" and "I Still Long For Your Kiss" by Lucinda Williams, and "Hurt" by Nine Inch Nails and Johnny Cash.

Trouble Clef

Try to avoid using passive titles in songs about overcoming adversity. When a singer stands up against adversity, the public is put on the singer's side.

Anyone who has tossed and turned or walked the floor till morning will identify with Kris Kristofferson's agonized plea of "Help Me Make It Through the Night" and Peter Frampton's "I Can't Stand It No More."

Titles that offer a cathartic release for people bruised by bad relationships will reach millions. The important thing to remember as a writer is this: Don't be embarrassed by what you feel. Be as frank with the world as you would be with your best friend or your psychiatrist. The more self-protective you are, the less power your lyrics will have. Say to yourself, "I'm not afraid to show myself, to be known."

When Richard Marx wrote the heartfelt title, "Right Here Waiting," he resisted putting the song on his album. He felt it was far too personal and it would expose his innermost thoughts to the world, like writing a love letter to his wife and having it printed in the tabloids. Later on, Marx realized that part of his job as a songwriter was to communicate with as many people as possible.

Title Triggers

Ideas for titles can come from anywhere—a favorite book, a snippet of overheard conversation, a weather report. No matter the sources, make sure you keep a record of potential titles; you never know when you might need them.

Find the Right Word

Sometimes one word says it all. The following songs with one-word titles all made number one:

"Emotions" by Mariah Carey

"Batdance" by Prince (Prince)

"Dirrty" by Christina Aguilera

"Smooth" by Santana/Rob Thomas

"Frantic" by Metallica

"Dumpweed" by Blink 182

"Bodies" by the Sex Pistols

"Come" by Prince

"Jump" by Van Halen

"Hurt" by Nine Inch Nails and Johnny Cash

Dance to the Music

Songwriters frequently hit the jackpot when they write dance songs. Some well-known dance titles are the following:

"The Twist" by Chubby Checker (H. Ballard)

"The Loco-Motion" by Little Eva (G. Goffin and C. King)

"Vogue" by Madonna (Madonna and S. Pettibone)

"Macarena" by Los Del Rio (A. Romero and R. Ruiz)

"Achy Breaky Heart" by Billy Ray Cyrus

"Hot Hot Hot" by Buster Poindexter

"Zoot Suit Riot" by Cherry Poppin' Daddies

Cover the Country

As I mentioned in the previous chapters, many songs describe a special place—whether real or fanciful. Don't be afraid to put the name of that place right in the title, as the following songs do:

"Penny Lane" by The Beatles (P. McCartney and J. Lennon)

"New York State of Mind" (B. Joel)

"Hotel California" by The Eagles (D. Felder, D. Henley, and G. Frey)

"It's Chicago, It's Not Chicago" by Soul Coughing

"Los Angeles" by X

"New York, New York" by Ryan Adams

In addition, modes of transportation are always popular themes with writers and with the public. Natalie Cole rode in a "Pink Cadillac," and Harry Chapin drove a "Taxi." Other transportation-based tunes: "Cars," by Gary Numan, "Land of Hope and Dreams" (Bruce Springsteen), "2-4-6-8" (Tom Robinson Band), and Lyle Lovett's "If I Had a Boat."

Keep Your Titles in the Trunk

Start thinking of titles immediately. Place a star next to the ones you like best, but don't throw out the others. Your composing priority one week may be a gentle country ballad, but six months later you might want to produce an up-tempo R&B song. Some of your earlier titles (even unstarred ones) might be perfect at that time.

Words That Work

Certain words are commercial magic, and they unfailingly touch a universal chord.

Trouble Clef

You can't copyright a title, so many songwriters use titles that have been hits in the past. Try to avoid reusing titles if possible. It creates confusion in the public's mind. Also, when identical titles are logged by ASCAP, BMI, and SESAC, payments might go to the wrong person.

Come On, Baby, Light My Fire

Candles have a particular attraction for writers. Elton John's "Candle in the Wind" was a tribute to Marilyn Monroe and then to Princess Diana. "Sixteen Candles" was a number-two smash for the Crests, and "(Lay Down) Candles in the Rain" made it to number six for Melanie.

Writers are also attracted to fire-themed songs. Some of the most popular include James Taylor's "Fire and Rain," Cult's "Fire Woman," Funky Green Dogs' "Fired Up!", and Bob Seger's "Fire Lake."

Cry Your Way to the Charts

Record industry executives cry tears of joy with they find good songs with "tears" or "crying" in their titles:

"96 Tears" by ? & the Mysterians (R. Martinez)

"Tears of a Clown" by Smokey Robinson and the Miracles and by Stevie Wonder (H. Cosby, W. Smokey Robinson, and S. Wonder)

"Crying" by Aerosmith

"Don't Cry" by Guns N' Roses

"Cry Me a River" by Justin Timberlake

"Tears in Heaven" by Eric Clapton

A Taste of Sugar

"Sour" pops up occasionally, as in "Sour Girl" by Stone Temple Pilots, but sugar is all over the charts. In fact, it's one of the most utilized concepts in popular music:

"Sweet Surrender" by Sarah McLachlan (S. McLachlan)

"Sweet Lady" by Tyrese (J. Austin, C. Farrar, and T. Taylor)

"Sweet Child o' Mine" by Guns N' Roses (S. Adler, D. McKagan, A. Rose, S. Hudson, and I. Stradin)

"Sweet Dreams Are Made of This" by Eurhythmics (A. Lennox and D. Stewart)

"Pour Some Sugar on Me" by Def Leppard (S. Clark, P. Collen, J. Elliott, M. Lange, and R. Savage)

One Is the Magic Number

Numbers are always popular in titles: "Two Hearts" (Phil Collins), "Three Times a Lady" (Lionel Richie), "Four Walls" (Jim Reeves); but none has the commercial impact of the number one. The following are just a few of the chartbusters with "one" in the title:

"The One I Gave My Heart To" by Aaliyah (D. Warren)

"One More Night" by Phil Collins (P. Collins)

"One More Try" by George Michael (G. Michael)

"One of Us" by Joan Osborne (E. Brazilian)

"One of These Nights" by The Eagles (D. Henley and G. Frey)

"One Last Cry" by Brian McKnight (B. McNight, B. Barnes, and M. Barnes)

"One" by U2 (A. Clayton, D. Evans, P. Hewson, and L. Mullen)

"One Way or Another" by Blondie (D. Harry and N. Harrison)

Hirschhorn's Hints _____

If you have a chance to write a song for a film, fight for the title you believe in. Al Kasha and I were asked to write a song called "The Poseidon Adventure" for the film of the same name. No song with "The Poseidon Adventure" as a title could have become a hit. Fortunately, Al and I convinced the producer to let us use "The Morning After" instead.

Only

Maybe because we all want to be someone's "one and only," the word "only" has potent title appeal. Neil Young summed it up best when he said, "Only Love Can Break Your Heart," and Melissa Etheridge sang "I'm the Only One." Hootie and the Blowfish scored with "Only Wanna Be With You." Ringo Starr sang "Only You," demonstrating the power of the emotion that "only" expresses, and "Only" was the title for songs by Ass Ponys and Static-X.

Kiss

Artists, publishers, and producers all pucker up when they see the word "kiss" on a lead sheet or hear it on a recording. Prince went to number one with "Kiss" and Faith Hill scored with "This Kiss." The Red Hot Chili Peppers sang "Suck My Kiss" and Aaron Tippin told his lover to "Kiss This."

First-Line Fever

Titles and first lines are the lure, the come-on to draw the audience in. If they're bland or colorless, you've lost your listeners. In an age of diminished attention spans and relentless bombardment by new stimuli, no one will give you more than a few seconds to score an impact. Movies succeed or fail after one weekend. If ratings for a television series are mediocre, it's instantly yanked from the schedule. The same goes for songs.

I've heard novice songwriters say, "I'm not going to be so blatant and commercial." This attitude is musical suicide in the popular music world or even in theater, where Andrew Lloyd Webber felt he had to dangle a monster-sized chandelier in front of his *Phantom of the Opera* audience to get its attention. Your title has to project power in order to outshine the competition.

A memorable tune, a rousing rhythm, or a superb vocal performance are all valuable assets, but spending extra time and energy in creating an outstanding title and a mesmerizing first line will yield surprising and exciting results.

The Least You Need to Know

◆ A title has to suggest a story or create a mood.

◆ Sexually oriented titles are always in demand.

◆ The best titles are powerfully emotional exaggerations of life. They offer a rich experience packed into a three-minute song.

◆ The audience's diminished attention span and increased exposure to new stimuli make captivating titles more important than ever.

◆ A dynamic title grips the audience, and a powerful first line mesmerizes them.

Chapter 4

Breathing Life into Your Lyrics

In This Chapter

- ◆ Concentrate on what you see
- ◆ Live the visual lifestyle
- ◆ Create drama with details
- ◆ Write with all your senses
- ◆ Connect colors and music

Lyrics have to be emotional. From the time pop music was new, they expressed such feelings as "I want you," and "I'll never stop loving you." Today the lines are equally intense: "Luv U Better" (LL Cool J), "Like I love you" (Justin Timberlake), and "The way I do" (Melissa Etheridge). Valid emotion will connect with audiences, particularly when conveyed by superstars, but newcomers—particularly in this MTV and video age—will have a better chance of being noticed if they spice up their lyrics with visual images.

Boyz II Men don't just say, "I adore you." They sing "On Bended Knee." We see their emotional need through action. Titles such as "Scar Tissue" by Red Hot Chili Peppers, and Morphine's "Cure for Pain," bring the story brilliantly alive. Other striking examples include Metallica's "St. Anger" (I'm madly in anger with you") and Linkin Park's "One Step Closer." You can improve your visual sense through awareness and practice.

A Unique Visual Personality

When I started, one of the first songs I brought to a publisher read like this:

> Nothing matters but your love
> Nothing matters but your kiss
> Without your touch my life is lonely
> How can I go on like this?

The publisher studied the song and said, "It's nice, but I see a hundred lyrics like this every day." When I pressed him for an explanation, he shrugged. "They have no special personality. How would I know if it's you or someone else?"

It all comes down to seeing with concentration. The majority of us walk through life with blinders on, more preoccupied with our private thoughts than with the external stimuli blazing around us. You can develop a visual sense effectively and rapidly by embarking on a whole new lifestyle.

The Visual Lifestyle

A visual lifestyle is a daily pattern, one that should kick off in the morning and be part of your schedule all day long. Tell yourself:

- This visual lifestyle is a new and permanent existence.

- Developing a visual lifestyle means success and recognition.

- A visual lifestyle is going to make me a much better writer and change my whole life.

Start with Cereal

As you're eating breakfast, try to think visually. Nothing interesting there, you think, just a plate of oatmeal with raisins and strawberries. But wait! The raisins and strawberries are much more like a painting than you ever imagined. The bowl is green and gold. You never noticed it before.

Read the newspaper for visual images, not simply for information. If the statement is, "President Bush stumbled off Air Force One, stooped forward with exhaustion, eyes lined as he told the press about his latest plan to deal with terrorism," forget "his latest plan" or "terrorism." Home in on "stumbled ... stooped forward ... eyes lined."

As you peruse every page, circle the visual phrases. Within a few weeks, your lyrics will gain color. Bland phrases will drop out of your writing, and everyone who hears your language will relate more deeply to it.

Live in the Visual Landscape

Take a walk every morning. While appreciating the walk's cardiovascular benefits, tell yourself, "I see everything around me." Notice the cars, trees, flowers, and the runners waving as they pass by. If you're in a suburban area, observe the homes. Are they one-, two-, or three-level? Are they painted in conservative black and white? Is the trim blood-red or blue? Are kids in the front yard? What are they wearing? What game are they playing?

Now you've reached the park. Other walkers and runners have joined you. Old people sit on the benches. What expressions are they wearing? Optimistic? Sad? Resigned? You might notice a water fountain you've never been aware of before or a fence that needs painting.

Backstage Banter

Madonna described how the words of the number-one hit "Like a Prayer" developed. "Originally, when I recorded the song, I would play it over and over again, trying to get a visual sense of what sort of story or fantasy it evoked in me. I kept imagining this story about a girl who was madly in love with a black man, set in the South, with this forbidden interracial love affair."

—From *The Billboard Book of Number One Hits,* by Fred Bronson

---

If you live in a big city like New York, with an apartment in Manhattan, you'll find yourself awash in imagery if you bother to look around. Move beyond the obvious high-rise buildings, speeding yellow cabs, and expensive restaurants and study the gray-haired, overweight vendor on the corner selling salt bagels or the sax player blowing his heart out while indifferent crowds push past him.

Driving through the Midwest may strike you as one long, open field or expanse of blue sky, but less conventionally beautiful sights, such as a broken-down truck or tractor, give character to the landscape. Whether in Texas watching rodeo riders or Miami observing surfers, the clue to visual imagery is noticing offbeat, eccentric details.

Twain and Conroy

Read incessantly, and *not* only the bestsellers. Today's writing is often fast, concise, and stripped for action. Few recent books can match Mark Twain's *Tom Sawyer* or *Huckleberry Finn* for language. But if you want to see modern visual writing at its finest, read Pat Conroy. *The Prince of Tides* and *Beach Music* are definitive demonstrations of how words can achieve the height of cinematic excitement.

Maya Angelou shows off her flair for employing visual color in her autobiographical *The Heart of a Woman*, setting the scene with "After a shower, I settled in my bed with a book, a drink and a package of cigarettes." It's impossible not to *see* and absorb the surroundings, especially when she continues, "specters of laughing black people, shouting and arguing, crowded around my bed."

The cemetery scene at the end of Stephen King's *The Dead Zone* is already a movie, and F. Scott Fitzgerald's concluding lines from *The Great Gatsby* ("So we beat on, boats against the current, borne back ceaselessly into the past") say more about the pain of lost dreams than many entire novels and plays.

When reading books for their visual impact, underline the words that transform thoughts from plain, bland statements to vibrant portraits. Repeat this procedure as you read novels and you'll find your visual sense immeasurably sharpened.

Hirschhorn's Hints

Country music singer and legend Tom T. Hall says that some songs require a mental picture of a train wreck. Some others require, melody-wise, a flower waving in the breeze. Allowing random mental pictures to float through your mind not only produces beautiful lyrics, but beautiful melodies as well.

The Drama in the Details

Watch movies for more than the car chases or the explosions. From this day forward, study how the characters dress, walk, talk, and gesture. Zero in on the set design, the architecture, and the furnishings of rooms ranging from the Middle Ages to today. Everything from the gardens of Venice to the ghettos of New York is in the movies, and you should be studying it all with an eye to re-creating details.

In the end, lyric writing is all about the details that individualize people and situations. It's often more vital to notice a food stain on a coat than the coat itself. A food stain hints at the type of person you're watching. This kind of observation protects you from settling for clichés.

Songwriter Sol Marcus, who wrote "Don't Let Me Be Misunderstood" for the Animals, once took a new writer to task for saying, in one line: "I love the morning sun and I wanna grab you, babe." These lines are certainly visual, but the same person would never speak both of them, particularly in one sentence.

Analyze Nonvisual Lyrics

A highly effective approach to jump-starting your visual sense is to analyze both good and bad lyrics and rewrite them by deleting generalities and finding ways to make them more specific. Many songs achieve popularity based on their well-produced tracks, powerful vocal performances, or basic ideas, but the lyric lines are banal and clichéd. You'll discover yourself improving quickly if you rework those throwaway lines and make them visual.

Remember the banal lyrics I quoted at the beginning of the chapter? In case you've forgotten them, here they are again:

> Nothing matters but your love
> Nothing matters but your kiss
> Without your touch my life is lonely
> How can I go on like this?

Now see how the same idea can be transformed by adding visual details:

> Nothing matters but the heat of your skin
> Your lips breathing deep in my ear
> Without your body in bed next to mine
> I drown in a dark cloud of fear

Look for Consistently Visual Writers

Some lyricists have a much more visual flair than others. Study the market to find out who these artists are and then give special attention to their work. Certain names spring immediately to mind:

Dave Alvin	Aimee Mann
Chuck Berry	Paul McCartney
Garth Brooks	Joni Mitchell

Kurt Cobain	Liz Phair
Iris DeMent	Bob Seger
Bob Dylan	Paul Simon
Eminem	Tim Rice
Dan Fogelberg	Bruce Springsteen
John Hiatt	Pete Townshend
Lauryn Hill	Bernie Taupin
Billy Joel	Lucinda Williams

Describe Everyday Experiences Visually

Another process that expands your visual sense is concentrating on ordinary, mundane activities. Paint them visually in ways that heighten the actions and bring them alive. Think of small details that give them individuality and freshness. It's been said that you can take an orange and find dozens of characteristics about it worth describing.

These seemingly static situations can lead to interesting lyrics. For example, the following lines describe the act of waking up:

> My legs were crooked, my top undone
> My hair was in my eyes
> My knees were stiff from too much sleep
> The sun took me by surprise

Taking a picture off the wall becomes an emotional experience in these lyrics:

> Tore your picture from the wall
> The tears ran down my face
> I stared into your evil eyes
> and cursed your last embrace

Describing the ordinary act of picking up a child at school creates an image all parents can relate to:

> My six-year-old was bundled up
> Shivering at the gate
> He ran to me, leaped in the car
> Angry I was late

Visual, but Not Verbose

Books sometimes have descriptions of sunsets, rivers, and mountains that are beautiful in themselves, but they slow the story down to a crawl. Expert writers use imagery to dramatize emotions and events, but never at the expense of pacing. All visual details must serve a purpose in the song. If they don't move the story and the emotions forward, discard them.

The Other Senses

Most people are oblivious to their visual surroundings, and they're even less aware of the sounds, smells, tastes, and tactile experiences that help to create our "take" on the world. Only by responding to everything around you with all your senses will you reach your highest potential as a lyricist. Seeing is the first but not the only step toward giving lyrics a pulse and making them breathe.

Sound

Sounds roar from every direction. Cars don't simply go by; they zoom, screech, groan, and rumble. A bus comes to a sharp, squealing stop. Two people in a bitter argument snarl at each other. Someone moans with pleasure.

Life has a soundtrack, but most of us have the volume turned way down. Adjust the dial and listen to everything. What you hear will make your lyrics more compelling.

Smell

Take a deep breath. Stop and smell the roses, a woman's perfume, the chicken or steak from a local diner, and the stench of garbage. Not every smell is pleasant, but all of them help to set a scene and make your words more vibrant.

Taste

I used to have a bad habit, one I overcame with superhuman effort. I would gulp down my lunch or dinner, and an hour later I wouldn't even recall what I'd eaten! All of us have been given the great gift of taste, so chew slowly and savor your food. Taste is a sense that can bring lyrics succulently alive, as demonstrated by extensive use in hit songs of such words as sugar, ice cream, candy, jam, Tootsie Roll, and pizza pie.

Touch

Skin-on-skin contact is certainly one form of touch. Yet touching is a sensual experience that extends far beyond contact between two human beings. We're rarely aware of all the things we touch. Consider the soft comfort of old blue jeans, the bristly stab of a beard, or the warm suppleness of a horse's back. A clean tablecloth has a gentle coolness; the mahogany finish of a piano is smooth and pleasing. Such titles as "Touch It" (Monifah), "Touch Me All Night Long" (Cathy Dennis), and "Touch Myself" (T-Boz) dramatize the constant, intense yearning for intimate contact.

Writing with All Your Senses

Writing is always more memorable when it encompasses the five senses. Consider this verse I wrote for "Hearing the Wind":

> Eating cherry pie
> Watching the sun in the sky
> Waiting for love to let me in
> Smellin' the fries
> Smoke in my eyes
> Touching your hand—and hearing the wind

Every sense—taste, sight, touch, sound, and smell—is engaged in this lyric.

Brushing your teeth is admittedly routine and boring. You've probably never bothered to ask yourself, what sensation am I experiencing when the toothbrush moves across my teeth? The same goes for combing your hair, buttoning your shirt, and tying your shoelaces. These are moments when your psyche switches to automatic, and you have to catch yourself and pay attention.

Look at Who's Talking

Pay attention to the way people talk. Both a forest ranger and a Philadelphia debutante speak English, but they might as well be speaking two different languages. Work to capture their specific expressions, slang, and attitude.

Write It All Down

As the impressions mount, as your senses begin to feast on the barrage of input you receive, one thing is absolutely crucial: Keep a record! You can do it the old-fashioned way by writing in a notebook; carry a tape recorder and speak about all you see, touch, hear, taste, and smell; or record everything of note in your Palm Pilot.

When you listen to music, jot down every interesting, unusual, original word or phrase you encounter. It sets the mental machinery buzzing. You won't necessarily use any of these lyrics, but they'll stimulate you to think of your own. The same applies to magazines. The authors who contribute articles to *Vanity Fair* and *GQ* are masters of writing that employs all the senses.

Music and Colors

Thinking in colors can stimulate musical composition. Let waves of purple, red, blue, green, and black flood your mind. Be receptive without straining for tunes. Gradually, if you're patient, the imagery will be accompanied by sound (this is called *synesthesia*), such as the tinkling of a distant piano, bells, a lone fiddle, drums, or bagpipes. Before long your brain will explode with sound, and that sound will channel itself into exciting melodies and rhythms you can utilize.

Trouble Clef

Don't trust your memory! It will let you down every time. You'll remember the broad outlines but not the specifics, and specifics are what make your lyrics magical.

Lyrical Lingo

Synesthesia is the process by which a certain color or colors provokes the hearing of certain sounds.

Hirschhorn's Hints

Thunder, deep voices, and drums often invoke dark images (think of Garth Brooks's "The Thunder Rolls," which actually employs the sound of thunder). The imagery is light when people hear squeaks from string instruments, flutes, or piccolos. High pitch makes the colors more powerful and vivid. If you see red with middle C, C-sharp will be a brighter red. You'll see a more brilliant color if D is played rather than C-sharp.

To encourage musical creativity, listen to music before you start to write and let your mind bring up imagery in a free-floating way. Psychologist Chuck Loch makes the following recommendation:

Imagine hearing music that deeply affects you emotionally. You close your eyes. A cloud or filmy veil of color begins to billow. Spreading sheets of color overlay each other. Bands or ribbons of color develop and flow with the music. (*Songwriter* magazine, June 1979)

Loch's research revealed that high-pitched music tends to produce small, sharp-edged images; low-pitched music brought on dark, round images. Graceful lines of color accompanied smooth music; syncopated music yielded jagged lines.

Don't be concerned whether your mental imagery conforms to the majority. For half an hour, give yourself over to the sounds and let your mind choose its own visual equivalents. After the power of your imagery dissipates, start to write. Your music will gain richness, color, and freedom.

The Least You Need to Know

◆ Experience your surroundings visually.

◆ Even mundane events can translate into exciting and visually appealing lyrics.

◆ When you write, think with all five senses.

◆ Thinking in colors can stimulate musical composition.

Part 2

It's All About the Music

Smooth rhyming, alliteration, and the proper use of vowels and structure are the building blocks of any superior song. Repetition and the right rhythmic groove are the lifeblood of popular songwriting; beyond that is the big H—the hook! "Give me a hit hook," is the cliché uttered by all publishers, producers, and writers.

In this part, you'll learn what a hit hook is and how to write one. You'll also study sample repetitions and rhythmic grooves until these elements become second nature to you. You'll become familiar with prosody—the seamless marriage of words and music—writing instrumental and vocal figures, thinking in terms of emotional intervals, and choosing the right tempo to show off your song to best advantage.

Rhyme and Structure

In This Chapter

◆ Rhymes that work and rhymes that don't

◆ Ways to build your rhyming skills

◆ Rhyme schemes and song structures

◆ Amazing alliteration and powerful vowels

Rhyme doesn't seem like a controversial word. It's love and above, moon and June, and sing and spring. Or is it down and around, shine and mind, and laugh and pass? It depends on who you're talking to. Some people feel strongly that rhymes have to be true, like the first three pairs of words; others find the so-called false soundalikes, as in the last three pairs, equally satisfying.

I prefer the true rhyme, but I'm not as locked into it as others tend to be because attitudes toward rhyme have changed. Still, learning the rules of rhyme and structure will prevent you from wandering formlessly and ensure that every thought comes across with emotional clarity.

The Importance of Rhyme

Fresh, original, interesting concepts matter more than any surface craft. But craft provides the key that expresses those thoughts clearly, and rhyme is one crucial way of achieving this clarity.

New writers frequently want to dispense with rhyme before they learn the basics, and the results are almost always chaotically self-indulgent. Rhymes also provide a flow that makes it easier for most singers to interpret the material. Just as certain chords give people a sense of relaxed familiarity, rhymes offer the same internal comfort.

Most of all, rhymes provide a structure on which you can build. Experienced composers can break rules of rhyme, but only after learning them.

Types of Rhymes

Most rhymes fall into one of the following categories:

◆ **Perfect rhyme.** The sounds are exactly alike, as in day/play, joy/boy, blaze/craze, and ease/knees.

◆ **False rhyme.** Still a matter of controversy among writers, this rhyme pairs words that contain similar sounds, such as time/mine, down/around, and hard/car.

◆ **Masculine rhyme.** This rhyme involves a single syllable. That syllable may be the entire word as in store/floor or the last syllable in longer words, as in venerate/segregate. In a masculine rhyme, the final syllable is accented, as in these words: resound, avoid, reply, and consume.

◆ **Feminine rhyme.** In this two-syllable rhyme, the stress falls on the first part of the word: walker/stalker. The final syllable of the word is unaccented, as in softness, careful, and fairest.

◆ **Inner rhyme.** "The wall is tall and close to the mall" illustrates multiple rhyming within a single sentence.

A Hit Mixture

In most cases, professional songwriters know how to rhyme. But more often today they go by what feels emotionally right, even if it means sacrificing the perfect, obvious rhyme word.

This combination of false and true rhyme is used in Celine Dion's "The Power of Love" as well as in "I've Waited All My Life."

> The morning sun is shining
> We made love through the night
> I pray the feelings still go on
> When I look in your eyes
> I've waited all my life for you
> And if you leave, I'll break
> You're everything I've waited for
> So stay here for my sake

"Night" and "eyes" don't even sound alike, except for the vowel sound of "i." Yet "break" and "sake" would satisfy any purist. Your intuition has to tell you when such false rhymes as love/touch or again/rain best serve your thought and when a true rhyme would make the point more effectively.

Endings That Set You Free

The following endings will give you maximum rhyming freedom:

-ay	-ee	-in	-ore
-ade	-eer	-ine	-ot
-ain	-el	-ist	-ote
-ake	-ence	-it	-ow
-ar	-ent	-ize	-ow (o)
-are	-ess	-ock	-ude
-ate	-ew	-oke	-y
-ean	-ide	-oom	
-eat	-ill	-oon	

These are by no means the only alternatives, but they make a writer's life much simpler. I'm not a person who shuns rhyming dictionaries. But sometimes you're in the midst of a song, and no rhyming dictionary is available. Train yourself to automatically know as many rhymes as possible by using these sounds and writing as many rhymes as you can think of.

Inner Rhymes

The best inner rhymes give songs rhythmic grace, smoothness, and professionalism:

> I see your face—it's everyplace
> I hear you talk—I see you walk—when I close my eyes
> The smile I wear is just a disguise
> I'm gonna crack—'cause I want you back
> The smile I wear is just a disguise

Listen to the classic record of "Ain't Nothin' Like the Real Thing" by Marvin Gaye and Tammi Terrell, and you'll see how perfectly the rhymes coast along, beautifully integrated into the overall structure.

Wayward Rhymes

When you're creating a rhyme, keep the word "flow" in mind. Whether a rhyme is false or true, it must maintain a comfortable, natural flow. That's the only thing that matters. Use words that offer dozens of rhyming alternatives and avoid lines that lack any rhyme, unless you feel that your thought is so brilliant it can survive without safety nets of craftsmanship.

Rhymes Without Reason

My advice is to learn to rhyme perfectly before you settle for false rhymes. If possible, avoid words that aren't rhymes in any sense of the word, such as new/knew or bare/bear. Combinations like these call attention to themselves and sound amateurish.

Another amateurish approach is twisting a line unnaturally:

> You're all that I've been thinking of
> Because I find, in you, my love

No one talks that way. Don't wrench words like pretzels for a rhyme.

Trouble Clef _____

Cole Porter, legendary Broadway composer of the '30s, '40s, and '50s) used *puberty* and *Shuberty* as well as *flatterer* and *Cleopatterer*. Show writers often employ this device, distorting words out of shape and then pronouncing the result witty, sophisticated, and playful. But we're not in the age of Lorenz Hart and Noel Coward. Unless you're a brilliant wordsmith, an attempt to bend words this way might sound more like a mistake than an inspiration.

Rhymes That Box You In

Although love is the main theme behind all songs, the word itself offers few interesting rhyming possibilities. Love/above was a dated combination in the 1930s, and love/of always sounds clichéd. What's left? *Glove* is not a pop word; *shove* sounds hostile rather than romantic; and *dove* sounds pristine in the rock era.

In Search of Colorful Rhyme Words

If you're hitting a brick wall searching for interesting rhyme words, these sources can sharpen your lyric writing:

- *Roget's International Thesaurus.* This invaluable resource was first printed in 1852, and has been a treasure chest of synonyms ever since.

- *Slang* by Paul Dickson. This book is packed with expressions relating to fields such as business, computers, the automotive industry, counterculture, the drug trade, fantasy, the future and science fiction, food and drink, medicine, sailing, performing, politics, real estate, sex, sports, and many other areas. Also check out *Dictionary of American Slang* compiled by Harold Wentworth and Stuart Berg Flexner.

- *The Dictionary of Cliches* by James Rogers. Over 2,000 popular expressions; their meanings and origins are listed in this book.

- *Instant Quotation Dictionary* will spark your lyric writing. Other quotation books include *Dictionary of Modern Quotations* by J.M. Cohen and M.J. Cohen, *The International Thesaurus of Quotations* by Rhoda Thomas Tripp, and *20,000 Quips and Quotes* compiled by Evan Esar.

- *A Dictionary of American Idioms* contains such expressions as "get down to brass tacks," "far out," "bolt from the blue," and "zero in on."

Rhyming Dictionaries

Many rhyming dictionaries are so detailed that they confuse rather than enlighten. I like the pocket-sized *Random House Rhyming Dictionary*, edited by Jess Stein. In a pinch, this tiny volume has never failed me.

These rhyming dictionaries are also useful:

♦ *The Songwriter's Rhyming Dictionary* by Sammy Cahn

♦ *The Complete Rhyming Dictionary* by Clement Wood

♦ *The New Comprehensive American Rhyming Dictionary* by Merriam-Webster

♦ *Merriam-Webster's Rhyming Dictionary* by Merriam-Webster

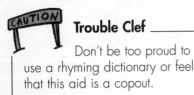

Trouble Clef

Don't be too proud to use a rhyming dictionary or feel that this aid is a copout.

♦ *Capricorn Rhyming Dictionary* by Bessie Redfeld

♦ *Webster's New Explorer Rhyming Dictionary* by Merriam-Webster

♦ *The Modern Rhyming Dictionary* by Gene Lees

Rhyme Schemes

Successful writers utilize a variety of popular rhyme schemes. This section points out several important ones.

My Oscar-winning song "The Morning After," written with Al Kasha, demonstrates the rhyming of lines 2 and 4:

> There's got to be a morning after
> If we can hold on through the night
> We have a chance to find the sunshine
> Let's keep on looking for the light

To add even more rhyme, you can rhyme lines 1 and 3 and lines 2 and 4:

> You've broken my heart
> Our bridges have been crossed
> 'cause he broke us apart
> It hurts to know I've lost

Another hit rhyme scheme is to rhyme lines 1 and 2 and lines 3 and 4:

> I want you more than I can say
> So promise you won't go away

If I can't have your love I'll die
So baby, please don't say goodbye

Some writers rhyme all the lines:

Baby I'll be there
You know how I care
There's so much to share
Love beyond compare

Or a writer may rhyme the first two or three lines and leave the last one without a rhyme:

I hate to sleep alone
It's painful on my own
I want you back
I just want you to know
I'll never let you go
I only want to show
That I need you

Yet another popular rhyme scheme is to rhyme lines 2 and 3:

I hate the rain
It just reminds me of my tears
How much I've cried through all these years
I hate the rain

Sometimes writers only rhyme the first line of verse 1 and verse 2:

I'll never be free
You've got me in chains
I'm praying that I can escape

You're part of me
When I try to run
I never get far

Or the last line of each verse rhymes, as in this example:

The minute we met
I wanted your love
And girl, I still do

> With each passing day
> This ache only grows
> My whole life is you

These often-used, thoroughly dependable rhyme schemes can work for all writers. If you're a new songwriter, stick with them until they feel comfortable and natural. When they seem automatic, stretch out and try others.

Other Hit Ingredients

Using rhyme effectively is basic, but other hit ingredients such as structure, alliteration, and the right vowel sounds will add form, flow, and vibrancy to your songs.

Structure

Without structure, your song would be shapeless and sprawling. Within it, however, there are a surprising number of variations.

Verse

A verse is the first portion of a song, always known as the "A" section, which sets up the tune and the story before hitting the hook (also known as chorus, but referred to as "hook" by most songwriters). A verse (or "A" section) repeats melodically, but the words are generally different when the song returns to it (now called the "B" section). Sometimes the bridge (the mid-section of the song, and melodically different from the verse or hook), goes right into the hook at the end of the tune. Other times it returns to the verse (at which time the melody is the same, but the lyrics are different).

Bruce Springsteen's "Born in the USA" uses this form:

> A (Verse) A (Verse) A (Verse)

The most accessible and familiar form is this one:

> A (Verse) A (Verse) B (Bridge) A (Verse)

"Raindrops Keep Fallin' on My Head" (H. David, B. Bacharach), "Saving All My Love for You" (M. Masser, G. Goffin), and "Just the Way You Are" (B. Joel) use the AABA structure. Al and I also used the AABA format on our two Oscar winners, "The Morning After" and "We May Never Love Like This Again."

Another familiar form is the following:

> A (Verse) B (Hook) A (Verse) B (Hook)
> A (Verse) B (Hook)

"Killing Me Softly with His Song" utilizes the ABABAB structure, as does the driving "Big Bad Leroy Brown." This structure has no *bridge* in it, just two sections alternating with each other.

B. J. Thomas's "Don't Worry Baby" has the following format:

> A (Verse) B (Hook) A (Verse) B (Hook) C (Bridge) B (Hook)

A variation on ABABCB would be this structure:

> A (Hook) B (Verse) A (Hook) B (Verse) A (Hook)

Sometimes the verse is repeated four times or more, without any chorus or bridge. Johnny Cash's "I Walk the Line" uses this structure.

The Eagles demonstrated that basic forms can be stretched, extended, or molded into any shape that makes sense. For "Lyin' Eyes," they did the following:

> A (Verse) A (Verse) A (Verse) B (Hook) A (Verse) B (Hook)

This structure is daring because it delays the appearance of the chorus until nearly halfway through. If you're a new writer, it's safer to stick with more familiar forms. The Eagles were powerful enough when they recorded "Lyin' Eyes" to experiment and buck commercially conservative trends.

Alliteration

Along with rhyme, *alliteration* (in which two or more words in a line start with the same letter) makes the line sweep along smoothly and effortlessly. And using long vowels such as "e" and "o" helps singers to achieve greater vocal passion and power.

See how alliteration makes the following lyrics flow smoothly:

> Tell me you'll be true
> Trust my love for you

Note the three *T* words: tell, true, and trust.

Alliteration is something to concentrate on. You can overdo it, as in "How wonderful to walk with you this Wednesday," but if kept in check, it's the best friend any lyricist can have.

Vibrant Vowels

A, E, I, O, and *U* are the magic letters, the vowel sounds that should be elongated and dramatized. Think how often you hear big, powerful notes on words such as *go* and *say* and *me.* Think how weak it sounds when you sock out a roaring note on *the* or *but.* When you're writing, write sustained, powerful, and emotional notes on the long vowel sounds of A, E, I, O, U, and you'll give singers exciting notes to dramatize.

Act Out Your Lyrics

When used properly, rhyme, alliteration, and vowels pay off the ultimate dividend: Your words will talk. Whether sung or spoken, lyrics should never sound stilted. After you've completed your lyric, give it the talk test. Be an actor. Read every word out loud, dismissing all music from your mind. Pretend you're speaking to a loved one or a friend.

Hirschhorn's Hints

Get sheet music of your favorite songs and speak the lines. You'll begin to see how the best ones sound like natural human speech.

Is there any phrase that sounds awkward when spoken? It will be equally awkward in combination with music. Speak the lyrics two, three, or four times. Your ear will latch on to the lines that sound real and reject the ones that seem artificial. You'll notice right away which words are fillers, throwaways, or pieces of a first draft that should have been discarded.

Once the talk test identifies your weak lines, be ruthless and get rid of the verbal dead weight. Don't rationalize, as so many beginning writers do, that the line "works," that the overall feeling is fine, or that it's the best you can do. You may be tempted to do that if you're tired or discouraged or bored by the process. If this is the case, stop working, and then return to the problem and deal with it in a renewed frame of mind. An absolute truth about all writing is this: As good as something is, there are always ways to make it better.

Before you play your material for anyone, make sure that you've done as much as you possibly can with your rhymes, alliteration, and vowels. When the lyrics speak to you, they'll speak to the listener as well.

The Least You Need to Know

- Try for pure rhymes first.
- Be constantly aware of inner rhymes.
- Keep in mind that the thought behind the lines counts most.
- Learn the basic rhyme schemes used by the pros.
- Alliteration gives your material a flow and polish.
- Lyrics have to sound like honest, colloquial human speech.

Chapter **6**

Repetition and Hooks

In This Chapter

♦ Simplify your style with repetition

♦ Factor in the tempo

♦ Improve your hook consciousness

♦ Add magic with riffs and figures

The core of all popular music is repetition. A song may repeat only one note or one lyric line or, more commonly, an entire section. The importance of repetition can never be emphasized too strongly, because composers, particularly new ones, tend to resist it. In their quest for originality, they drop basic form, as though adopting a structure will compromise their art. They often come up with tuneful themes and then replace them, never to return to the melody they started with!

When people complain that they can't sing a song, it's because the tune is difficult or even impossible to remember. Repetition can make your songs more memorable and, as a happy consequence, more likely to become hits.

Styles of Musical Repetition

You can work miracles within a tight, organized framework. Some familiar ways repetition can be applied include the ones illustrated in the following figure.

Samples of repetition.

(© Joel Hirschhorn)

Hirschhorn's Hints

Generally, the title phrase is repeated. There are a few exceptions to this rule: Bob Dylan's "Rainy Day Women #12 & 35" never repeats the title, even though another line within that song, "everybody must get stoned" is emphasized repeatedly. John Denver's "Annie's Song" also avoids the title. But most of the time, the title is hammered home, because it represents the song's main theme and idea.

As a new writer, I once told Irwin Schuster, an A&R (artists and repertory) man at Screen Gems Music, that I was afraid I would bore the audience if I repeated the title too much. His answer: "You can *never* repeat it too much, not in pop music."

The Strength of Simplicity

Simplicity allows people to hum, whistle, and sing songs after one or two listens. Simplicity equals *repetition*. This formula pertains equally to a Broadway standard and a rock song, whether the song is Webber and Rice's "Jesus Christ Superstar" or an early 1950s hit such as "Maybe Baby," with this catchy opener:

> Maybe baby, I'll have you
> Maybe baby, you'll be true
> Maybe baby, I'll have you for me

Lyrical Lingo

Repetition can refer to one note, full lines, or a complete verse. When an entire section is repeated, this section is known as the song's hook.

A **hook** is also known as a chorus, but professional songwriters prefer to call it a hook. The hook can be a catchy main section without the title, but most of the time the title is part of it. Secondary elements can serve as additional hooks—a repeated instrumental figure, a repetitive vocal line from the background singers, a sound such as oob la di oob la da or sha na na. But the main hook is a full section following the verse that almost always contains the title.

Paul McCartney made sure listeners would remember his title when he sang the phrase "band on the run" four times in a row!

Repeat Hits

When repetition is skillfully utilized, it can produce songs that become hits two or three times. Goffin and King's "The Loco-Motion" was a gold record in 1962 for newcomer Little Eva (their daughter's baby-sitter) and reappeared at the top of the charts 12 years later with Grand Funk Railroad. A third version by Kylie Minogue reached number three in 1988. This rousing dance record kept repeating, "Come on, baby, do the Loco-Motion." Diana Ross and Phil Collins benefited from the repetition of the title "You Can't Hurry Love," which was a number-one smash for both of them.

Repetition and Tempo

When a tune races ahead quickly, keep the lyrics simple. That's why there are so many repetitive sha-na-nas, tra-la-las, and doo-wop-doo-wops when tempos pick up steam. On a tune such as "Stayin' Alive" by The Bee Gees, the rhythm plunges ahead rapidly, so the words are simple, and the title repeats unceasingly. The words can be more varied and sophisticated when the tempo is slow, because listeners have time to digest them.

Hooking the Audience

It doesn't matter if the material is pop, country, R&B, hip-hop, hard rock, soft rock, punk rock, Latin, or adult contemporary: The lifeblood of a song is its *hook*. Hook is a perfect word for pop writing. A pop song doesn't seduce, coax, or invite; it hooks people with an assertive, repeating demand.

You don't have to open a song with a hook, but for chart insurance, Berry Gordy, founder of Motown, used to urge his writers to jump in hook first. Number one was Gordy's goal, and he once referred to number nine on the charts as a major disappointment and number twenty-eight as "dismal."

A hook is often based on a sound, such as "Hi-De-Ho" by Blood, Sweat and Tears, "Be-Bop-a-Lula" by Gene Vincent, and Al Green's "Sha-La-La." Other songs with outstanding hooks include 50 Cent's "In Da Club" (Give me a hug), Hanson's "MMMBop," Beck's swinging guitars and keyboards throughout "The Devil's Haircut," the "voopah voopah voopah—Slim Shady!" noise in Eminem's "My Name Is …," and the "Stacy's mom has got it goin' on!" chorus in Fountains of Wayne's "Stacy's Mom."

The ideal hook contains three elements:

- ◆ A danceable, pulsating rhythm

- ◆ A melody that sticks in people's minds after one listen

- ◆ A lyric that propels the story forward

Hooking the Emotions

A hook line has to connect with all the senses. If you were to take a sentence such as "I should brush my teeth" or "It's time to do the dishes" and base your song around that phrase, no great performance or explosive orchestration could rescue it. An outstanding hook always puts across the song's basic, overall point of view. Hooks should represent the most powerful part of your lyric and melody. For example, "Dancing in the Street" by Martha and the Vandellas sought to combine exuberance, a sense of celebration, and a feeling of future hope; the pounding hook captured all three.

It doesn't matter what kind of emotion you're projecting, as long as that emotion deeply affects people. In Sting's "Every Breath You Take," the hook line, "I'll be watching you," conveys suspicion and paranoia. The melody here is more low-key and insinuating. It portrays the feeling of a lover's desperation and creates a strong setup for the rest of the song.

"Killing Me Softly with His Song," written by Charles Fox and Norman Gimbel, is gentler and more subdued than the previous two songs, but the effect is just as forceful. The spare, guitar-driven arrangement and Roberta Flack's sensitive vocal brought out all the emotions felt by someone who finds herself falling in love at first sight.

Lyricist Gimbel knew that the words in a hook had to be vivid. When Johnny Mercer commented, after first hearing the song, that the word "killing" was too shocking and tonally

Trouble Clef

Don't let your focus on a hook mislead you into thinking that the rest of the song doesn't matter. Writers often give short shrift to the second verse in particular, figuring the hook will compensate. Keep this in mind: Every part of the song has to be worked over and made as strong as possible.

Hirschhorn's Hints

Listen to songs in your car (or when you're walking or riding the bus). Gerry Goffin felt he could tell if a song had a hit hook and lyric if he listened to it on the car radio. He never listened at home. It was just something about the resonance of the car that caught the sound of a hit single.

Hirschhorn's Hints

To emphasize and hammer home the hook, writers like to attach a strong, rising section right before it begins. This section is called a pre-chorus. It's not mandatory, but pre-choruses are riveting announcements that the big musical wave is coming. Whenever you feel a pre-chorus works comfortably within your song's context, you should consider using it.

harsh, Gimbel obeyed his instincts and used the word he believed in. He had enough confidence not to emasculate the hook and make it tame.

Marvin Gaye's "What's Goin' On" is a definitive example of the hook as chant. "What's Goin' On" he cries over and over again, with increasing despair, to a world brimming with prejudice and hostility.

The test of a top-notch hook is its ability to exist without verses, bridge, or orchestral icing. A good hook should have tremendous impact and stand completely alone.

If you write a hook first, you know right away if you have something special. You've established the story, the rhythmic feel, and the song's crucial repetitive element.

Developing Your Hook Consciousness

Try thinking in hooks. As a practice exercise, listen to the radio and ignore everything except the hook. Treat the radio dial as you would your television remote; stay on a pop station for a couple of songs, and then switch to country for a few more. After that, move to R&B. Scan an oldies program. Cover all genres. Do this for an hour a day, listening to nothing but the hooks.

This exercise will develop and sharpen your hook consciousness. It will simplify any tendency you have to wander and ramble. Then listen to CDs you have, one or two in each style. Play the hooks over and over again. Listen to them a couple of times, without analyzing anything. Once the general hook is in your head, concentrate on individual notes and words. What is repeated? How many times? If you can write music, write the hooks down. If you can't notate music, write down the lyrics from each hook you hear.

Ask yourself what the hooks contain that catch your ear most powerfully. What, in your opinion, makes them special?

Creating and Testing Your Hooks

Sing the hooks you've heard without backing yourself up on an instrument. Get a sense of how simple they are and how little they depend on chords and arrangements to be appreciated. In writing your own hooks, do the same thing. Never think this thought: It may not sound perfect just now, but when it's produced or an arrangement is added, it will be just right. If the hook doesn't work without embellishment, you need to re-examine it, rewrite it, or discard it.

Verse vs. Hook

The verse and the hook (chorus) are from the same family, but you must never make them so similar that no distinction exists. It's always better to hear the complaint, "I can remember the hook, but not the verse," than to hear someone express the opposite thought. Make sure the chords don't fall in exactly the same places, and that the rhythms differ. The lack of contrast between verse and hook will cost you a hit, even if you're lucky enough to land an important artist and get top promotion.

Instrumental Breaks

Instrumental breaks allow musicians to let loose. Sometimes these breaks are spontaneous creations in the studio. Other times the composer works out every note with care. But either way, the instrumental break allows room for another hook. It can be utilized in the intro or repeated at the end. It can become part of a background chorus. When writing your song, keep its value in mind.

Sleep on It

In the rapturous rush of a completed first draft, you'll tend to love what you've written. My advice is to get away from it for a while and re-evaluate your masterpiece the next morning. You may still be impressed with your own brilliance; you may even feel that the work is better than you originally thought. But you may also notice notes, words, or chords that could benefit from rewriting. When that happens, don't be depressed. With the clarity of distance, you'll be able to make the song far better.

What Hooks Your Friends?

When your friends listen to music, what hooks them? What do they respond to? Your job, as a commercial songwriter, is to develop a keen awareness of what appeals to other people. Even though you must stay true to yourself, you're also writing for the public.

Keep in mind that before your song reaches the ears of the public, it has to win the approval of radio program directors who decide what music will be aired and emphasized. The song must be immediately singable or it will never be added to a Top 40 playlist. Occasional exceptions are made for icons like Whitney Houston or Madonna, but even superstars have a tough time if they don't offer a memorable hook. Today, more than ever, program directors are conscious of ratings. They were never risk-takers, but in this era, the word *risk* is poison.

Tell Yourself the Truth

Remember: Your friends and family are your public. So are your children and your nieces and nephews. You don't want intellectual reaction or analysis of your work; you want to judge the emotional response. If you're honest with yourself, you can always tell the difference between "It's nice" and genuine excitement. Don't be so self-protective that you program your pals to react the way you want them to. Don't start out by saying, "I wrote a new song you're going to love." People, particularly family members, take their cues from the need you project.

Criticism is tough to take. We all want our work to receive unqualified praise. I used to think, after I won my Oscars, that I would have less difficulty accepting negative reaction, that success had insulated me against hurt feelings. My shell is a little tougher now, but if friends give me a less-than-ecstatic reaction, I still feel as though one of my children has been criticized. When that happens, I try to keep my main goal in mind: I need the truth so I can improve my work and win world acceptance for my songs.

Instrumental Icing: Figures and Riffs

A song is a blend of melody and lyrics, and many songs have succeeded by coasting on these two components alone. But the real magic comes when you add *figures* and *riffs*. Publisher Irving Mills of Mills Music once referred to them as "the golden glue."

Lyrical Lingo

Figures and **riffs** are both short melodic or rhythmic phrases. A figure is nearly always repeated throughout the song, often serving as an extra hook. A riff, on the other hand, can be utilized once or twice without appearing throughout.

Don't make the mistake of saying, "Figures and riffs aren't my job. They're the job of the arranger or producer." Anyone who studies hooks and develops an acute case of hook consciousness will be cured of that attitude.

Figure on Catchy Figures

Stevie Wonder's "Superstition" supplies a rocking guitar intro that repeats after every line in the song. This record wouldn't have had half the impact without Wonder's superb guitar riff.

Lennon and McCartney based many of their early tunes on riffs. Think of "Day-tripper," and you'll hear the repetitive 11-note riff in your mind before you hear the melody. "You Keep Me Hangin' On" achieves immortality through its SOS figure.

These records all have unforgettable, built-in background figures:

> "Enter Sandman" by Metallica (J. Hetfield, L. Ulrich, and K. Hammett)
>
> "Smells Like Teen Spirit" by Nirvana (K. Cobain, K. Novoselic, and D. Grohl)
>
> "All Night Long (All Night)" by Lionel Richie (L. Richie)
>
> "Fame" by Irene Cara (M. Gore and D. Pitchford)
>
> "Live and Let Die" by Paul McCartney (P. McCartney and L. Eastman)
>
> "Take My Breath Away" by Berlin (G. Moroder and T. Whitlock)
>
> "Livin' La Vida Loca" by Ricky Martin (D. Child and R. Rosa)

Sampling

Sampling means taking a part of one record and using it again as an integral part of another. Puff Daddy got rich snipping Sting's "Every Breath You Take" chorus. The Primitive Radio Gods sampled B. B. King's "How Can You Get" chorus, and made a huge modern-rock hit out of "Standing Outside a Broken Phone Booth with Money in My Hand." The drum line of Led Zeppelin's "When the Levee Breaks" showed up in songs by Erasure, The Beastie Boys, and Mike Oldfield.

Write Cool Riffs

Rock fans treasure the wailing sax in Leiber and Stoller's comedic Coasters recording "Yakety Yak." Whether it's a movie tune such as "What's New, Pussycat? (wa-wa-wa-wa)"; or George Harrison's "My Sweet Lord," with its repetitive and romantic guitar riff; added words, notes, and sounds become fresh, delightful hooks of their own.

In other words, you can't have too many hooks! After a while, it becomes an enjoyable game to see how many you can include. Try writing a tune that contains the following hook elements:

Backstage Banter

A famous music publisher used to give his staff writers an assignment: to write a song and think of as many hooks as possible, both lyrically and melodically. He wouldn't accept less than 10, and someone on the staff would occasionally come up with 15 or more.

- The hook verse itself
- A vocal part that keeps repeating in every verse
- A bass part that repeats every other bar
- A guitar part that opens the record and then repeats in every hook section
- A recurring piano figure
- The lead vocalist doing a high, recurring falsetto part

The following figure illustrates how it can be done.

"Nobody Knows How Much" (Joel Hirschhorn). A 32-bar computer-generated song demonstrating four hooks, a recurring piano figure, and a recurring falsetto part for the lead vocalist.

(© Joel Hirschhorn)

Always remember what people say when they like something: "I can't forget it." "I can't stop singing it." "I heard it in my dreams." "I found myself whistling it." If you can write unforgettable, repetitive hooks, your songs will always attract the attention of artists and producers.

The Least You Need to Know

◆ Repetition of lyrics, notes, or whole sections of the song simplify the song and make it more memorable.

◆ Keep the hook simple.

◆ When the tempo of the tune is rapid, keep the lyrics simple.

◆ Put as many figures and riffs in your songs as possible.

Chapter 7

Melodies and Chords

In This Chapter

♦ The elements of an appealing melody

♦ Chord progressions of Top 100 songs

♦ Rhythms that drive the chords

♦ Prosody, the marriage of words and music

What is a good melody? Opinions and tastes vary, but a melody with popular appeal is usually …

♦ Singable.

♦ Easy to remember.

♦ Based on a pleasing chord pattern.

♦ A combination of creatively arranged notes on top of a captivating rhythm.

♦ A blend of intervals that mix innovation with a sense of the familiar.

Successful popular melodies can be different, but not *too* different. A few adventuresome, daring chords can be included that take the listener by surprise. These chords are a dash of color that make the melody special, but the rest of the chords should be comfortably familiar to the listener's ear. The same applies to rhythm. You can slip in a 5/4 or 7/4 bar rather than the more typical 2/4 or 4/4. But put in too many of them, and you have jazz, not pop music. Danceability is always a major factor in commercial songs.

What Makes a Tune Singable?

A melody consists of intervals, which are the distances between one pitch and another. The choice of appealing intervals determines whether your song makes an impression with the mass audience. A major second (C to D) leaping to an augmented octave (C to C-sharp) would be likely to alienate your public. But a major third (C to E) moving to a perfect fifth (C to G) is something listeners can greet with enthusiasm.

Record buyers automatically embrace certain chord progressions. These buyers don't intellectually know why particular chord patterns draw them in; the response is emotional.

The following chord progressions are used in Top 100 songs. Without attempting to analyze which songs they provide foundations for, write your own tunes over them. Do this with other progressions you hear on the air or have on sheet music. It will sharpen your commercial ear immeasurably.

- G Em Am Am C/D D7
- C C/Bb Am7 D7/F# C/G (F/G G7) C
- F F F/E Dm7 G7 C F F/E Dm7 G7 C
- Ema7 Ema7 F#m7 F#m7 C
- Ema7 Ema7 F#m7 F#m7 A B A B A B E
- Am Dm G Cma7 Fma7 Bm7-5 E7 E7
- C Cma7 F C Cma7 F
- C G (Am F) (C G) (F C/E Dm7 C)
- D D G A A7 A7 D
- Cma7 Cma7 Am7 Am7 A7 A7 D
- Cma7 Cma7 Am7 Am7 Dm7 Dm7 Fm7 F/G
- C Em7 Fma7 Fma7 Em7 Fma7 Fma7

- C C G G G G C C

- C7 F Bb C7 F

- Gm C7 F F Gm7 C7 F

- Eb F7/Eb Fm7 Bb7 Eb

- D D/F# G Bm Em D/F# C G

- G A7 D7 G

- Eb Fm7 Bb7 Fm7 Bb7 Eb

- D A7 Bm D/A Gma7

- C G7 C G7 C E7 Am E7

- C#m C#m B C#m

- F F Fma7 Fma7 Bb Bb C C

- Eb Ab Ab Gm Eb Ab Gm Ab

- D A/C# G A D

- F#m D A F#m D A

- Db F7 Bbm Gb Db Ab7 Db

Reliable Rhythms

Chords and intervals are two thirds of the puzzle; rhythm is the support system that gives those chords a groove and makes them pulse with excitement.

The following figures show examples of frequently used, always reliable rhythms. These rhythms should be studied, played, and internalized. When you're running through them, learn the range of moods they can convey by picking varying numbers on a metronome and getting to know how the rhythms sound in all tempos.

Hirschhorn's Hints

Readers who want to learn more about chords should check out the *Complete Idiot's guide to Music Theory*, by Michael Miller. Miller provides a complete, concise, and helpful overview of the subject.

Hirschhorn's Hints

A good rhythmic groove can be used in dozens of ways. If you play certain beats slowly, they convey an entirely different mood than if you play them in an upbeat manner.

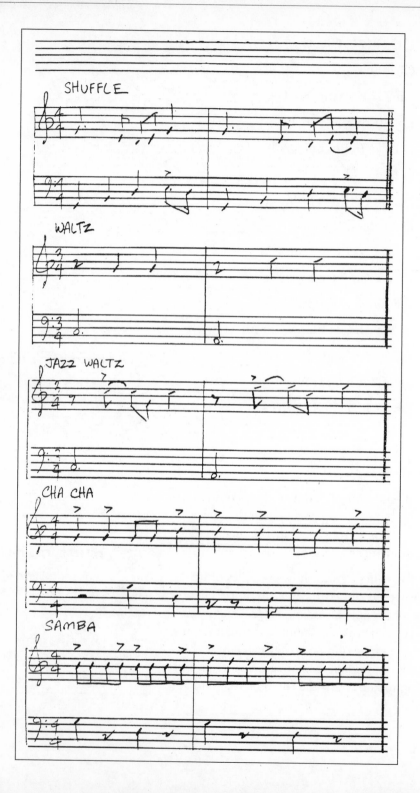

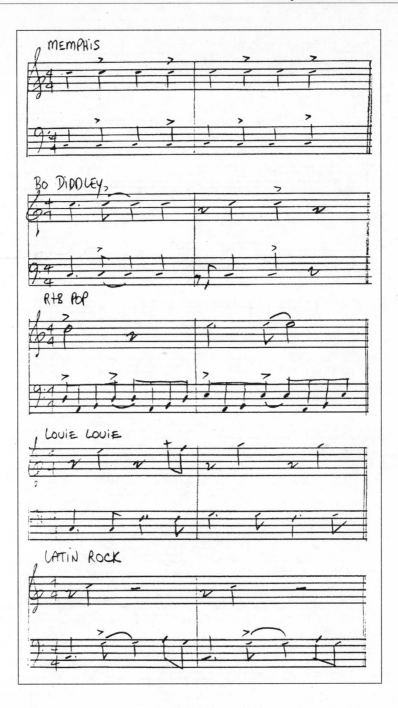

Frequently used grooves.

(All © Joel Hirschhorn)

Prosody

Now you have a tune that incorporates all the vital elements. But how does it match up with the lyrics? *Prosody*, the union of words and music, is like a marriage. When a powerful emotion is being expressed, it makes no sense to drop the notes or to keep them on one repetitive level.

Lyrical Lingo

Prosody is the proper, seamless blending of words and music.

Music's basic function in a song is to dramatize the words that are being sung. When lyrics are put to a melody, the same applies in reverse: The words dramatize the melody.

Consider the song "When You Wish Upon a Star," and how effectively it uses octave leaps. The octave leap on *you* has a plaintive, yearning quality. Then again, on the word *no* in the phrase "Makes no difference," the octave leap appears again. The emotional level of the song and the lyric is powerfully heightened by these two perfectly chosen dramatic intervals. The following figure illustrates some examples of logical, effective prosody.

You Gotta Shop Around

What's the most intense thought in a line? Make sure you emphasize that emotion. Don't place your most powerful interval leaps on undramatic words. For example,

Hirschhorn's Hints

Think of yourself as a singer at all times. Imagine yourself onstage, facing a huge audience. Unless your words and music project excitement, you'll quickly lose the audience's attention. Sing each line individually when you've completed a draft. Do it several times. Each line is crucial to the overall impact.

"I went shopping today," doesn't scream out for melodic melodrama, unless, of course, someone robbed the store while you were at the checkout stand. Use common sense.

There are no hard-and-fast rules in prosody, just your own artistic judgment. Sometimes the sadness in a heartbreaking line is dramatized best by going up, rather than down. Other times, a sense of joy can come across more vividly if the interval dips. The true test is if the prosody moves you. If you're not personally moved by what you're writing, no one else will be, either.

Examples of prosody.

(All © Joel Hirschhorn)

Do a Prosody Search

Analyze all the current hits. How are the emotional effects achieved? After listening a few times, make note of the most emotional lyrics in the song. How does the melody highlight them? Do the notes go up or down? Ask yourself why the composer and lyricist made the choices they did. This exercise will help you to improve your prosody with amazing speed.

The Least You Need to Know

- ◆ The more interesting your chord progression, the better your chances are for a hit.

- ◆ Rhythm is just as vital as melody.

- ◆ Prosody is a key element to the overall emotion of the song. Develop a habit of analyzing prosody whenever you hear a new song.

Part 3

Working with Genres

All good songs follow certain rules, but each genre has its own individual characteristics. This part shows you what elements go into outstanding country, R&B, and rap songs, as well as Christian and Latin pop. You'll gain understanding of the elements that go into commercials, children's songs, and theater musicals, and learn how to write film tunes that work within movies *and* function as hits outside the picture.

Chapter 8

Pop and Rock Music

In This Chapter

- ◆ Hooks in pop music
- ◆ Styles of pop classics
- ◆ The optimism of pop lyrics
- ◆ Mixing and matching genres
- ◆ Heavy metal, grunge, adult contemporary, and dance music

Pop is a catch-all phrase for a genre that appeals to the largest possible audience. Many people try to pin it down to a clear definition, but the beauty of the form is its eclectic, elusive appeal.

Before the dawn of rock music, pop songs were products of Broadway and Hollywood, or the brainchildren of freelance Tin Pan Alley composers and lyricists. By the '50s, however, the arena had grown large enough to encompass rock and roll, and a new kind of pop was born—a simple, intensely driving blend of rock, blues, and country.

In the '60s, such terms as pop rock, country rock, and folk rock started to surface. Pop was like a huge wave, flowing out and embracing every other genre. Pop's rock cousins continue to make a significant impact: heavy metal, grunge, dance pop (listed as Adult/Club Play in *Billboard*) and Adult Contemporary (now listed by *Billboard* as Adult Top 40).

The Elements of Good Pop

Good pop songs usually share several characteristics, as explained in the following sections.

Hooks

All commercial music genres require a hook, but nowhere is it as vital as in a pop song. Whether you're listening to records by such varied artists as Christina Aguilera, Mary J. Blige, Justin Timberlake, Linkin Park, Metallica, 50 Cent, Maroon 5, Norah Jones, Beyoncé, or the Dixie Chicks, the hook section jumps out at you.

Overall Style

Pop is geared to a huge audience that likes its music exciting, but without a raw, harsh edge. The top songs of each decade illustrate this: "Hey Jude" (The Beatles, '60s); "You Light Up My Life" (Debby Boone, '70s); "Physical (Olivia Newton-John, '80s); and "One Sweet Day" (Mariah Carey & Boyz II Men, '90s).

Hirschhorn's Hints _____

More than any other genre, the lifeblood of pop is hit singles. Groups who write for themselves and produce their own albums can stretch out beyond pop boundaries, and sometimes their CDs succeed brilliantly without singles to drive them forward. But a pop album must have hit singles, which further emphasizes the necessity for pop stars to have three or four cuts in each album that are accessible to practically every taste.

Lyrics with Universal Appeal

The Grammy nominations of several love songs demonstrate that the most successful pop music takes on topics with widespread emotional appeal, such as loneliness, heartbreak, desperation, and enduring love: "Unbreak My Heart" (Toni Braxton), "I Will Always Love You" (Whitney Houston), "I Swear" (All-In-One), and "Harder to Breathe" (Maroon 5). "I love you," "I want you back," and "I can't live without you" are staple themes in pop.

Although angry protest is not as prevalent as it was in the '60s, it still flourishes in the form of Toby Keith's country hit "Courtesy of the Red, White and Blue." But generally, anything too startling, shocking, or sordid is the province of non-pop productions, or in albums by metal and punk groups. This is not to say that music with a harsh, raw edge such as that of Nirvana, Metallica, and N.W.A. hasn't made an impact, but pop (particularly pop singles) undergoes a softening process to make it palatable to the vast public. Even the tragedy of Marilyn Monroe is diluted in Elton John/Bernie Taupin's "Candle on the Wind."

Titles from *Billboard*'s Top 25 hits from the 1990s show the relatively safe, audience-friendly nature of pop.

Recommended Listening

The following are selections from number-one pop records from the 1990s. They are worth studying because they had such impact on so many millions of listeners:

- "Smooth" by Santana featuring Rob Thomas
- "(Everything I Do) I Do It For You" by Bryan Adams
- "The Sign" by Ace of Base
- "End of the Road" by Boyz II Men
- "Waterfalls" by TLC
- "I Swear" by All-4-One
- "Dreamlover" by Mariah Carey
- "Jump" by Kris Kross
- "I'll Be Missing You" by Puff Daddy and Faith Evans
- "Take a Bow" by Madonna

> **Backstage Banter**
>
> "I Don't Want to Miss a Thing" was a pop smash for rock group Aerosmith and equally successful on the country chart when sung by Kenny Chesney. Country star Tim McGraw had a hit with Elton John's "Tiny Dancer."

Combining Genres—a Hybrid of Styles

You'll find Latin, R&B, gospel, and country influences in pop records. Although *Billboard* divides pop music into separate genre-specific charts—Hot R&B/Hip-Hop, Hot Latin, Hot Dance, Hot Country, many of the cuts on these charts also occupy a prominent place on the Hot 100, *Billboard's* weekly chart of the 100 most popular hits.

Pop offers writers the freedom to mix and match styles any way they please, as long as the melodic hooks and lyrics are powerful. The pop songwriter has to develop an innate sense of how far he or she can go. Pop songs can't be too long, nor can they ramble self-indulgently. They can certainly have a touch of edginess, but nothing that will divide or offend the vast buying public.

Backstage Banter

Motown Records' Berry Gordy was a master at juxtaposing the funky and the slickly traditional, often pairing driving bass lines with rich, melodic strings. He gave his records a "safe" label, "The Sound of Young America," and consciously minimized the tougher aspects of blues and gospel. He made his records appealing to every record buyer. The Motown formula triumphed even when The Beatles and the British invasion came along. It stands as a perfect example of pop thinking and an understanding of the broad requirements of the pop market.

Rock Genres

Rock 'n' roll is a musical umbrella that incorporates a variety of genres such as: heavy metal, grunge, adult contemporary, dance pop, punk rock, reggae, and disco.

Hirschhorn's Hints

When you write an album, don't just think in terms of singles, concentrating on one piece of material and allowing the rest of the songs to be throwaways or carbon copies of each other. Rick Nielsen of Cheap Trick points with pride to the fact that his group has always been an "album band," with each cut of superior quality.

Heavy Metal

The powerfully amplified electric guitar was a superstar from the beginning in heavy metal, a genre that took the rock world by storm in the late '60s. Led Zeppelin was an early pioneer, building and sustaining its position as one of the classic metal bands. Metallica, Guns N' Roses, Black Sabbath, Linkin Park, Limp Bizkit, and Korn kept the pace going. Long after the public thought Metallica, among other metal bands, had peaked, they showed their amazing endurance and popularity with a record-breaking 2003 summer tour, provoking Rick Franks,

Regional VP of Clear Channel Entertainment, to label them "the best hard rock band on the planet."

Although metal hits have occasionally made it on the Hot 100, metal and pop typically kept to themselves. The metal genre often tackles themes such as obsession with death, drug tragedies, and mental illness. Metallica's debut album, *Kill 'Em All*, makes this image clear, as do lines like "veins that suck with fear." The group's "Disposable Heroes" is a wrenching study of a soldier dying in battle.

Embodying the basic attitude of most metal groups is rebellion against conformity, exemplified by Metallica's "Damage, Inc" with the words "following our instinct, not a trend—go against the grain until the end."

Musical Characteristics

Beyond the chaotically fast-paced, gymnastic guitar parts and solos, high-pitched, wailing vocals, and walloping backbeats, metal bassists offer thunderous riffs and drummers let loose with protracted solos.

Feedback is an ear-splitting given, and any device necessary to distort the sound is utilized.

Recommended Listening

- AC/DC: *Back in Black*
- Iron Maiden: *Peace of Mind*
- Judas Priest: *Screaming for Vengeance*
- Guns N' Roses: *Appetite for Destruction*
- Metallica: *Master of Puppets*
- Ozzy Osbourne: *Diary of a Madman*
- Venom: *Black Metal*
- KISS: *Destroyer*
- Black Sabbath: *Paranoid*
- Slayer: *Reign in Blood*
- Korn: *Untouchables*
- Queens of the Stone Age: *Songs for the Deaf*
- Megadeth: *So Far, So Good … So What!*

Grunge

One of Seattle's proudest musical claims is the emergence of Nirvana, three punk rockers who came to be known as definitive representatives of the grunge music scene to American adolescents, from their 1991 debut album to the present day.

Nirvana's album, *Nevermind*, shot to number one and yielded "Smells Like Teen Spirit." They also scored with "Come As You Are," and "Lithium." "Smells Like Teen Spirit" was, in the words of the group's bassist Krist Novoselic, "a call to consciousness." Built on a four-chord sequence, it was written rapidly, and after three takes, the group chose the second take as the master release.

Musical Characteristics

Grunge is an explosive, dissonant pairing of metal and punk. Along with the provocative and tragic image of Nirvana's Kurt Cobain, grunge's legacy is maintained by Stone Temple Pilots, Pearl Jam, Smashing Pumpkins, Mudhoney, Local H., and Audioslave. A genre that features slamming, powerful drums and nasty, hyped-up guitar, it expresses an angry, contemptuous attitude toward middlebrow culture and values.

The influence of 1970s hard rockers such as KISS and Black Sabbath can be heard when listening to grunge music.

Backstage Banter

Whenever Kurt Cobain would write straightforward, conventionally beautiful melodies, he refused to put them on tape. He wanted to hide and squash his pop sensibility, but despite the efforts he made to present only punk rage and alienation to the world, his melodies come across loud and clear, particularly in *MTV Unplugged in New York*, an all-acoustic album that shows off Cobain's best songwriting and melodies.

Recommended Listening

- Nirvana: *In Utero*
- Stone Temple Pilots: *Purple*
- Alice in Chains: *Greatest Hits*
- Alice in Chains: *Dirt*
- Pearl Jam: *Ten*

- Soundgarden: *Superunknown*
- Nirvana: *Nevermind*
- Stone Temple Pilots: *Core*
- The Melvins: *Stoner Witch*
- Mudhoney: *Superfuzz Bigmuff*

Adult Contemporary

The mellowest form of pop and rock, adult contemporary (AC) selections are targeted toward those millions who prefer their pop on the mellow side.

Musical Characteristics

Adult contemporary stresses accessible melody and easily remembered hooks, but it's far more biting now than in the '60s when Frank Sinatra, the Carpenters, Barbra Streisand, and Bread were typical representatives of the form.

Pop, soul, and country, once off-limits to adult contemporary playlists containing Ray Conniff and Ferrante and Teicher are now vital parts of AC programming.

Recommended Listening

- Michelle Branch: *Are You Happy Now?*
- Kelly Clarkson: *Miss Independent*
- Jewel: *Intuition*
- Live: *Heaven*
- Josh Kelley: *Amazing*
- John Mayer: *Bigger Than My Body*
- Liz Phair: *Why Can't I?*
- Santana featuring Chad Kroeger: *Why Don't You and I*

Dance Pop

When it comes to dance pop, the beat is everything. If you have a hot, exciting track, some of the most surprising artists can get on the dance charts.

Jennifer Lopez, Beyoncé, and Justin Timberlake are likely dance record contenders, but when a groove is properly nailed, the featured performer can be a theatre star like Linda Eder (*Jekyll and Hyde*), who made the Top 20 with "I Am What I Am" (Dance Mixes), or Sarah Brightman (*Phantom of the Opera*).

Also worth noting as representatives of Electronic dance pop are Basement Jaxx, Moby, and Fatboy Slim.

Trouble Clef

Jewel warns new singers and bands that the producer/artist relationship is an individual thing, and the chemistry has to be right. She wants her own ideas, sensibilities, and tastes on the entire record, and insists on working with someone who doesn't fight with her creatively about the spotlight.

Musical Characteristics

Such hit dance titles as "Crazy In Love" and "All Night Long" make it clear that the words have to be direct, uncomplicated, and emotional. An infectious hook is a must, with a couple of catchphrases that are hammered out over and over.

If you want to write a dynamite dance record, hang out at clubs and watch people move. It will get your heart jumping and rev up your sense of rhythm to the highest pitch. Then listen to dance albums.

Study the mixes carefully. This is a case where words may go by the wayside. Tune your ear to the drum and guitar, and balance your own demo mixes the same way.

Recommended Listening

- Junior Senior: *Move Your Feet*
- Milky: *Just the Way You Are*
- Madonna: *Die Another Day* (Remixes)
- Jewel: *Intuition* (Remixes)
- Jennifer Lopez: *I'm Glad* (Remixes)
- The Postal Service: *The District Sleeps Alone Tonight*
- Paul Van Dyk featuring Hemstock & Jennings: *Nothing But You*
- The Roc Project featuring Tina Arena: *Never (Past Tense)*
- DJ Icey: *A Little Louder*
- Sting: *Send Your Love*
- Fatboy Slim: *The Rockefeller Shank*

Other Genres

The following genres aren't commercially dominant enough to be awarded special *Billboard* charts, but their influence is still strongly felt in contemporary music.

- **Punk Rock.** Represented by The Sex Pistols, The New York Dolls, The MC5, The Clash, The Ramones, The Talking Heads, The Strokes, The Vines, The Yeah Yeah Yeahs, The Donnas, The Libertines, Bad Religion, Social Distortion, Green Day, and Offspring. A loud, repetitive musical anti-reaction to assembly-line rock forms and what punkers considered a dead, meaningless rock establishment.

- **Reggae.** The foundation of reggae music is rasta, music which combined Caribbean styles and R&B. Other ingredients include drum bands, plantation work songs, and a form named *mento*. Some well-known reggae songs include "Africa Is Paradise" and "Deliver Us." The genre is largely identified with Bob Marley, the first world-famous reggae superstar. Classic reggae artists include Burning Spear, Jimmy Cliff, Toots and the Maytals, and Lee "Scratch" Perry.

  Reggae, over the years, has morphed into "dancehall," responsible for many international smashes. Newer reggae pop artists with big recent hits include Shaggy and Sean Paul.

Lyrical Lingo

Mento is a Jamaican style blending African rhythms with Cuban rumba.

- **Disco.** An outgrowth of dance pop and funk that reigned throughout the 1970s. Disco was known for its powerhouse pop hooks and driving beat. Designed as party music, it reached statospheric heights of popularity with The Bee Gees' *Saturday Night Fever* score and soundtrack, and Donna Summer's singles, "Hot Stuff" and "Bad Girls." Other disco superstars: Loleatta Holloway and Jocelyn Brown. Disco has mutated over the years into house and dance music, then techno and electronica. It's still viable, represented in songs by Basement Jaxx and Junior Senior.

The beauty of pop is its versatility, its absorption of every musical form through the years. Pop songwriters from the pre-rock era were hemmed in with far more rigid guidelines, and today the top-selling pop artists range from Maroon 5 to Jagged Edge, Trapt to John Mayer, Luther Vandross to Clay Aiken. As long as these multiple genres are handled with craft, imagination, and a wide-open grasp of public taste and need, creative opportunities are limitless.

The Least You Need to Know

- ◆ Catchy, memorable hooks are a pop must.

- ◆ Pop lyrics must have a universal appeal.

- ◆ A pop writer has the freedom to mix rhythms and melodies from many genres when writing pop music.

- ◆ In addition to pop music, other successful rock genres are heavy metal, grunge, dance pop, and adult contemporary.

Country

In This Chapter

♦ Country goes pop

♦ Realism reigns

♦ Country's chord patterns stay simple

♦ A country collection that holds everything from honky-tonk to rock

Barbara Mandrell once sang, "I was country when country wasn't cool." Today, country is cooler than ever, from both an artistic and a financial point of view. If country music calls to you, then go for it! The opportunities to write songs and have them recorded have never been greater.

Country *Is* Cool

Country music, in its efforts to compete with rock for multiplatinum sales, has gone partially, and in some cases completely, pop. Garth Brooks initiated the process with his phenomenally successful songs, and records such as Faith Hill's "Breathe" are so completely pop that they're causing country purists to cry foul. Objections still linger about country's use of lush strings and synthesizers.

Hit-songwriters such as Diane Warren now concentrate on country songs as much as they do on rock music. Warren's acceptance by Nashville clearly announces that writers from Los Angeles, New York, or anywhere else can make their mark on the country charts. Her "How Do I Live?" became a simultaneous smash for Trisha Yearwood and LeAnn Rimes, and she has followed up with Mark Chesnutt's "I Don't Wanna Miss a Thing."

A Little Background

Scottish, Irish, and English settlers brought their folk music to the South in the eighteenth and nineteenth centuries, and these folk songs became the basis for country music. The first country recordings were released in the 1920s. Radio stations recognized the genre's appeal and brought it to a wide audience, courtesy of such artists as Jimmie Rodgers and the Carter Family.

A pack of independent recording labels opened up in late 1940s Nashville: Nashboro, Republic, Excello, Dot, Bullet, and Tennessee. As recording activity proliferated and the *Grand Ole Opry* achieved fame, booking agencies and music publishers made the city their base of operations. The area on the southwest side of town that spawned this accelerating country world got the name Music Row.

Lyrical Lingo

The **Grand Ole Opry,** which started in 1926, is the longest-running radio broadcast in history. An invitation to play the Opry certifies country performers or performer/writers as superstars. Great names associated with it include Minnie Pearl, Roy Acuff, and Bill Monroe.

Country sales were modest at first, and they sharply diminished with the advent of rock 'n' roll. Three producers, Columbia's Don Law, Decca's Owen Bradley, and RCA's Chet Atkins, decountrified much of the music by subtracting steel guitars and fiddles. Vocal choruses, rhythm sections, and eventually strings took the twangy edge off the sound, broadening country's national appeal.

Hirschhorn's Hints

Garth Brooks was the first country artist to sell a million copies. He brought country to a mass audience. Brooks's album, *Ropin' the Wind,* made its debut at the top of the pop charts. But at the beginning of his career, every label in Nashville refused to sign him. He had to make a living singing recordings of songs by other writers until Capitol Records recognized his potential. The message in his story is this: Don't give up. If you have something special, it will eventually be recognized.

Traditional country stylings featuring honky-tonk and mountain music still exist, but the pop influence, spearheaded by Garth Brooks, is unlikely to disappear. Nashville records always stayed firmly rooted on the country charts in the past. Now dozens of them are represented on *Billboard*'s Top 100.

The Currents of Country

To write country, you should be as familiar with Merle Haggard, Johnny Cash, and the Gatlin Brothers as you are with the Dixie Chicks, Kenny Chesney, Toby Keith, Tim McGraw, and Vince Gill. You should also have a basic understanding of the many ideas and emotions that make country what it is:

♦ **Honesty.** Whether pop-flavored or flat-out country, honesty is the key ingredient to Top 10 country music. This music is for the man on the street, without pretension and slickness. Country artists have no interest in lyrics and music that sound forced or fake.

♦ **Raw reality.** Country classics often reflect struggle. "Guitar Man," by Jerry Reed, follows the efforts of a guitarist to find success and the bitter rejections he receives. He sleeps in hobo jungles and bums a thousand miles of track. In another part of the lyric, Reed talks about nearly starving to death in Memphis, having run out of money and luck.

♦ **Down-to-earth drama.** Country is no place for fantasies. Tim McGraw contemplates the question of aging with his memorable "The Next 30 Years," and in "Middle-Age Crazy," the protagonist is 40 going on 20, with a "young thing beside him that just melts in his hands." The man in Bob McDill's "I May Be Used but I Ain't Used Up" strikes a positive note for older folks who still want to feel the pleasures of youth.

There's no self-delusion in country breakup songs, either. "Two Story House" tells of a couple who achieved fame and fortune, but despite the surface splendor, "there's no love about." Love is no simple matter in "When She Cries," because the protagonist has tried and failed to fulfill the dreams of his loved one, and sometimes in the night, he hears her crying. He wants to be the man that she deserves, and he dies a little each time she cries.

♦ **Honky-tonk heartache.** Stories of honky-tonk nightlife are *Grand Ole Opry* staples. In "Honky-Tonk Attitude," we hear about "tight pants, line dance, Stetson hats and cowboy boots" and the Friday nights when a man goes out with a honky-tonk attitude. Hank Williams Sr.'s classic "Honky-Tonk Blues" tells of a man who went to a dance, wore out his shoes, and then woke up in the morning wishing he could lose the honky-tonk blues. As he concludes, "Lord, I'm suf-ferin' with the honky-tonk blues."

♦ **Turning to the Lord.** Spirituality is a current that runs strongly through coun-try songs, as exemplifed by Clay Walker's "Jesus Was a Country Boy" and Rebecca Lynn Howard's "Jesus, Daddy and You."

♦ **Feelings that touch everyone.** Like pop music, country's lyrics often have a universal appeal and play to emotions that most of us experience at some time in our lives. "I'm Not Lisa," by Jessi Colter, touches that chord in all people who can't quite replace the person their lovers cared about before. Garth Brooks reminds us about our capacity for revenge when he sings, "Friends in Low Places," in which a rejected suitor shows up at his former girl's wedding and proceeds to wreak havoc.

♦ **Street poetry.** Country lyrics rely on visual imagery to shine. A good example is Johnny Russell's "Rednecks, White Sox, Blue Ribbon Beer." "Country State of Mind," by Hank Williams Jr., is a definitive example: The protagonist is chewin' on a hickory twig, asking someone to pass a bottle so he can have a swig. He ain't got a lot, but he's got it made in the shade, because he's in a "country state of mind."

The majority of country songs are miniature motion pictures. You, as a country writer, must draw every detail of the scene for the listeners so that they can see cracked paint on the walls, hear the railroad whistle, taste the food, and touch the people.

♦ **Dramatic overstatement.** Country lyrics don't hold back. When you're writing them, be as vividly emotional as the following:

Hirschhorn's Hints

You can't connect with country publishers or the public unless you dig deep down into yourself and the sources of your own pleas-ure and pain. Bob McDill, writer of 28 number-one country hits, says that country songs are more about loss and hurt than music, beat, or groove.

I was lying in the dark
Screaming to the wall
Praying I'd hear her footsteps in the hall
Dying for her touch
Aching for her smile
Desperately I grabbed the phone and I began to dial

♦ **Exquisite simplicity.** The greatest education country can give you, as a writer, is to avoid generalities and write specific visual details and actions. Country lyrics are stories, and your job is to create realistic, five-sense pictures. It can also teach you how to edit out over-blown phrases and shave your sentences down to exquisite simplicity. Lee Greenwood's "Going Going Gone," and "God Bless the USA," are perfect examples of this kind of simplicity.

◆ **Spoken dialogue.** When the words sound as though they just sprang into the protagonist's mind, you've reached the pinnacle of country composing. With urgency and immediacy, people in country songs confess, confide, share intimate feelings, and open up their souls to close friends or loved ones.

Trouble Clef _____

Just because country is frank, don't go overboard. A conservative, puritanical streak still runs through the country world. Garth Brooks wrote "kiss my ass" as part of a last verse for "Friends in Low Places," but the phrase never made it into the final song. "I'll Try," by Alan Jackson, originally said, "We both know damn well." The line eventually became "We both know too well."

◆ **Get loose and playful.** The lyrics in country music have a looseness and freedom about them. Alan Jackson's hit "Right on the Money" uses free-flowing imagery with "She's a three-point jump shot" and "She's the best cook that ever melted cheese." Tracy Byrd's "I'm from the Country" is verbally playful when he talks about sleeping in the hay because he's from the country and he likes it that way.

Many country titles have the same far-out playfulness. Consider "I'm Gonna Hire a Wino to Decorate My Home," in which the protagonist tells her alcoholic husband that she's made this decision so he'll be comfortable and won't feel the need to roam. Another product of an inventive imagination is "God Must Be a Cowboy." These off-center, tongue-in-cheek approaches are typical of much country music. A country writer doesn't say, "She's leaving me for him," when he can just as easily say, "That ain't my truck in her drive."

◆ **Turning clichés inside out.** A characteristic of country lyric writing is taking common expressions and bending them in a clever way. Dean Dillon's "Nobody in His Right Mind Would've Left Her" is a perfect example with its "right" and "left" references. Another good example is "If I Said You Had a Beautiful Body Would You Hold It Against Me?"

◆ **Say it straight out.** Country songs have an appealing, down-home directness. When you're coming up with ideas and titles and you want to break beyond conventional thinking, remember these classics: "Please, Daddy, Don't Get Drunk This Christmas," "Ruby, Don't Take Your Love to Town," and "You Make Me Want to Be a Mother."

Musical Elements of Country

Country music is a combination of different genres. You should be familiar with the ones in this list:

◆ **Honky-tonk.** This music is what most people think of when country music is mentioned; it uses steel guitars, fiddles, acoustic guitars, and vocals. Stars that kicked off the movement were Ernest Tubb, Al Dexter, and Hank Williams. George Jones and Lefty Frizzell were also highly admired practitioners of honky-tonk.

◆ **Country gospel.** This genre describes the sound of traditional country wed to spiritual lyrics.

◆ **Bluegrass.** The roots of modern country grew out of bluegrass, a style of music that blended fiddle, mandolin, and banjo with string bass and guitar accompaniment. Bill Monroe kept this traditional string music alive and flourishing. His band, The Blue Grass Boys, was responsible for the term "bluegrass." Earl Scruggs, Ricky Skaggs, and the Osborne Brothers are other bluegrass performers. Other notables: Alison Krauss, Del McCoury, and Ralph Stanley. Today's bluegrass is a diverse compilation of styles, incorporating Celtic music, rock 'n' roll, fusion jazz, and Southern gospel. Certifying the genre's current popularity was the hit bluegrass soundtrack that accompanied the surprise film hit, *O Brother, Where Art Thou?*

◆ **Hillbilly.** This term was the first definition used for country music derived from Tennessee, Kentucky, Virginia, West Virginia, and Southeastern Ohio. "Fiddlin'" John Carson, Henry Whitter, and Vernon Dahlert recorded hillbilly songs.

◆ **Alt Country.** An alternative genre spearheaded by rock musicians blending their rock 'n' roll roots with country. Alt-country representatives include Jeff Tweedy of Wilco, Son Volt, Lucinda Williams, and Steve Earle—all some of the best practicing songwriters today.

◆ **Western swing.** This music is a combination of string band music, blues, folk, jazz, and traditional pop melodies. Lyrics concentrated on the lives of cowboys and reached a zenith with Gene Autry and Roy Rogers. This genre attained a new popularity in the 1990s. Contemporary examples are Hot Club of Cowtown and Asleep at the Wheel.

- **Rockabilly.** This music served as the root for rock 'n' roll. A combination of rhythm and blues and hillbilly songs, Jerry Lee Lewis, Carl Perkins, Buddy Holly, and the Everly Brothers made it popular; Wayne Hancock and the Stray Cats carried on the tradition. Punk also had a serious rockabilly phase with the Blasters, X, Social Distortion, and Los Lobos in the early 1980s.

- **Country rock.** Country played by rock bands, with pop melodies, a strong backbeat, and powerful amplification typifies this genre. Neil Young, Gram Parsons, the Byrds, and Ryan Adams increased this genre's popularity.

- **Traditional country.** This country music has a distinctive twang and uncomplicated instrumentation. Ernest Tubb, Eddy Arnold, Hank Williams, and Roy Acuff played it and helped launch the *Grand Ole Opry*, the weekly radio program that came to represent country music to the world.

- **Country pop.** Here's a genre that consists of country-flavored rock 'n' roll songs such as "I Don't Wanna Miss a Thing" sung by Mark Chesnutt, "How Do I Live?" by Trisha Yearwood, and "Wide Open Spaces" by the Dixie Chicks. The advent of rock 'n' roll and its wildfire success encouraged country to absorb more pop influences. This pop Nashville sound smoothed out the rough edges of the earlier country records, and by the 1970s country recordings were more accessible to a wide noncountry audience.

- **Outlaw country.** David Allan Coe, Merle Haggard, Willie Nelson, Waylon Jennings, and Johnny Cash are representatives of this genre, which emphasizes smaller bands and acoustic instruments. A 1980s influx, featuring Steve Earle, Lyle Lovett, and Randy Travis, led to the Garth Brooks revolution of the early '90s.

- **R&B, gospel, and folk.** These music genres are mixed into the country brew for color, as demonstrated by Ray Charles's classic album, *Modern Sounds in Country and Western Music*.

- **Old-time country.** This style was heard in the nineteenth century and first recorded in the 1920s. Originally British folk songs played on the fiddle, the same folk songs were later played on banjos, Spanish guitars, bass, *dobro*, and washboard.

Lyrical Lingo

The **dobro** is a guitar with amplification made of steel or wood. Musicians also know it as the Hawaiian guitar.

Chord Patterns of Country

Country is simple, although not as simple as it used to be. But behind the new, often lushly orchestrated country pop hits is a fundamental simplicity that can't be sacrificed. The songs build excitement, but they don't veer into strange, wild syncopations.

A look at country hits from the last few years confirms their chordal simplicity: Tracy Byrd's "I'm from the Country" begins with D D G G D D A A D D. The melody is buoyant and infectious. "Wide Open Spaces," a hit for the Dixie Chicks, has a hook based on four chords that recur four times: E F#m7 A B.

Musical progressions that move stepwise, whether up or down, allow for driving rhythm. They also offer room for the musicians to improvise. An uncomplicated but memorable progression underscores Vince Gill's touching ballad, "Kindly Keep It Country": Bb Bb Bb Bb7 Eb Eb Bb Bb. Looking at those chords, you might be tempted to think that they're dull or unimaginative. But when you listen to Gill's record, you encounter a rich, moving melody.

Trouble Clef ____

Too many chords weigh down a tune. Once you find a pattern, stick with it as the melody develops.

Trouble Clef ____

Although Nashville has opened its doors to outsiders, a prejudice against outsiders still lingers. One studio owner commented, "If you heard a country record cut in L.A., you knew it. It never seemed authentic." Your chances of doing recordings that inspire enthusiasm in the country music industry will improve if you go to Nashville and stay there, at least part of the time.

In the past, country chords rarely included major and minor sevenths. Today, with pop so much a part of hit country cuts, these chords are more acceptable. "For You I Will," sung by Aaron Tippin, features D Bm7 F#m7 A. "They're Gone," a smash for Diamond Rio, has a prominent major seventh with Am Fma7 G Em7 F F G G.

"They're Gone" also utilizes an augmented chord, a chord much more frequently employed in show songs than country tunes. It adds beauty and flavor to the melody, even though the use of this chord in country songs is still rare.

Here are other hit country chord progressions:

"Nothing but the Taillights": D7 C G G D7 C G G C C G G

"Husbands and Wives": F F/E Dm7 F/C F F/E Dm7 F/C Gm7 C7 Gm7 C7

"Keepin' Up": E B C#m C#m E B C#m C#m A A B B

"Then What?": A E B E A E B E

Keeping the Nashville Flavor

When you're writing country songs, try to keep a sound and an arrangement concept clearly in mind. Even though country and pop overlap somewhat today, the balance still has to retain its Nashville tone. Think of those steel guitars and fiddles. Imagine a country voice doing the song. It makes all the difference, because country phrasing is altogether different from pop. Madonna and Faith Hill are both blond and beautiful, but musically they have nothing in common beyond the fact that they sing.

Another little exercise has helped me through the years. I do more than imagine artists vocally; I close my eyes and picture them physically. How do they move? What are they wearing? What environment surrounds them? Seeing a country band with your mind's eye gives you a specific slant. This picture is your own, private form of a video you run in your mind to fuel your creative ideas and keep you on the right atmospheric track.

Recommended Listening

To get an overall feel for country, you must be familiar with a wide variety of artists. This sampling of CDs will make you an all-around connoisseur of the music:

Garth Brooks (contemporary country): *No Fences* (1990, Liberty)

Brooks and Dunn (contemporary country): *Brand New Man* (1991, Arista)

Buffalo Springfield (country and folk rock): *Buffalo Springfield Again* (1967, Atco)

Johnny Cash (traditional country/rockabilly): *The Sun Years* (1990, Rhino)

Floyd Cramer (instrumental, Nashville sound): *Essential Series* (1995, RCA)

Diamond Rio (bluegrass/contemporary country): *Diamond Rio* (1991, Arista)

Dixie Chicks (contemporary country): *Shouldn't a Told You That* (1993, Crystal Clear)

The Eagles (country rock): *Hotel California* (1976, Asylum)

Merle Haggard (Western swing): *Tribute to the Best Damn Fiddle Player* (1970, Koch)

Jerry Lee Lewis (honky-tonk): *18 Original Sun Greatest Hits* (1984, Rhino)

Earl Scruggs/Doc Watson/Ricky Skaggs: *The Three Pickers* (2003, Rounder)

The Oak Ridge Boys (country pop/country gospel): *Y'All Come Back Soon* (1978, MCA)

Elvis Presley (rockabilly): *The Complete Sun Sessions* (1987, RCA)

Bonnie Raitt (country blues/rock): *Nick of Time* (1989, Capitol)

Linda Ronstadt (country rock/country folk): *Heart Like a Wheel* (1974, Capitol)

Merle Travis (traditional country): *The Merle Travis Story (24 Greatest Hits)* (1989, CMH)

Ernest Tubb (honky-tonk): *Country Music Hall of Fame* (1987, MCA)

Alison Krauss & Union Station (bluegrass): *Live* (2002, Rounder)

Hank Williams (traditional country): *40 Greatest Hits* (1978, Polydor)

Steve Earle (bluegrass): *The Mountain* with the Del McCoury Band (1999, Warner Brothers)

Gram Parsons (country-rock): *Grievous Angel* (1973, WEA)

Uncle Tupelo (country rock): *Anodyne* (1994, Sire)

The pop world has become such a slave to technological advances that sounds and theatrics take precedence over many of the songs. Fortunately, country music has never succumbed to this trend. The attitude in Nashville is "song first." The guitars and drums may thunder more loudly than they used to, but the meaning of the lyrics and the tune predominate.

The Least You Need to Know

- If you write country music, avoid all pretension and slickness. Write with down-to-earth realism and deal in universal problems.

- Country lyrics are rhymed dialogue that blend street honesty with visual color.

- Country styles include honky-tonk, country gospel, bluegrass, hillbilly, Western swing, rockabilly, country rock, traditional country, and country pop.

- Chord progressions in country should be simple and uncluttered.

- Study all the country genres, from hillbilly and bluegrass to country pop.

Chapter 10

R&B and Rap

In This Chapter

◆ R&B roots

◆ Blues, gospel, and doo wop

◆ Soul, Motown, and funk

◆ Rap and hip-hop

Atlantic Records president Jerry Wexler coined the term "rhythm and blues," but the best definition of rhythm and blues is the one offered by the late Screamin' Jay Hawkins:

> Rhythm and Blues is music about the pain you have suffered. It's about having a good time, feeling passion, experiencing humiliation. It's about your mother dying, your woman walking off, even a bottle of wine. Rhythm and Blues is a slave who picked cotton. It's a black man who ran from a lynch mob. It's something of pain, something of bliss, something of love, something of hate, revenge or laughter. Whatever the emotion, all great music is based on things you actually experience through living." (Quoted in *The Rhythm and Blues Story*, by Gene Busnar [Jules Messner, 1985])

Rap/hip-hop is dance music, featuring singers who speak in rhyme to pulsating rhythms. It first caught on strongly in New York City's African

American neighborhoods, developing in the early 1970s and heating up to an explosive point by the 1980s. Sex, partying, and radical politics are recurrent rap themes. Rap records sample sections from other tracks, and edit pieces of different songs together as well.

Birth of the Blues

Heartache has always given life to great music, and the birth of the blues is a great example of this truth. Black people were taken by force from their homeland in Africa and brought over in chains to America. Many died; those who survived their ocean crossings were sold as slaves upon arrival. Blues began as a music of despair, of slaves crying out for liberation.

Music was the powerful bond that gave them strength to face their heavy burdens. The rhythms and chants of African music were a means for people to communicate with each other, a communication more eloquent than words. A call-and-response style evolved as one person sang lead against a chorus. Modern R&B owes its existence to these pain-soaked blues.

Lyrical Lingo

A **12-bar blues** consists of four bars of tonic (first chord of the scale), two bars of subdominant (fourth), two bars of tonic, one bar of dominant (fifth), one of subdominant, and two of tonic. A modern example of 12-bar blues is Leiber and Stoller's "Kansas City": C (4 bars) F7 (2 bars) C (2 bars) and G7 (1 bar) F7 (1 bar) C (2 bars). The jazz of Count Basie focused on 12-bar blues.

From a musical standpoint, blues are marked by a hammering beat and a melody built on flatted thirds, fifths, and sevenths. These slurred, flatted notes have built-in emotion, a sobbing, prayerful quality. The standard blues form is a *12-bar blues*.

A characteristic of all R&B music is hitting beats 2 and 4. Instrumentation generally includes a rhythm and horn section. The rhythm section has bass, piano, drums, and guitar. Trumpets and saxophones are staples of the horn section, with trombones participating every now and then. Strings became part of many R&B records in the 1960s.

From Minstrel to Motown

In the 1800s, whites were attracted to black minstrel songs. These upbeat blues songs and tunes bore a resemblance to Anglo-American jigs and reels and utilized tambourines and fiddles. At the time of the Civil War, white minstrels gained great success in Europe and America playing these songs in a black style. White audiences reacted enthusiastically to the watered-down performances.

By the 1920s, the record industry had become a powerful force, and blues were reaching the masses. Jimmie Rodgers established his reputation as the singing brakeman from Meridian, Mississippi. The father of bluegrass, Bill Monroe, invested powerful blues feelings in his playing. Country and blues music were blended in the performances of Western swing bands.

Despite their tolerance for bluegrass and Western swing, major record labels rejected R&B, denigrating it as "race music," and newly formed independent companies such as Chess, Modern, Specialty, and Atlantic rushed in to fill the gap. R&B records first reached a large public in 1948 via WDIA, a radio station in Memphis.

The Johnson Influence

Singer, guitarist, and composer Robert Johnson was one of the greats of early R&B. His contemporaries of the 1920s and 1930s claimed that his vocals, guitar playing, and stomping feet had the power of an entire band. His early, primitive recordings (his first recording was in 1936) featured the tinkling piano fills, driving bass line, and powerful drum of a four-piece electric blues band. Following Johnson were Muddy Waters and blues singing great B. B. King.

> **Backstage Banter**
>
> One-verse songs with a song structure of AAA (the verse repeated three times) caught on in the first quarter of the twentieth century. The AAA structure evolved into AAB structure (verse, verse, chorus), which was called the blues.

Jordan's Jump

In the late 1930s, Decca Records got behind bluesman Louis Jordan and promoted his group, The Tympany Five. The Tympany Five specialized in a style that came to be called jump blues. Jordan's arrangements strongly emphasized horn riffs that repeated, and his hit songs such as "Choo Choo Ch'Boogie" found favor with black and white record buyers alike.

Crooner Nat Cole showed the world a more mellow blues form when he sang and played club blues. Club blues also reached a wide audience, as did the vocal sounds of The Ravens, The Ink Spots, and The Mills Brothers.

The Gospel Truth

God-fearing African Americans regarded blues as low class. The deeply religious were horrified when they heard the overt sexuality of "Honey Love" by The Drifters and

"Work with Me, Annie" by The Midnights. Many perceived blues as "the devil's music."

Gospel music took a controversial commercial turn when secular lyrics were attached to gospel melodies. In 1955, Ray Charles turned "This Little Light of Mine" into "This Little Girl of Mine." "I Got a Woman" was Ray's rewrite of "My Jesus Is All the World to Me."

Doo Wop

In the 1950s, R&B songs started centering on the lives and problems of teenagers. In "Charlie Brown," the Coasters expressed an adolescent sentiment, "Why is everybody always picking on me?"

The most popular form of R&B at this time was doo wop. The characteristics of doo wop are medium tempos and close harmonies. These songs are doo wop classics:

"Story Untold" by The Nutmegs

"Come Go with Me" by The Dell-Vikings

"Silhouettes" by The Rays

"You've Got the Magic Touch" by The Platters

"Barbara Ann" by The Regents

"Poison Ivy" by The Coasters

"Since I Don't Have You" by The Skyliners

"Stay" by Maurice Williams and the Zodiacs

"In the Still of the Night" by The Five Satins

"Little Darlin'" by The Diamonds

Early R&B Hits

Listening to and studying early R&B classics, which were known as "race records," will give you a basic rhythm and blues background. All lovers of rhythm, blues, and gospel should know these Top 10 R&B hits:

"My Song" by Johnny Ace

"3 O'Clock Blues" by Ruth Brown

"Lawdy Miss Clawdy" by Lloyd Price

"Hound Dog" by Willie Mae Thornton

"Crying in the Chapel" by The Orioles

"Baby Don't Do It" by The Five Royales

"The Things I Used to Do" by Guitar Slim

"Honey Love" by Clyde McPhatter and The Drifters

"Earth Angel" by The Penguins

"Only You" and "The Great Pretender" by The Platters

"Long Tall Sally" by Little Richard

"Fever" by Little Willie John

"I'm in Love Again" by Fats Domino

"Rip It Up" by Frankie Lymon and the Teenagers

R&B's approach to sex and relationships was raw and direct, and these sentiments were reinforced by the blaringly sensual rhythm. Originally, the term "rock 'n' roll" was a euphemism for sexual intercourse.

The Motown Sound

Sam Phillips of Sun Records visualized how R&B could be expanded when he said, "If I could find me a white boy with a black sound, I could make a million dollars." That boy turned out to be Elvis Presley.

Lyrical Lingo

Rolling Stone's definition of the **Motown sound**: "While the vocalists provided emotion, the band mounted a nonstop percussive assault highlighted by a 'hot' mix, with shrill, hissing cymbals and a booming bass—anything to make the song jump out of the car radio. With tambourine rattling to a blistering 4/4 beat, the music came to epitomize what Motown called 'The Sound of Young America.'"

Despite the fact that audiences were becoming more and more fascinated by R&B, the small independent labels that produced R&B records still felt that they were a minority enthusiasm. It took Atlantic Records and the *Motown sound* to change that thinking.

The Many Faces of R&B

Jump blues, club blues, and doo wop led to soul, funk, disco, and hip-hop.

The Sound of Young America

With his Motown record label, Berry Gordy softened the harder blues and gospel edges of soul and made it accessible to everybody. The Holland Brothers, Eddie and Brian, and Lamont Dozier (a team later identified as HDH) turned out exactly the kind of records Gordy wanted, with such stars as Diana Ross and the Supremes, Marvin Gaye, Gladys Knight, Smokey Robinson, Martha and the Vandellas, Mary Wells, The Jackson Five, and Stevie Wonder.

These Motown classics are a must-listen for any aspiring R&B songwriter:

"Can I Get a Witness?" by Marvin Gaye

"Baby I Need Your Loving" by The Four Tops

"Come See About Me" by The Supremes

"Uptight" by Stevie Wonder

"Ain't Too Proud to Beg" by The Temptations

"What Becomes of the Brokenhearted?" by Jimmy Ruffin

"You Can't Hurry Love" by The Supremes

"Ain't No Mountain High Enough," "You're All I Need to Get By," and "Ain't Nothin' Like the Real Thing" by Marvin Gaye and Tammi Terrell

"I Heard It Through the Grapevine" by Gladys Knight

"My Girl" by The Temptations

"Twenty-Five Miles" by Edwin Starr

> **Backstage Banter**
>
> Berry Gordy Jr. began as a prize-fighter and then became a hit songwriter, turning out Top 10 hits for Jackie Wilson such as "Reet Petit," "Lonely Teardrops," and "To Be Loved." But he had a bigger vision, a vision that led him to form Motown and become the most successful owner of a black label in record history.

"ABC" by The Jackson Five

"If I Were Your Woman" by Gladys Knight

"Mercy Mercy Me (The Ecology)" by Marvin Gaye

"I Just Want to Celebrate" by Rare Earth

"Dancing in the Street" by Martha and the Vandellas

Chicago Soul

Chicago soul was defined by a gentle, sensitive musician named Curtis Mayfield. Curtis and I wrote some songs in the early 1960s, and he confided his intention to write music that inspired people. He and his group, The Impressions, contributed such hits as "People Get Ready" and "Amen." The Impressions gained recognition for their memorable falsetto and for using strings on their records. As a solo artist in the 1970s, Curtis reflected the realities of inner-city life in such songs as "Freddie's Dead."

Southern Soul

Ray Charles was the king of southern soul, a style spotlighted on Stax and Atlantic Records. Isaac Hayes, Otis Redding, The Staple Singers, and Sam and Dave were major Stax artists. Here are some of the best examples of southern soul:

"Theme from Shaft" by Isaac Hayes

"Cold Feet" by Albert King

"Knock on Wood" by Eddie Floyd

"Sweet Soul Music" by Arthur Conley

"In the Midnight Hour" by Wilson Pickett

"Hold On, I'm Comin'" by Sam and Dave

"Respect Yourself" by The Staple Singers

"B-A-B-Y" by Carla Thomas

"Walking the Dog" by Rufus Thomas

"Your Good Thing (Is About to End)" by Mabel John

Funk: Forerunner of Rap

James Brown scraped away any sweetness from R&B and spearheaded the funk movement. Funk subtracted melody and played up rhythm. Chords virtually disappeared, and the rhythms became increasingly complex, knitting together a series of different instrumental parts.

Listen to these funk classics:

"Shining Star" by Earth, Wind & Fire

"Ladies' Night" by Kool and the Gang

"Flash Light" by Parliament

"I Wanna Testify" by Parliament

"Express Yourself" by Charlie Wright and the Watts 103rd Street Rhythm Band

"One Nation Under a Groove" by Funkadelic

"Funky Broadway" by Dyke and the Blazers

"I Got You (I Feel Good)" by James Brown

Disco and Dance

In the 1970s, disco went heavy on synthesizers and strings and was heartily embraced by African Americans, as well as Latino and gay audiences.

Listen to these disco classics:

"Stayin' Alive" by The Bee Gees

"Dance, Dance, Dance (Yowsah, Yowsah, Yowsah)" by Chic

"I Will Survive" by Gloria Gaynor

"Get Down Tonight" by K.C. and the Sunshine Band

"Love Train" by The O'Jays

"Will It Go Round in Circles" by Billy Preston

"You'll Never Find Another Love Like Mine" by Lou Rawls

"Car Wash" by Rose Royce

"We Are Family" by Sister Sledge

"Hot Stuff" by Donna Summer

"Boogie Oogie Oogie" by Taste of Honey

"I'm Gonna Love Ya Just a Little More Baby" by Barry White

"Play That Funky Music" by Wild Cherry

Disco put dance in the limelight, but dance has always been a crucial element of R&B and rock. Who can forget kids on Dick Clark's American Bandstand saying, "But can you dance to it?" Now, videos have made danceability a must for most records, and Michael Jackson's MTV classics, "Beat It" and "Billie Jean," underscored this musical fact of life. Disco went underground in the late '70s/early '80s, first as house music in Detroit and Chicago, later as techno/rave music and more recently as "electronica."

Rap and Hip-Hop

Like R&B, rap has taken the world by storm because it clearly conveys what African Americans are thinking and feeling. Rap was launched in the South Bronx, a dangerous neighborhood. Disc jockey DJ Kool Herc introduced the basic sound. As rock journalist Alan Light recalls …

> He would set up two or more turntables and mix only the hottest sections of several records together, switching back and forth between isolated, hyper-propulsive beats. The earliest *rapping* consisted of simple chants and call-and-response rhymes over the deejay's cutting and scratching, and it became one part of an emerging cultural phenomenon called "hip-hop." (Quoted in *The Rolling Stone Illustrated Story of Rock and Roll,* by Anthony DeCurtis, James Henke, and Holly George-Warren [Random House, 1992])

Bobby Robinson, who established several labels including Red Robin (1952), Whirlin' Disc' Records (1956), and Enjoy (1962), put it out on the grapevine that he was looking for the best rap acts. Right away he was contacted by the Funky Four out of the Bronx, what he calls "a dynamite little group," and released "Rappin' and Rockin' in the House" by the Funky Four (Plus One More), which became an instant hit.

Kids watched television, lusted after the better things in life shown on the screen, and used rap as a vehicle to make their emotions known. Synthesizers and drum machines made it easier and less expensive to do a rap record. No live musicians were necessary.

Hip-Hop to the Top

Hip-hop can be defined as a progression of events including deejaying, emceeing, break dancing, and graffiti that started in the early 1980s. Early exponents of the hip-hop form are Afrika Bambaataa and Grandmaster Flash. The music's evolution, in the words of the *Chicago Tribune*'s Michael Kilian, "produced the remarkable rhyme schemes of Rakim and Slick Rick, the feminist flavor of Salt N' Pepa (endorsed by no less an intellectual than Pauline Kael), MC Lyte, Monie Love, and Queen Latifah; the agitprop poetry of Public Enemy and the gangsta sounding track of N.W.A."

Hip-hop is now a dominant force in current pop music. Jay-Z, the late Tupac Shakur, G-Unit, Ice Cube, LL Cool J, Queen Latifah, Eminem, Beyoncé Knowles, and Will Smith have crossed over from hip-hop to become popular movie stars. Many pop hits by Mariah Carey, Christina Aguilera, and Mary J. Blige feature guest-rappers.

Going to Extremes

Mos Def, age 26, a Brooklyn, New York, rapper, told *Newsweek:* "Sex, violence, the underbelly, with junkies, prostitutes, alcoholics, gamblers … the new trend is depravity." Eminem's "Kim" tells a story in which he cuts his wife's throat and locks her in the trunk of a car. This violence alienates many songwriters, but most of them would also agree that Eminem is a brilliant songwriter and artist.

Rap will survive because of its honesty, and how it reflects the longings and feelings of a culture, emotions that millions from different worlds also share. It is, as Public Enemy proclaims, "black America's CNN."

Regan on Rap

Russ Regan did more than turn Elton John, Neil Diamond, Barry White, The Beach Boys, Olivia Newton-John, Alan Parsons Project, Irene Cara, and the DeFranco Family into stars. He operated a rap label (Quality Records) and became a devotee and expert on the form.

What Regan says about rap …

- Beats. Great beats. Beats are the key to rap. That's why *samples* are so important.

Lyrical Lingo

A **sample** is the reuse (in all or in part) of an already successful track to serve as the foundation for a rap production.

- Then the message—whether it's a message about love, about violence, if it's real, it works. There's a difference between rapping and rhyming. Rhyming guys don't make it. If you try to do rhymes, trying to be poets, it's phony rhyming. Rap is a real art. It's not something you can just do in a false way. I equate it to a lounge act and a recording act: a lounge act comes off plastic; a recording artist goes into the studio and comes off from the heart.

◆ Delivery—how the rapper delivers his rap. I think Dr. Dre is incredible; Eminem is fabulous. Eminem is raw and real. I loved Tupac Shakur when he was alive. Snoop Dog, also brilliant. LL Cool J is excellent.

◆ I think rap caught on because the urban community was ready for a new art form. Most of the great musical trends have started in the urban communities. The African Americans start the trends and are very creative. Now, 60 to 70 percent of the rap music buyers are white. The same thing happened when Motown hit in the 1960s. A lot of rap talks about a way of life, what they see every day.

Rapturous Albums

Here's a list of some of the best rap albums you can listen to:

Public Enemy, *It Takes a Nation of Millions to Hold Us Back*

Eric B. and Rakim, *Paid In Full*

Eminem, *The Marshall Mathers LP*

Boogie Down Productions, *Criminal Minded*

Missy Elliott, *Under Construction*

Beastie Boys, *Paul's Boutique*

Run-DMC, *Raising Hell*

EPMD, *Strictly Business*

Jay-Z, *Reasonable Doubt*

Rhythm and Rap

If you write R&B or rap, just keep in mind that these genres are the musical result of passion. The reason Fontella Bass's "Rescue Me" is played over and over again in motion pictures is because of its urgent emotional cry. "I Will Survive" is the ultimate survivor's stance, an announcement by Gloria Gaynor that she won't be destroyed.

The Least You Need to Know

♦ A 2/4 backbeat is the basis to rock; flatted thirds, fifths, and sevenths spell blues.

♦ R&B and rap are dance phenomena.

♦ Gospel tunes became hits when "Lord" was changed to "baby."

♦ Rappers think of their music as black America's CNN.

♦ R&B and rap is music of passion.

Chapter 11

Latin Pop

In This Chapter

- ◆ Latin lyrics
- ◆ Latin musical elements
- ◆ Recommended Latin albums
- ◆ Chord progressions

The Latin pop explosion became official in 1997 with the establishment of the Latin Academy of Recording Arts and Sciences (LARAS). The year 2000 saw the first Latin Grammys at Staples Center in Los Angeles. This event featured such nominees as Carlos Santana, Marc Anthony, Enrique Iglesias, Jennifer Lopez, and Ricky Martin, artists who racked up enormous sales.

Latin pop is musically identified with a wide-range of instruments, including bongos, conga drums, timbales, cowbells, claves, maracas, guiros, and cabazas. It is an outgrowth of such Cuban and Caribbean rhythms as the mambo, rumba, conga, merenge, and cha cha.

Latin Music Basics

A great portion of Latin music is based on a rhythm pattern called the clave. Played with two sticks, it provides a centerpiece for the rest of the

Be open to artists and writers who aren't necessarily in your chosen genre. Colombian artist Juanes, who scored a hit with the CD *Fijate Bien,* a blend of salsa, R&B, vallenato (accordian music), and funk, lists Patti Labelle, Celia Cruz, Stevie Wonder, Led Zeppelin, Aretha Franklin, and Metallica as important influences.

band. Two voices often improvise phrases, batting call-and-response phrases back and forth.

But Latin pop takes off in multiple directions from the basic formula. Shakira, a Latin pop music star by the age of 12, hit it big internationally, with recordings in Central America, Chile, Argentina, Spain, Colombia, and the United States. Her music, according to Nobel Prize–winning author Gabriel García Márquez, has a personal stamp and doesn't resemble material done or created by anyone else. You can hear disco flavoring, steamy ballads, new wave, Beatles-influenced arrangements, and the echoes of such bands as Nirvana and the Cure. At bottom, though, is a pulsating Latin undercurrent.

Latin Pop Lyrics

Latin lyrics are sensual and visual, but above all, they have an earthy, honest quality. Some of the best examples, ones that apply to every successful Latin pop record, can be found on Enrique Iglesias's *Escape* CD. Let's look at some of the themes that album explores:

- **Love without strings.** In "Love 4 Fun," Iglesias doesn't suggest a permanent relationship. He's frank about saying that he wants a good time, and if his partner is willing to go along and let him do his thing, they can enjoy the moment.

- **Someone to lean on.** In "Hero," Iglesias explores another successful Latin music topic: lifelong commitment. He promises to stand by his girl forever. But he wants to know, in sweepingly romantic Latin style, if she would die for the one she loves. There's no halfway emotion in Latin lyrics.

- **Survive and triumph.** "I Will Survive" was Gloria Gaynor's anthem, and Enrique Iglesias's new song of the same name expresses the thought in current terms. "I will survive," Iglesias says, "no matter what you do." He takes a tough, combative stance, warning the girl in his life not to laugh behind his back. Once again, there's a virile directness throughout.

- **The sexually liberated woman.** In "One Night Stand," heroine Jenny is getting dressed at 6 P.M., preparing to leave. The male in the relationship wants more, but Jenny, it turns out, was only searching for a one night stand. She leaves her underwear and perfume, but it's likely he won't ever see her again. This clearly showcases the modern woman, who claims equal sexual privileges.

- **Sexual enslavement.** Once again, there's a sexually aggressive woman, but this time we get the intimate details: "she bring you up and this time you know you want it." She's a drug that's taking him high and low; she makes him nasty, makes him feel pain, and then he's elevated, transformed, made to feel born again.

Every song on Shakira's *Laundry Service* LP expresses honest and vivid opinions about sex and romance. Songs on this album cover the following topics:

- **Visual sexuality.** Shakira, more than most writers, is fearless in her choice of words. In "Whenever, Wherever" (with lyric co-written by Gloria Estefan), she claims she would climb the Andes solely to count the freckles on her lover's body. Her lips "spill emotion like a fountain." Her expansive, all-encompassing emotion is conveyed when she says she never imagined there were only 10 million ways to love somebody.

- **Claiming her rights.** The modern woman is never passive. In "Rules," she sets forth the following conditions: Her lover can use his eyes only to look at *her*, use his lips only to kiss *her*, laugh only if he laughs at *her*. Don't forget, she warns, you're condemned to me. Sentiments like these are a strong demonstration to writers that they can't hold anything back if they want to seize the public's attention.

- **Masochism.** When a Latin lover is hung up on someone, that attachment is complete. In "Fool," Shakira taunts her sadistic boyfriend, telling him to slap her on the face and find new ways to hurt her while she keeps chasing the soles of his shoes. She claims she can't help it if she's a fool, but you always feel that her masochistic decisions are choices, rather than acts of a helpless victim.

- **Total devotion and abandonment.** "Eyes Like Yours (Ojos Asi)" shows a woman who has one overwhelming aspiration—to live forever in her lover's eyes. She travels the world, from Bahrein to Beirut, never finding eyes that would compare with his.

- **Kitchen sink realism.** Shakira insists on realism in her lyrics. In "The One," she talks of shaving her legs in the morning and losing her kitchen phobia. In "Ready for the Good Times," she refers to roaches that used to climb her door. More than most writers, she's able to express the beauty and the ugliness of life. There's a stark truth to her CD's title, *Laundry Service*.

Trouble Clef

Don't give up. Life can change in an instant. After Marc Anthony gave a great performance, it's said that a disc jockey called out to his colleagues, "Find this kid's CD. I threw it in the trash this morning. Find it and play it."

Musical Elements

Latin pop/rock production is vividly represented in the following examples:

- ◆ **"Pero Me Acuerdo De Ti"—Christina Aguilera.** A fine example of a romantic Latin pop ballad. The verse repeats twice, but it's strong enough to sustain interest until the hook arrives. When the hook does come, it lifts and continues to build, stretching its intervals three times. A modulation and inventive guitar work keep the track moving, as Aguilera continues to reach. Many tunes by beginners don't stretch and build enough. This melody is a definitive example of a tune continuing its ascent to an urgent climax.

- ◆ **"El Album"—Aterciopelados.** This is an excellent example of Latin pop production. A five note figure sets the mood and supports the minor key melody for 20 bars. A second figure replaces the first, and then the hook gets a lift by switching to a major key. A brief spoken part gives the track flavor.

- ◆ **"Fijate Bien"—Juanes.** A driving bass figure alternates with guitar, followed by an instrumental melody. Listen to the lead vocal, and how it interplays seamlessly with a figure. Try not to think only in basic tunes. Whenever possible, link them up with related instrumental figures, the way it's done here. The pre-chorus builds to a catchy, singalong hook. This is the kind of tune that lends itself perfectly to solos, including a solo by accordion.

> **Backstage Banter**
>
> Christina Aguilera was named one of today's most fascinating women on a *Ladies' Home Journal* CBS TV special.

- ◆ **"Lo Hare Por Ti"—Paulina Rubio**. Rapid-fire drums, trumpets in harmony, and a verse section where the words race in a rage of 32nd notes. If you're going to write lyrics that race ahead, make sure they fit comfortably—as here—with the speeding rhythm. This feel is guaranteed to kick up excitement and get the crowd dancing. The setup gives singer Paulina Rubio a chance to speak and sing parts.

- ◆ **"Celia's Oye Como Va"—Celia Cruz.** A standard by which all Latin tunes are measured, from the opening figure to the distinctive brass fills and rhythms. Worth playing over and over again to catch all the background vocals and weaving percussion parts.

Recommended Listening

The following albums all contains examples of Latin songs and vocal performances that convey the flavor and excitement of the music:

- *Un Dia Normal* by Juanes

- *No Es Lo Mismo* by Alejandro Sanz

- *Siempre Arriba* by Bronco: El Gigante de America

- *25 Exitos Originales* by Los Originales de San Juan

- *2003 Latin Grammy Nominees (Pop/Tropical)* by various artists

- *Almas Del Silencio* by Ricky Martin

- *Corazon Latino* by David Bisbal

- *Thalia's Hits Remixed* by Thalia

- *Yahir* by Yahir

- *Confesiones* by Obie Bermudez

- *Sincero* by Chayanne

- *Quien Contra Mi* by Yandel

- *La Historia* by Control

- *Estrella Guia* by Alexandre Pires

- *The Last Don* by Don Omar

- *Grandes Exitos* by Shakira

- *Belinda* by Belinda

- *Cuatro Caminos* by Café Tacuba

- *Libre* by Marc Anthony

- *Salsa Around the World* by Various Artists

Latin Chord Progressions

Writing to established chord progressions is an effective way of becoming accustomed to the flavor of each musical genre. Play these chord patterns and you'll develop an automatic sense of Latin melody:

- G D7 Am Em C Em Am7 Dsus D7

- Dm A7 Dm A7 Gm7 Dm A7 Dm – Gm7 Dm A7 Dm

- D A7 G D

- E B7 E B7 E B7 E B7

- G F#m7 Bm7 G

- D C Em D

- Gm Gm D7 D7 D7 D7 Gm Gm

- Gm D7 D7 Gm Gm D7 D7 Gm

- C Am/F# Dm7 F/G C Am/F# Em A7

- Am7 Dm G7 C Am7 Dm G7 C

To get the chordal flavor in your fingers, get into the habit of writing tunes over sheet music progressions. As the basic sound becomes more automatic and familiar, you can begin to alter the chords, with full assurance that the Latin authenticity is preserved.

Do the same with rhythms. Listen to CDs and write down the rhythms. Play them over and over at first, without trying to create your final melody.

Make notes of certain intervals that recur repeatedly. Notice, for example, when a hook is built around an octave leap. Zero in on the parts of the melody that are the most exciting, and make note of the rhythms and intervals in those particular sections. There's a reason certain sections grab you emotionally, and it's easy to jot down those reasons and utilize them in your own composing.

The Least You Need to Know

- Latin lyrics are sensual, visual, and earthy.

- Listen to the current Latin stars, but also to greats from the past: Perez Prado, Sergio Mendes, Tito Puente, Richie Valens, Luis Miguel, Selena, Los Lobos, who have had crossover hits in America for decades.

- Writing tunes over tried-and-true Latin chord progressions will make your composing more and more genre-specific.

Chapter 12

Christian Music

In This Chapter

- ◆ Basic elements of Christian lyrics
- ◆ Musical characteristics
- ◆ What groups and songs to listen to
- ◆ Christian chord progressions

Modern Christian music began to make national inroads 30 years ago, and from gentle pop it has branched out and preached the word through surprising sources, such as the heavy metal band Stryper and the rap group Gospel Gangstas.

Starflyer 59 hits hard with roaring guitars, and Sixpence None the Richer represents Christian pop's sensitive side. The Christian umbrella has also reached out to cover disco and reggae.

Christian pop's vast expanse ranges from Amy Grant's soothing style to the theater-flavored "Jesus Christ Superstar." And not all Christian music is performed by singers or bands who can easily be pegged as "Christian musicians." P.O.D., U2, Bruce Cockburn, and Van Morrison are artists who present their Christian values in a more secular framework.

Basic Elements of Contemporary Christian Writing

Christian pop is not an area for the cynically motivated, who may view it as a potentially easy entry into the music business. More than any other field, the work springs from deeply personal involvement, and writers can't come across as slick or synthetic. Contemporary Christian pop songs address the following themes:

♦ **Genuinely spiritual feeling.** Christian pop/rock does much more than preach to the choir and appeal to those who share its principles and emotions. It should have the power to influence and attract millions of non-Christians and non-religious individuals searching for personal answers. The song "Thy Word" recorded by 4HIM, contains the emotional depth that would draw audiences when it talks of people feeling afraid and losing their way, then gaining reassurance at the knowledge that the Lord is with them:

> Thy Word is a light unto my feet
> and a light unto my path
> When I feel afraid—Think I've lost my way
> Still, you're right there beside me.

♦ **Dramatic intensity.** Christian singers and songs are explosive, urgently intense. Michael W. Smith doesn't refer to God only as loving or supportive, he refers to him as an "Awesome God" in the song of the same name.

♦ **Power Words.** Words in Christian songs are wildly colorful and fiery. "Exalt," "amazing," "ocean's tides," "mighty mountains," "bursting," and "wondrous" are some of the expressions that give charge to Christian lyrics.

Trouble Clef

Christian writer/artists get into trouble when they don't practice what they preach. Bill Buchanan of Fusebox stresses the importance of setting a positive example, claiming, "You're a role model whether you want to be or not." Rebecca St. James preaches sexual purity until marriage and lives by her words.

♦ **Single-mindedness of purpose.** Big Daddy Weave sums up the mindset of Christian believers in "Audience of One," when he says he has one desire: "to bring Glory to your name." Praising Jesus, extolling his virtues, is central to Christian singers, writers, and believers.

♦ **Poetic imagery.** Jars of Clay refers to "open fields of wild flowers" and "she will come running, fall in his arms, the tears will fall down." It's not sufficient to simply put forth a spiritual passion. The best writers find inspiring and innovative means of expression.

♦ **Directness.** All popular music benefits from simplicity, but nowhere is this characteristic more prevalent than in Christian pop and rock. Nothing should be permitted to blunt the message. An excellent example of clarity is "Breathe," performed by Rebecca St. James.

♦ **Idols.** Christian songs stress love for God and discourage the worship of false, fleeting, or unworthy symbols. Billy Preston sang "never glorify false idols," in which he dismissed the worship of movie stars, rock stars, or other ephemeral figures.

Backstage Banter

Christians are as vulnerable to worshipping false idols as anyone else, but they try to be aware of it and emphasize the need to keep focused on the Creator. Jason McKinney of SpinAround told Christian Music Central, "As Christians, we have our idol of the day. We put our trust in a job or our money or our family, then when that thing fails us, we run back to God and declare our undying love for him, until the next idol comes along to replace him."

♦ **Gratitude.** Millions look upon Jesus as Savior, a force that has brought them from the brink, rescued them from utter despair, weariness, and a sense of over-whelming futility. Some of the finest Christian songs convey gratitude toward a God that has literally brought them back from the brink. "The Happy Song" by Delirious talks of a Lord that wiped away the past. "I Stand Amazed," by Glassbyrd, refers to broken dreams lost along the way.

♦ **Euphoria.** Beyond gratitude, Christian songs are about a bursting, absolute, and all-encompassing joy, an ecstatic "Hallelujah." They talk of people willing to shout the message from the rooftops, from mountaintops, from the heavens.

♦ **Facing problems.** A major theme of Christian songs is encouraging people to face up to their problems, rather than hiding from them.

♦ **The emptiness of success.** Being what Madonna called a "Material Girl," is directly counter to the Christian music message. Christian lyrics repeatedly tell us that money and power can never bring lasting satisfaction if they serve as substitutes for spiritual commitment.

♦ **Don't be square.** Many are drawn to spirituality and Christian messages, but fear that the world will label them square. Christian lyrics ask seekers to ignore teasing and ridicule and embrace Jesus without self-consciousness or embarrassment.

♦ **Frank admission of flaws.** We're all flawed, and Christian songs urge spiritual completion through a union with Jesus. Don't be afraid, while writing this material, to expose your imperfections, your frailties. Hold nothing back for fear of how you'll be perceived. "The Heart of Worship," by Passion, says, "though I'm weak and poor, all I have is yours."

◆ **Willingness to sacrifice.** Some of the most compelling Christian lyrics speak of sacrifice, of a willingness to do anything that will please and satisfy Jesus. Nichole Nordeman says it beautifully with her recording of "You Are My All in All."

◆ **A growing, evolving connection.** As close as committed Christians feel to Jesus, they seek an ever-stronger connection with their Lord. Jeff Devo's "More Love, More Power" is an eloquent illustration of a person who wants an evolving bond with the Creator. This is a subject millions of Christian devotees relate to, because so many of them seek the most powerful connection possible.

◆ **It's never too late.** A constant Christian theme in song is to tell people who have basically given up that it's never too late to accept Jesus and place their hearts and fates in a higher power.

◆ **Be humble.** The least desirable quality in a Christian song is arrogance, a sense of superiority to others who haven't yet found the light. In "Audience of One," the lyrics speak of living for the lord with a song of humility. Bob Dylan cautioned, "you've got to serve somebody." Spiritual devotion rules out sanctimonious self-righteousness.

Lyrical Lingo

There's a common misconception that the word "Jesus" must appear in every Christian song. This might have been true in the past, but now the message can be conveyed more subtly, utilizing a writer's uniquely imaginative means of expression.

◆ **Total dedication.** Christian lyrics are not half-hearted, never a matter of "I'll try this and see if it works." Listeners want a message of such consuming dedication that they can trust in a solution to their problems or gain new insights. Total dedication in Christian lyrics means "with all my heart," pledging love forever.

Storytelling

Jason McKinney and Alan Moore of the popular SpinAround believe that storytelling is a vital ingredient of Christian music. "That's why so much of the Bible is in story form," says Moore. He and McKinney focus on telling modern day parables that people can see mirrored in their own lives. They see this approach as fulfilling their goal to draw people closer to Christ. The songs they've recorded deal with stories of wives, children, broken homes, parental conflict, and the need for forgiveness.

Musical Characteristics

Christian music today freely embraces every style, from pop to soul, Christian metal, contemporary Christian, punk, hardcore, hip-hop, ska, swing, and rap. Multiple contemporary sounds and genres are combined with Christian lyrics.

The compulsively memorable pop hook is a regular staple of Christian material. Many of these tunes are anthems. Repetitiveness in melody, lyric, and message are essential to sock across the point: that love of Jesus is the way to overall love, peace, and happiness.

I've listed groups and single artists worth checking out in three major Christian categories:

Contemporary Christian

- Michael W. Smith
- Amy Grant
- Michael Card
- 4HIM
- Plus One
- Stacie Orrico
- Point of Grace
- Twila Paris
- Kathy Troccoli
- Jars of Clay

Christian Metal

- Aria Below
- Dwell
- Embodyment
- Guardian
- InadA
- Laing Groove

- Pure Defiance
- Stryper
- Warfare

Punk and Hardcore

- 7 Method
- Ace Troubleshooter
- Ghoti Hook
- Harrison 4
- Lucy's Demise
- McPx
- Relient
- System Seven
- Value Pac

Ten Contemporary Christian Songs Worth Studying

- "Awesome God"—Michael W. Smith
- "Majesty"—Caedmon's Call
- "You Are My All in All"—Nichole Nordeman
- "You Are My King"—Newsong
- "Redeemer"—Nicole C. Mullen
- "Here I Am to Worship"—Tim Hughes
- "Come, Now Is the Time to Worship"—Phillips, Craig, and Dean
- "He Is Exalted"—Twila Paris
- "Oh, Lord, You're Beautiful"—Keith Green
- "I Stand Amazed"—Glassbyrd

Gospel

Many of the same elements that mark outstanding contemporary Christian writing are present in good gospel music—power words, spiritual fervor, poetic imagery, frank admission of flaws, humility, and a desire to spread the word.

Gospel music caught on in a big way with composer Thomas A. Dorsey. He was born in 1899 and in 1920 composed his first song, "If You Don't Believe I'm Leaving, You Can Count the Days I'm Gone." His work once again gained popularity when Mahalia Jackson sang his memorable "Precious Lord, Take My Hand."

"Oh Happy Day" by the Edwin Hawkins Singers became the first gospel gold record. The Soul Stirrers was arguably the most popular male quartet. As Lady Soul, Aretha Franklin blended gospel with R&B and broadened its limited core audience to include a vast segment of the general public.

Ten Outstanding Gospel Albums

The following CDs offer stirring samples of contemporary gospel, and should be studied and analyzed carefully. Others to seek out and analyze beyond this 10 are classic works by Mahalia Jackson, the Soul Stirrers, and Rev. C. L. Franklin, as well as gospel excursions by Johnny Cash, Marty Robbins, and Run DMC.

◆ Kirk Franklin: *The Rebirth of Kirk Franklin*

◆ Virtue: *Free*

◆ Mary Mary: *Incredible*

◆ James Bignon & the Deliverance Mass Choir: *God Is Great*

◆ Donald Lawrence & the Tri-City Singers: *Go Get Your Life Back*

◆ Yolanda Adams: *Believe*

◆ Luther Barnes & the Sunset Jubilaires: *It's Your Time*

◆ Christ Tabernacle Choir: *Inhabit the Praise!*

◆ The Blind Boys of Alabama: *Higher Ground*

◆ Vickie Winans: *Bringing It All Together*

Hirschhorn's Hints

Current events are a crucial source of material for Christian pop and gospel music. Singer Shirley Caesar told *Gospel Today* magazine that her aim was to sing about relevant issues: "Drugs, black on black crime, a lot of hurting women who have been abused, young girls who have had children out of wedlock. I want to let them know about Jesus so that they might just get up and straighten out their lives."

Chord Progressions Worth Writing To

The following are chorn progressions from Christian songs. Writing melodies utilizing these chords will result in authentically Christian tunes and will give you practice in composing songs that appeal to devotees of this genre.

Build a melody on these chords:

- Bb Fsus Cm7 Eb Bb Fsus Cm7 Eb
- Eb Bb E/B Bb Cm Eb/Bb Bb Eb
- Bb Gm7 F Eb Bb Gm7 F Bb
- G D Em C C Am Bm Em – G D Em C – G Am Bm D G
- G C/G D7 C D G C/G D7 G
- F F Bb Bb F F/A Bb C
- C G G D Dsus G G C Dsus D7
- G C G/B D7 G C G/B Dsus Em C G
- G C D7 D7 – G C D7 D7 Em C G
- G C D7 D7 G C D7 D7 C D G
- D A7 D A7 Bm7 G G D/F# A7

The Least You Need to Know

- The best Christian lyrics have a genuinely spiritual feeling, dramatic intensity, power words, poetic imagery, directness, and a frank admission of flaws.
- Storytelling, more than ever, is prized in Christian writing.
- Christian music embraces a variety of styles: pop, Christian metal, punk and hardcore, hip-hop, rap, and rock.
- An effective way to learn Christian composing is to write melodies over chord progressions.

Chapter 13

Commercials and Children's Music

In This Chapter

◆ A songwriter's role in an ad campaign

◆ The importance of understanding the consumer's psychic needs

◆ How to write a successful jingle

◆ Children's music that adults will also enjoy

"Buy me! Buy me!" This cry, packaged in new jingles or classic hit songs, floods daily into millions of living rooms through TV and radio. Many of these pleas are ignored. But if the commercial has a memorable catch-phrase, an unforgettable tune, or a captivating visual, we find ourselves hypnotically drawn in.

Good jingles are simple, but writing them isn't. Composers of commercials need an intuitive understanding of human psychology, of common desires and dreams.

Companies are spending increasingly huge sums on commercials targeted to children, knowing that if they can capture children's lifetime loyalty to their particular soft drink or toothpaste, the investment will pay tremendous dividends. More children's videos, CDs, and songbooks are also being sold every year, which means more work for songwriters.

Commercial jingles and children's songs are both areas rich with opportunity for songwriters who can master the brisk, compact style and uncomplicated lyrics and chords that work best in these forms.

Composing Commercials

Before an ad agency hires a composer for an ad campaign, much of the planning has already taken place. A typical national ad campaign includes the following steps:

1. An advertiser contacts an ad agency to launch a national campaign for a new product.

2. The creative director (with input from his or her staff) decides what the campaign's objectives are.

3. A storyboard is worked out, and if the advertiser approves, the campaign moves ahead.

4. Budget suggestions are presented, analyzed, and approved.

5. The creative director puts out the word to production houses and asks to hear demo reels.

6. The casting director alerts actors for upcoming auditions and starts examining videotapes.

7. The composer is selected, and a recording date is chosen.

Getting Engaged

You're hired for the campaign. At the first meeting, you get a general sense of the product and what the client would like to put across to the public.

Trouble Clef

Don't bother sending unsolicited material to ad agencies. You have to access them through a connection or an agent.

You make a bid, after ascertaining the following facts:

♦ How large an orchestra the client wants

♦ How much time you have to create and complete the spot

Even though you're a songwriter, you might be given the following things to work with:

◆ A complete lyric

◆ A concept for words written to a known melody

◆ A copy line and the concepts of the commercials.

◆ A description of the mood that the client and agency want to capture

Like film directors trying to explain to scorers what they want in a scene, advertisers can't always convey ideas clearly. You have to be a detective and figure out their needs. Just because they're inarticulate doesn't mean they don't have a sense of what they want. They also know what they don't want, and you need to listen with an unprejudiced ear.

Pressing the Right Buttons

The product may be a company, perfume, soap, or cereal. The viewer may be a 35-year-old housewife, a high school senior, or a fourth-grader. There are countless millions of people, but they all have few needs in common:

◆ **We need love, love, love.** Why do we need a new perfume? Why is a new car mandatory, when we still have a perfectly good one? Because television and radio tell us we have to be more attractive and more able to impress people in order to find love.

◆ **D'ya think I'm sexy?** As with love, we're never totally convinced we have enough sex appeal. But if we had the right shoes, the right earrings, the right suit, we would become, according to ads, irresistible to everyone who meets us. Buying someone the right drink will ensure a lifetime of happiness. It doesn't matter that the conscious mind questions this message. On a deeper level, we accept it—if the jingle is properly crafted.

> **Hirschhorn's Hints**
>
> On your own, you might take the initiative and write jingles about current, popular products; record the jingles and have your agent submit them. Creative directors may be drawn to your work if it has freshness and imagination.

> **Backstage Banter**
>
> Former *New Yorker* magazine film critic Pauline Kael once asked the question, "What person, what creature, ever felt they were loved enough?" The answer is "No one." We have that space inside that never quite feels filled, and jingles rush to tell us that if we use a certain product, we'll find all the love we want.

♦ **A safe harbor.** No matter how much we pose and swagger, we know it's an act. Most of us are insecure, and commercials remind us that the right product can give us confidence. No social situation will be threatening if we wear designer jeans. If you tap into a person's fears, and subliminally let them know that these fears can be conquered, you've made your sale.

♦ **I'm a big shot!** Give people a sense that they can be famous and important, and you have their attention and their dollars. If wearing an Armani suit will bring a $50,000 raise, the suit will find its way to many a closet. We crave recognition; we want a top job that will knock out our friends (and every woman or man who crosses our path).

♦ **What's in a name?** Whatever the product, whether it's Budweiser beer or Tommy Hilfiger shirts, keep repeating the name! Repetition is the key to popular songs, and the same is true of jingles. Your goal is to sell a product. Advertisers pay billions a year to induce customers into stores, and a subtle, indirect commercial won't do the trick.

Ready to Write

More and more, hit songs are being used to sell a product. To compete, your tune must be compulsively catchy and singable. It must be one of those "I can't get it out of my head" melodies, such as "It's a Small World" by Richard and Robert Sherman. Don't submit a melody to an ad company until you're convinced it has a memorable hook.

Hirschhorn's Hints

Don't think of jingles as a stepchild of pop songs, something you're marking time with until your song-writing career explodes. Jingles and pop tunes are art forms in their own way.

Analyze the Objective

Before you start to write, analyze all the angles:

♦ What is the main theme of your commercial?

♦ What group of people is being targeted?

♦ What age are they?

♦ Where do they live?

Give Me "Yesterday"

Suppose the client gets an inspired idea: He or she wants to use a Beatles song. Fine, but the publisher sometimes won't allow those tunes to be cleared for commercials, and if it does, the price may be exorbitant. But the boss is mentally married to the idea. You'll probably be called upon to provide a melody that resembles the one the client favors.

Don't Be Obscure

Dig for that one clear idea and hammer it home. With attention spans at an all-time low (and remote-wielding viewers who click away from commercials whenever they can), you have to state your case instantly. Don't wander and don't make people guess or speculate about what you're conveying.

Trouble Clef _____

You can't take a song such as "Ain't No Mountain High Enough" and alter the tune or lyric without permission from the company that owns the copyright.

Personality

You want your jingle to sound unique and original. What good is a jingle if it sounds like every other commercial on the air? You're fighting to be heard above the pack, and the way to achieve that is to offer a new sound, an offbeat way of touting the product.

Play with Words

One way to approach jingle lyrics is to find a well-known cliché and turn it inside out. When my partner Al Kasha and I were hired to do our first commercial for Lloyd's Bank, we tested such phrases as "You'll Love Lloyd's," "You Can't Avoid Lloyd's," and "Lloyds—the Family Bank." Finally, we came up with "You Can Always Bank on Lloyd's," and it was enthusiastically accepted. With this one statement, we promised security, protection, and a family-type friendliness. We used the key word "bank" and found a way to merge it with a well-known expression.

Trouble Clef _____

Don't make the mistake of being too fancy. Use layman's language. Appeal to the guy on the street. Jingles are not the area for complex, show-off rhymes or complicated chords. Avoid gymnastic musical leaps and keep the melody within a sensible range.

Think Showtime!

If you have a sense of theater, think of your commercial as a small musical show. If the tone is comic, be playful with your piccolos and tubas. If it's funky and street-oriented, let your bass and drum explode. It's not enough to write the best jingle; you need to emphasize its qualities with a theatrical, flavorful arrangement.

Trouble Clef _____

When a copywriter presents words that don't sing easily, you must, with tact and diplomacy, point out that the lyrics need changing. Tell that to the client right away; nobody likes surprises, even when your substitutions are an improvement.

Don't Bury the Singer

In pop music, the "feeling" is what counts. How many people do you know who love a song and remember the lyrics? Very few. The mix usually covers up half the words. In a jingle, every word counts. Let the singer be heard. This emphasis on the singer sometimes upsets arrangers and songwriters, who hate to lose a precious note, but if it's a contest between a guitar solo and a lead singer, the singer has to win.

Offer a Choice

Once you've worked out the idea and the jingle, do a recording of it. Offer three different versions. If you submit one, the client might love it, but like most people in show business, the client might be somewhat fearful of trusting his or her judgment. With three versions to pick from, the client feels more secure.

Don't Wing It

A lot of the work in pop music is spontaneous, even with an arrangement. Such creativity is not welcomed in the ad game. Pre-plan everything and get approval for everything, or your recording date could turn into a disaster.

What's the Deal?

Budgets vary widely in the jingle world, from a mere thousand dollars to seven figures. A deciding factor is whether the jingle is for radio, cable, a local spot, or a national one. A television advertiser who wants to keep costs low will acquire music from a stock music house. These stock houses offer canned tracks for radio and television spots. Unlike the conservative expenditures for local broadcast spots, national agencies frequently spend lavishly.

Publishing

It's always best to try to keep full ownership of the copyright for anything you write, but ad agencies recognize publishing as a huge source of income, and they aren't willing to automatically surrender copyright. If you can't get all the rights, negotiate for a split, but be prepared to give it up altogether in many cases.

Getting Paid

Most deals, whether for commercials, television, or film, involve part payment up front and the remainder when the project is completed. If you're fortunate, you might get the whole payment up front, but this kind of deal is rare. The agency might also want to divide your payment into thirds.

Package Deals and Their Drawbacks

Like many composers, I'm not crazy about *package deals* because you often end up with very little or no money at all. Say you receive $5,000 to handle everything: composing, scoring, conducting, studio costs, mixing, and delivering the master tape to the client. To walk away with more than artistic satisfaction, you have to budget down to the minutest detail. Your eye must be on the clock at all times so you don't go overtime.

Lyrical Lingo

A **package deal** is a fee that covers all elements of a recording: composing, scoring, conducting, studio costs, mixing, and delivering the master tape to the client. You're totally responsible for accomplishing everything without exceeding that overall payment.

The Market for Children's Songs

Opportunities to write for children are at an all-time high. Beyond writing for motion pictures and television, you can compose for direct-to-video productions, an outlet that continues to grow and surprise companies with its public acceptance. Videos featuring nursery rhymes, versions of classic stories, and sequels to hit films are racking up gigantic sales. Sales records for children's CDs, DVDs, and songbooks continue to be broken each year.

Do Your Research

Check your local record stores and ask the salespeople which children's videos and CDs have recently sold the most. Buy them and study their form and structure. Then immerse yourself in Saturday morning shows. Videotape and watch each series at least three times. Note the fantasy and freedom of the programs on Disney, Nickelodeon, Cartoon Network, Fox Kids, Kids WB, and PBS (particularly *Sesame Street*).

Educational Productions

Schools and other organizations use a wide variety of audiovisual (AV) productions for educational purposes. These DVDs, videos, filmstrips, or slide shows offer numerous employment opportunities for scorers and songwriters. Colleges, libraries, and industrial firms are just a few of the available outlets.

Demonstrate your skill by doing an educational film of your own and write music that shows off your abilities and highlights the key points of the subject under discussion. Let your local advertising agency see it. Connect with other educational outlets in your area and circulate your video. Familiarize yourself with AV houses by combing the Yellow Pages.

Hirschhorn's Hints

A website can be a perfect way to show off your talents and skills. Just make sure that it's polished and professional-looking. Study the competition, and make sure your website's visuals and catch-phrases are unique and memorable.

You won't get rich doing educational films, although if you do them regularly you'll probably make a decent living. Fees for audiovisual work are in the $300 to $3,000 range. As your reputation grows, the fees will become higher, and you'll have the choice of freelancing or taking a full-time job for one company.

Respecting the Minds of Children

When films and shows are tailored for adults, the creators treat their audience with respect. Why do kids deserve less? No one should write down to children or patronize them.

Backstage Banter

Christina Aguilera and Britney Spears appeared on Walt Disney's *Mickey Mouse Club,* which gave them early training and put both on the road to stardom.

I've composed scores for a lot of family and children's movies, including several Disney feature films. When working on all of them, I kept a line by James Thurber in mind: "If a story is good, it can be enjoyed by adults as well as youngsters." As a matter of fact, I've often found that children catch on to the subtleties of a story or a lyric before the adults around them do.

Make It Modern

No matter how young they are, kids are fully aware of Christina Aguilera, Britney Spears, the Dixie Chicks, *NSYNC, Toni Braxton, and Shania Twain. Younger children may enjoy classic ditties like "Skip to My Lou," but they also respond eagerly to the sounds of today.

Keep It Moving

Would you write a ponderous, slow-moving musical for adults? Then don't move sluggishly when writing for children. Attention spans today are a quarter of what they were 30 years ago. If a song, no matter how well written, slows down the action, remove it.

Create Characters, Not Caricatures

Characters, whether they're animated or live action, should be real. If not completely real, they should have certain human characteristics everyone can identify with. Cartoon villains without dimension won't scare anyone, and cartoon heroes make kids yawn. When writing a children's show or song, think of the characters as flesh-and-blood people. Give them fears and frailties. No one is 100 percent courageous or 100 percent evil.

As a child, I remember a critic saying that Prince Charming in the Disney film *Cinderella* was a bore because he was a handsome Mr. Perfect. On the other hand, the zany, Disney-invented mice who loved and defended Cinderella walked away with the picture.

Thou Shalt Not Preach

No one, from toddlers to the elderly, will tolerate being preached to for long. When you have to get a message across—whether it's "Don't do drugs" or "Brush your teeth after every meal," you need to find a way to make your point without preaching.

It's best to avoid a holier-than-thou tone, or give orders in an authoritative voice. Use humor to make your point. Put a positive spin on your message—rather than point out the cavities you might get as a result of not brushing your teeth, why not mention how beautiful your teeth will look, how shiny and white, and how popular you'll be as a result?

> **Backstage Banter**
>
> There's always a way to handle delicate material. In *The Original Top Ten*, an animated musical about the Ten Commandments that my partner Al Kasha and I worked on, adultery was the trickiest subject. We worked on it and finally devised, "Be Loyal to the One You Love," which makes the point without being heavy-handed.

Match the Songs to the Story

One of the prime-time animated musicals that Al Kasha and I worked on, *The Magic Paintbrush*, was based on a popular children's book and centered on a young boy with an ability to paint pictures that came to life. As in all animated songs, we made sure that every lyric line could be translated into a visual scene. We also wrote a song called "Keep on Believing" to express the theme of the show. It's important to know what overall point you're trying to make and include a song that clearly conveys that point.

Some people feel that songs, no matter how effective, interfere with the action. Disney's *Beauty and the Beast* proves otherwise. Every Manken/Ashman song in *Beauty and the Beast* propels the story forward. "Belle" defines the heroine's character, and "Gaston" comically points out the evil intentions of the villain. This movie has a perfect children's score; it's a textbook example to study when you're writing for young people. Nothing feels shoehorned in; the songs carry audiences along.

Don't Be Afraid to Be Dark

As Disney has proved time and again, children don't mind being frightened, and an extreme effort to protect their sensibilities by being safe and cute will encourage a mass exodus to the popcorn stand.

Another point to remember: If you're doing a children's musical and basing it on a classic, resist altering elements that made the classic famous in the first place. It's highly improbable that you, as the composer or the librettist, can spin a better yarn than Dickens did. You can make small changes, subtract a character or two, but be sure the structure and the spirit of the original are preserved.

Free Your Mind

When you write for children, let your mind run loose. If you do, you'll hit upon zany, inspired titles, such as "I'm an Aardvark and I'm Proud" and "Captain Vegetable" from *Sesame Street*. Or an offbeat term may occur to you, such as the Turkish word "Pachalafaka." In "The Alligator King," by Donald Hadley and William Luckey, a typically madcap line refers to seven statues of girls with clocks where their stomachs should be. Children's tunes also lend themselves to audience participation and antics such as juggling, mime, and clowning.

The beauty of writing music for children is the room this audience offers for creativity. Before long, it will seem natural to think of a dragon in someone's living room or a bird that turns into a lion. The joy of composing for kids is how completely it allows you to shed adulthood and be a child again.

Hirschhorn's Hints

When writing for children, think of yourself as eight years old. Let your beats be buoyant and your words have a playful spin. Concentrate on being funny whenever possible—whether you're doing "Supercalifragilisticexpialidocious" (from *Mary Poppins*) "Passamashloddy" (from *Pete's Dragon*), or "Hakuna Matata" from "The Lion King." When you're done, test the songs on children, and you'll immediately know if they work.

The Least You Need to Know

♦ Jingles and children's music should be clear and direct, with a musical hook.

♦ Writing commercials is not demeaning work; it is a highly developed skill.

♦ To be successful at composing commercials, you must understand the consumer and be open and receptive to the client's ideas.

♦ Good children's music also appeals to adults.

♦ Writing for kids can be a creative and joyful experience.

Chapter 14

Movie Scoring and Songwriting

In This Chapter

◆ Scorers can become songwriters

◆ Early jobs that can get you where you want to go

◆ The director and other key players

◆ Music that fits the needs of the movie

◆ How to build your scoring knowledge and experience

Scoring and writing songs for movies are two of the most artistically challenging and commercially satisfying careers a composer can pursue. Sometimes, both score and songs are most effective when they stay in the background. But when they're the focal point and need to dominate, composers must know when to come on strong and when to lay back and not compete with the action on screen. The key to success in motion pictures is knowing when you can be a star and when the effectiveness of the piece depends on your willingness to remain a supporting player.

Scorers as Songwriters

Legendary composers such as Max Steiner (*Casablanca, Gone with the Wind*), Erich Korngold (*Robin Hood*), Franz Waxman (*A Place in the Sun*), and Aaron Copland (*The Heiress*) handled only *underscoring* during the 1930s and 1940s.

On rare occasions, scorers crossed the line into songwriting. Alfred Newman's matchless melodic sense was utilized in such hit compositions as "The Best of Everything," from the film of the same name. But in most of these cases, the songs became hits outside the movie after lyricists added words to the tunes.

The songs in MGM musicals such as *Easter Parade*, *An American in Paris*, and *Singing in the Rain* were written by Irving Berlin, George Gershwin, and Herb and Nacio Brown. Other musical hit-makers such as Rodgers and Hammerstein, Jule Styne, Frank Loesser, Yip Harburg, Sammy Fain, Paul Francis Webster, and Livingston and Evans supplied the tunes for nonmusical pictures. Scorers rarely, if ever, wrote the songs for either musical or dramatic motion pictures until the 1950s.

Lyrical Lingo

Underscoring is background music that is meant to support screen action. It is used to heighten dramatic and comedic sequences.

Backstage Banter

Max Steiner wanted to write his own song for *Casablanca;* Warner Brothers said no. "As Time Goes By," the song finally used in the film and performed by Dooley Wilson, was written by Herman Hupfield.

Henry Mancini, Michel Legrand, and Marvin Hamlisch brought about a permanent change to Hollywood. Their melodic flair was so extraordinary that they were allowed to compose songs for the pictures in addition to underscoring them. Freelance songwriters found their positions threatened after studios decided that many scorers could handle both roles with equal skill. This trend became more commonplace in the mid-1950s with *The High and the Mighty* (co-written by the film's scorer, Dimitri Tiomkin) and increasingly widespread after Henry Mancini did *Breakfast at Tiffany's* in 1961 and won an Oscar for song and score.

As a songwriter, you can follow two routes to getting your songs in the movies. If you have arranging talent, you can learn orchestration and scoring and thereby gain greater power to put your own music into the movie. Or you can work independently and submit your songs to producers for consideration in their films. In the end, producers are out to make money, and they'll choose material that best promotes their picture, whether it's written by the scorer or someone else. Few scorers, no matter how well educated, have the commercial musical flair of a Mancini.

Make It Happen

You must make yourself known and heard. Perform your material everywhere and circulate your demos. Eventually, people will start to recognize you and admire your work.

Cut a CD of your best material and get it to all the producers in town. Heads of studios should be on your list, along with music supervisors and music publishers. Make sure your CD features a variety of moods so people see how versatile you are. And be a nuisance! The squeaky wheel gets the grease.

In addition, music agents are giving increasing attention to songwriters. These agents include the Carol Faith Agency, Gorfaine-Schwartz Agency, and the Kraft-Benjamin Agency.

Hirschhorn's Hints

Songwriters want more than hits; they also want to be acknowledged. That recognition will never happen if you don't make yourself visible. Harry Warren hated to attend parties, yet he expressed bitterness that no one knew him or credited him with his list of great songs, a list as long as Irving Berlin's. Warren wrote "The More I See You," "An Affair to Remember," "The Atchison, Topeka, and the Santa Fe," and "You'll Never Know." All his life, he lamented his anonymity without doing anything to change it.

Read the Hollywood Bibles

Daily Variety, which was launched in 1905, is the bible of show business activity. Read it to find out what pictures are being made, who the producers are, and which studios are doing them. The *Hollywood Reporter* reports the same information. Study both papers and make notes. Memorize the names of every important person in the music and movie industry. You can be certain that your competition is thoroughly familiar with all aspects of motion picture production.

Hirschhorn's Hints

Pay particular attention to films done by independent filmmakers and other films being shot on a reasonable budget. The producers of these modest features would prefer to hire someone whose price hasn't reached stratospheric heights. If you're relatively new, your odds of being considered increase tremendously.

Variety and the *Reporter* contain information about films that are in pre-production. At this early point, songwriters haven't been chosen yet, and you have a chance to jump in and volunteer your services. Everything depends on being the early bird, getting in on the ground floor before the job you covet has become general knowledge.

Respect Your Material

No matter how unpromising the movie material looks at first, you must do the best possible job with it. Never slough off an assignment because it seems unimportant; don't treat anything as though you are slumming. You never know how the movie will turn out in the end. Hollywood history is packed with films everybody figured would fail, and these movies then turned into sleepers and won Academy Awards.

A Successful Disaster—On Spec

When a publisher friend, Happy Goday, suggested to Al Kasha (my collaborator) and I that we submit a theme for Irwin Allen's upcoming disaster blockbuster, *The Poseidon Adventure*, everyone we spoke to said, "Don't bother. They're turning down the biggest names in the business. If they don't want Henry Mancini, they're certainly not going to use a song by Kasha and Hirschhorn."

But a career isn't just talent, it's timing. It's knowing when to seize an opportunity. Something in my gut told me: Take the chance. And my advice to all writers is the same: Take the chance. What have you got to lose?

We showed up with dozens of other composers, and Irwin Allen said, "Go home and write a love song. We'll listen to it at eight tomorrow morning." Again, a friend (?) of ours commented, "Not enough time. You'll never be able to do a good job." But we obeyed our instincts, stayed up all night, and wrote "The Morning After." Maureen McGovern's magnificent rendition of the song became a worldwide number-one song, and it won an Oscar.

Hirschhorn's Hints

No matter what the circumstances are, perform. With *Pete's Dragon*, Al and I were handed an outline of the story and told to write five songs, without pay, for evaluation. Fate almost sabotaged us when I broke my arm while ice skating and had to play the score with one arm in a partial cast. But we performed for 40 people (employees were recruited from all over the Disney lot to give their opinions). Miraculously, the reaction was positive.

Taking a chance without firm promises is only one aspect of a writer's life. Another is simply this: Your job, your passion, is to write no matter what the circumstances. You write because you can't help it, because the desire to write is a relentless drive that won't let you rest.

Have a Strategy

Drive is essential, but so is working out a practical strategy. If you're a lyricist, it makes sense to link up with the composers who score films. I recognized the wisdom of this and made an effort to develop relationships with motion picture scorers. These efforts resulted in fruitful, creatively stimulating collaborations with Nelson Riddle, Marvin Hamlisch, and Alex North.

Underscoring

Many outstanding books have been written on the subject of underscoring. From my point of view, Henry Mancini's *Sounds and Scores* ranks at the very top. I learned to orchestrate almost entirely from this particular volume. Mancini supplies generous examples and explains things clearly. Best of all, his music is so tuneful and accessible that the instrumental parts are easy to absorb in the first lesson.

Another extraordinary orchestration book is *On the Track* by Fred Karlin and Raymond Wright. The following books are also good:

> *The Techniques of Orchestration* by Kent Wheeler Kennan, Prentice Hall, Inc., New Jersey, 1970
>
> *Music Arranging and Orchestration* by John Cacavas, Bellwin-Mills Publishing Corp., New York, 1975
>
> *Scoring for Films* by Earle Hagen, Criterion Music Corp., New York, 1971
>
> *Modern Harmonic Techniques* by Gordon Delamont, Kendor Music, 1971

In the Scoring Game

When you're hired to write the score for a motion picture, you first have to understand the relationship between the score and the film. You also become part of a collaborative effort, which means that it's essential to develop a good working relationship with the film's director and music supervisor.

Follow the Right Leader

In his classic book *The Season*, novelist/screenwriter William Goldman stresses the importance of finding the "muscle" in a production, the actual decision maker. That might be the director, the producer, the editor, the executive producer, or the music supervisor. If you pay close attention, you'll figure out quickly who has the final say; then make sure that this individual's desires are fulfilled.

Many directors have little or no musical knowledge and lack the vocabulary to convey what they want. You can't afford to be snobbish and tune them out because they're not educated musicians. They might still have an instinctively correct sense of how to heighten the scene with music, and it's your job to figure out what they want.

Provide Reassurance

In the past, composers would write an entire score, and neither director nor producer would hear it until the day of the recording. That's no longer the case. Synthesizers have made it possible to make recordings of cues and try them out before final orchestrations are written.

Scorer David Shire says …

> On *The Color Purple*, with Quincy Jones's army of synthesists and keyboard players and arrangers, Spielberg wanted a Synclavier mock-up of every cue so that he could get a feel of exactly what the music was going to do … But one can get in trouble with them, I think, because the sound of a Synclavier imitating a symphony orchestra is still not an orchestra.

Backstage Banter
This music business story has now become legend: A director, eager to capture the correct atmosphere for his film, told his arranger, "Use French horns so we can get a French background." That's about as sensible as using English horns for an English background.

Nevertheless, this procedure protects against the disastrous possibility of a director disliking the music when it's too late to change it. The composer, too, can feel more relaxed, knowing that his or her work has been approved in advance and won't be thrown out, which has happened to even the best scorers.

Ask Questions and Do Your Research

Directors have many ideas, some of which they don't express. It's to your advantage to ask questions in order to pin down some of these ideas. Try to find out what instrumentation the director or producer favors. What does he or she want the music to say emotionally? Avoid technical queries, such as "Would you like the chords to go from C to E minor?" Such questions may only make the person feel uneasy or embarrassed and thus incur his or her resentment.

Marvin Hamlisch believes in research. When he was hired to score the James Bond thriller, *The Spy Who Loved Me*, he watched every prior James Bond picture. His score was totally original and representative of his delightful tongue-in-cheek approach, but doing the research gave him an understanding of what had worked with earlier Bond films.

Work Closely with the Music Supervisor

Music supervisors have gained tremendous power and influence in recent years. Their responsibilities include the following:

◆ Devise the budget

◆ Find composers and lyricists and recommend them to producers

◆ Seek out recording artists and record producers

◆ Negotiate soundtrack deals

◆ Coordinate artists' schedules with film release dates

◆ Attend dailies (screenings of the footage shot the previous day)

◆ Attend screening of the film prior to spotting. (Spotting is covered in detail in the following section.)

◆ Be present at spotting sessions

◆ Attend scoring sessions

◆ Function as liaison between composer and director

Backstage Banter

A temp track is the temporary music cut and dubbed into the film prior to scoring. Composers often don't like them because directors become attached to this temporary music and want it kept or reproduced. The director and producer become used to hearing the temp cues and can't imagine their scenes without them. The best you, the composer, can do if the director loves the temp music, and you don't, is keep an open mind about it and still carefully integrate musical themes and thoughts of your own. If you've previously written music of your own that you can incorporate into the temp track, you can achieve a partial solution.

Talking About Titles

When you're hired to write a song for a motion picture, you have a choice: to use the film's exact title or to come up with something more singable and commercial. Certain titles present a challenge beyond the capabilities of any mere mortal: *The Rules of Engagement*, *Being John Malkovich*, *The Cider House Rules*, and *Drowning Mona* are just a few examples. Or going back a few years, how would one possibly incorporate *Death of a Salesman*, *Breaking the Sound Barrier*, or *The Brave Bulls* into a song title?

Suppose producer Irwin Allen had insisted our song be titled *The Poseidon Adventure*. It would have killed any chance for a hit. *Breakfast at Tiffany's* is quite a mouthful, but Johnny Mercer and Henry Mancini came up with "Moon River" instead.

Spotting the Picture

Once the placement of music in a movie is decided upon, the music editor writes up a music breakdown, called *spotting* notes. He or she lists the cues and numbers them so that the first digit represents the reel number and the next digits offer the cue number within the reel. Therefore, 1M1 (or M11, or 1/1) means Reel 1, Cue 1. Composers should make their own notes as well.

Common spotting abbreviations include the following:

BG	Background
CU	Close-up
Cut	Direct cut from one shot to another
Dial	Dialogue
Ext	Exterior
FI	Fade in from black
FO	Fade out to black
Int	Interior
LS	Long shot
MS	Medium shot
MX	Music

Lyrical Lingo

Spotting is the process of watching the film and deciding where music should be placed.

O.S.	Off-screen (voice, sound)
Pan	Panorama shot, which means camera rotates, revealing sweep of scene
Pix	Picture
POV	From the point of view of named actor
Super	Superimposing one image over another (a double exposure)
2-Shot	Two subjects in frame
3-Shot	Three subjects in frame
V.O.	Voice over, a voice that doesn't lip sync with subject in frame
ECU	Extreme close-up
ELS	Extreme long shot
Zoom in	Effect of coming closer to a subject
Zoom out	Effect of subject receding

Practical Scoring Tips

A scorer must heed certain general rules when writing music for the movies:

◆ Concentrate, first and foremost, on the central character. What are that character's hopes, goals, and fears? Learn about the character until you understand him or her as completely as you understand a member of your own family.

◆ Certain scenes don't function well on their own. They may have undercurrents the director or writer failed to clarify for an audience. That's when a scorer should ride to the rescue. Suppose a character is shoveling snow or pumping gas. Your job is to get inside the person's mind and musically dramatize his or her emotions. The right cues can turn dead spots into exciting moments.

◆ Choosing the proper instrumentation is crucial. Insecure directors and producers might want you to go crazy with a huge, crashing orchestra. That kind of overkill can ruin a scene. If you sense that a three- or four-piece band or just a piano would accomplish the job more effectively, point it out. Be ready to justify your idea.

◆ A character might be pretending to feel one emotion when he or she is actually feeling another. If your hero is laughing but inwardly terrified, project that fear through your music. If the heroine is pretending to love someone but actually hates him, it might double the impact of the moment if you suggest it with your cues.

♦ Sometimes it helps to play against the events occurring onscreen. Happy music with bells and piccolos over a moment of horror can make the horror even more intense. You're skating on thin ice when you make these kinds of decisions, but they often heighten a scene's power.

Trouble Clef

When you score a love scene, guard against sentimentality. The right music can jerk tears, but the wrong music can make people feel manipulated and can turn off directors.

♦ Max Steiner, who scored *Casablanca* and *Gone with the Wind*, was a strong believer in writing individual themes for each character. Some directors favor that kind of musical emphasis. Others consider it corny. Check with your director before proceeding.

♦ Writing a single melody and playing it endlessly helps to sell the theme and frequently results in a hit record. Find out how your director and producer feel about this technique. They might prefer a score that catches a scene's every nuance. Requirements vary for each film. A love story usually benefits from a beautiful tune constantly featured with different instrumentation and rhythms. A thriller might suffer from the same treatment.

Hirschhorn's Hints

Will Jennings, lyricist for the Oscar-winning songs "Up Where We Belong" (from *An Officer and a Gentleman*) and "My Heart Will Go On" (from *Titanic*), feels that a song should have an organic connection to the film, not just be placed there for exploitation purposes. He also approves of a song being utilized at the end, if the theme has been featured before. "That way it comes back with more emotional power than if you'd never heard the tune."

Get Into It

Orchestration—the composing of instrumental parts of a movie that stand alone or blend into other sounds—requires a combination of formal study and practical experience. The following are some valuable roads to follow in pursuit of that goal:

♦ Play classical works and follow along by reading the orchestral scores. Memorize every sound, color, and range. After you gain an overview with your first lesson, zero in on one instrument at a time. Go through the entire violin part, then switch to viola, cello, bass. Do this with each instrument involved. Copy the parts until they feel like second nature, until you're thoroughly familiar with each instrument's capabilities. Work with a copyist; learn to copy and transpose parts yourself, and consider it a temporary (or possibly permanent) career.

◆ Find a private teacher to teach you orchestration, as I did, or if you prefer, attend a school like Juilliard. Pore over every arranging book you can get your hands on.

◆ Study conducting.

◆ Perform with an orchestra or band to familiarize yourself with arrangements. You'll see what works and what doesn't. Some instruments move more quickly than others. You can't move as rapidly on a bassoon as you can on a piccolo. A bass isn't as flexible as a violin. As a musician, you'll automatically absorb this information.

If you want to become an all-around movie orchestrator, study every conceivable kind of score. Never restrict yourself to classical, jazz, or rock, or tell yourself that you're only good at certain kinds of things. If you decide, for example, that you can't do a rustic, country score because your specialty is sophisticated city arrangements, this attitude will become a self-fulfilling prophecy. Remember that John Williams did *Fiddler on the Roof, The Reivers*, and *Star Wars*—three wildly different scores—and he did a brilliant job with each one.

The Least You Need to Know

◆ Do whatever it takes to gain experience and opportunities in writing songs for films and television.

◆ Bond with decision makers.

◆ Learn to read the director's mind.

◆ Stay close to music supervisors.

◆ Study conducting and orchestration and learn about every instrument.

Musicals for the Stage

In This Chapter

- ◆ The illusion of reality in an abstract space
- ◆ Types of musicals
- ◆ Ways of getting your musical to the stage
- ◆ Special material for artists and performers
- ◆ Work with, not against, the book writer
- ◆ Study the viewpoints of your choreographer and arranger

Writing songs for stage musicals involves many of the same skills required by every other genre: strong, visual titles, the use of repetition, memorable hooks, exciting rhythms, and fresh ideas. In addition, the songs have to tell a story, develop characters, and contain polished rhymes.

Belting to the Balcony

Write songs that have energy, spirit, and that always sought-after "edge." To be successful, your songs have to reach viewers in the last row, which, in many theaters, seems like a mile away.

Hollywood songwriters who set their sights on Broadway have been criticized for writing songs that are too sweet, too pleasant. This assertion has

Hirschhorn's Hints

Feel free to write as many songs as you consider necessary when composing for the stage. As you start working on a show, you'll keep some songs, eliminate some, and save some for re-evaluation at a later time. You'll be composing up to the last minute, because change and rewriting is the name of the game in theater.

some truth to it; those who are used to the camera tend to compose overly mellow music. After years of working in film, they are accustomed to the ever-present camera doing the work for them. In film, close-ups are able to furnish the necessary power, highlighting the tiniest expressions on the faces of the cast. That's why a movie can carry the weight of more ballads, whereas one or two are sufficient in a theatrical enterprise.

Modern audiences want songs that dig deep and penetrate outer layers of personality. For an example of a musical with a contemporary, powerful score, check out *Rent*, composed by Jonathan Larsen.

Dialogue vs. Music

Book writers—writers of the nonmusical dramatic text, also called librettists—generally want more dialogue, and songwriters want more music. Yet, for a musical to be successful, the book writer has to resist any impulse to dominate. His role is to set up scenes so the songs can make a maximum impact. That's not to say that dialogue isn't important. Crisp, character-driven dialogue helps the action flow and provides setups for the songs, but the balance must favor the music.

Musical book writers frequently resent this situation. They feel it renders them anonymous, and they're right. The more successfully they do their job, the more they'll be allowing a composer to shine at their expense. You, as a composer or lyricist, must make every effort to work harmoniously with the book writer. Be open to his or her suggestions and avoid a competitive situation. At the same time, make sure your lyrics furnish as much information as possible while not duplicating points the dialogue has made.

Nailing the Characters

What kind of numbers suit the different characters? You have to ask yourself this question over and over again. What defines each of the people involved? Your job, as composer and lyricist, is to bring these characters alive, to let the audience see their dreams, desires, and goals.

Where Songs Belong

Placing songs properly is one of the first and most vital aspects of creating a musical. Numbers have to move the plot forward and should never simply be tossed in at random.

Songs also need to move the story along. Deleting a tune you're attached to from a spot you've already chosen can be difficult, but if it's serving no purpose, it has to go.

Backstage Banter
On stage you don't have a camera moving freely around, capturing every detail of lavish locations. Julie Andrews can spin across the hills of Salzburg in Robert Wise's Oscar-winning film version of *The Sound of Music*. On stage, her movements would be comparatively restricted. In the 1940s and 1950s, sets were large, often elephantine. They were usually opulent, with every detail spelled out. Going from one sequence to another was more a feat of heavy labor than a feat of the imagination. Today, such literal monstrosities arouse the ire of critics and have been replaced with sets that zip in and out or revolve quickly. Such sets suggest a background or an atmosphere rather than recreate it on the stage. So don't conceive your theater piece as a series of short scenes, each with elaborate set changes.

The Performers and the Song

This might sound like a no-brainer, but for leading parts, try to choose people who can sing. Many people believe performers without singing ability can "act" the songs, but nothing can match the pleasure of hearing well-sung melodies. Aside from the aesthetic satisfaction, the tunes have a much greater chance of becoming hits when sung by successful singers. In the music industry today, where soundtracks are bigger business than ever, this consideration is tremendously important.

Backstage Banter
Richard Rodgers hated the fact that Gertrude Lawrence sang out of tune in *The King and I*, even though she acted the role convincingly. Sammy Cahn, who wrote the music for the 1970s Broadway show *Look to the Lilies*, said, "We had Al Freeman, Jr. and they kept telling us, 'he's an actor.' But I said, 'Can he sing?' Jule Styne answered, 'What good is a show if the book doesn't come off? He'll bring it off.' But I figured this way: let the book writer handle the book, I'll handle the songs." Cahn was proved right when no successful songs emerged from the score. Conclusion: Get someone who can sing *and* act if possible.

Every Job Is Your Job

Never think: Choreography is her job; mine is to write songs. In writing a musical, visualizing yourself as choreographer, director, or actor helps you gain a creative overview that will make your songs come more brilliantly alive.

Arranger and Best Friend

When you work on a musical, the *arranger* is an incomparable ally. Many outstanding tunes have been distorted, weakened, or ruined by arrangers who don't understand how to do them justice or who have a concept that differs too widely from the composer's.

Meet with the arranger beforehand and establish a strong personal rapport. Tell him or her clearly what you're trying to do with your tunes. If you envision guitar and a harmonica accompaniment to a particular song, make it clear that 40 violins would be a major mistake. However, don't close yourself off to the arranger's suggestions. A guitar and a harmonica might be too sparse and might not give your song the emotional charge it requires.

Lyrical Lingo

An **arranger** is often another word for orchestrator, the individual who writes out parts for the various instruments. Sometimes an arranger provides themes without furnishing the specific instrumental parts, and an orchestrator is then recruited to take these themes and translate them into fully fleshed instrumental terms.

Think Like a Choreographer

When you write songs for musicals, always check the lyrics afterward to see how danceable they are. An imaginative choreographer will do wonders with your material, but you can make the numbers twice as exciting by putting yourself in his or her place and saying to yourself, "How can I make this dance?"

Important Musical Categories

Musicals have always fallen into certain categories. Some of the most well-known types are adult fairy tales, revues, historical musicals, musical fantasies, and musical biographies. Musical adaptations are also popular; novels, plays, movies, works of Shakespeare, and Bible stories have all been turned into successful musicals. Some of the most memorable musicals, however, have been complete originals.

Adult Fairy Tales: Love Heals

For the romantic, sentimental composer who loves happy endings, adult fairy tales are a fertile musical area. The following musicals exemplify the adult fairy tale genre:

◆ *Beauty and the Beast* (Alan Menken and Howard Ashman). Among Disney's most popular animated musical films, it is just as successful on the Broadway stage. A mismatched pair, a lovely young girl and a ferocious beast, discover that love transcends appearances and true beauty lies within.

◆ *The Unsinkable Molly Brown* (Meredith Willson). The road from rags to riches is always romantic, and in this backwoods fable, Molly Brown rises from uneducated tomboy to society belle. She even rescues people on the doomed *Titanic*.

◆ *Seven Brides for Seven Brothers* (Joel Hirschhorn and Al Kasha). Two different points of view clash when a spunky waitress marries a chauvinistic mountain man and teaches him how to treat a woman with respect. (A new score was written for the stage version.)

◆ *Annie* (Charles Strouse and Martin Charnin). An orphan winds up as the cherished ward of a fabulously wealthy figure. This situation becomes plausible through Strouse and Charnin's buoyant, tuneful score and a need we all have to believe that love can triumph over any adversity.

An underlying theme of all these adult fairy tales is the miraculous power of love to transform one's personality. In *Seven Brides for Seven Brothers*, for instance, all seven men become courteous, considerate, well-mannered Prince Charmings.

Hirschhorn's Hints

Audiences can be counted on to cheer for a hero or heroine who rises to wealth, conquers snobs, and winds up with the love of her dreams. In Alan Jay Lerner's *My Fair Lady*, a guttersnipe named Eliza overcomes adversity and marries her professor. In Shaw's *Pygmalion*, the basis for *My Fair Lady*, Eliza didn't land Professor Higgins; but Lerner understood that audiences would reject the work if the two didn't get together. He went so far as to say that Shaw's ending was wrong.

Adult fairy tales are perfect for romantics. Yet within their fanciful plots and wide-eyed, optimistic viewpoints, they have a core of realism. The key to all good adult fairy tales is that they make people feel good.

The Revue

Revues are generally composed of vignettes and skits with an overall theme, whether sexual, social, or political. Sometimes they're compilations that define the life work of a creative artist or a writer's literary contributions. Here are some hit revues:

- ◆ *Cats* (Andrew Lloyd Webber and T. S. Eliot). The longest running musical in history, *Cats* is a series of T. S. Eliot poems set to Andrew Lloyd Webber's music. The story is merely a slim excuse for Webber's tuneful score, which includes the standard, "Memory."

- ◆ *A Chorus Line* (Marvin Hamlisch and Ed Kleban). A ground-breaking musical documentary, this show utilized the lives, hopes, and dreams of Broadway dancers as a foundation for a Tony-winning musical revue.

- ◆ *Fosse.* Bob Fosse's choreography is the focal point of this revue, with excerpts from such shows as *Pajama Game*, *Pippin*, and *Chicago*.

- ◆ *Jerome Robbins's Broadway.* This show features most of Robbins's dances from such masterpieces as *On the Town*, *A Funny Thing Happened on the Way to the Forum*, *Fiddler on the Roof*, *Peter Pan*, and *West Side Story*.

- ◆ *Smokey Joe's Café (Jerry Leiber and Mike Stoller).* Jerry Leiber and Mike Stoller's hits provide the pulsing rock magic for this revue.

- ◆ *Ain't Misbehavin' (Fats Waller and various collaborators).* This revue consists of 30 songs written or performed by Fats Waller.

- ◆ *Sophisticated Ladies (Duke Ellington and various collaborators)* This revue celebrates Duke Ellington's big band classics such as "Satin Doll" and "Mood Indigo."

Trouble Clef

Before you decide to use a property owned by someone else, get the rights! Carol Hall, composer of *The Best Little Whorehouse in Texas*, admitted that she never got rights to many properties she wanted to work on early in her career. "I was totally ignorant," she says. "I mean I'd just do a musical I had no rights to, if it struck my fancy."

The Historical Musical

The historical musical allows composers and lyricists to musically portray an era and its people. When historical musicals succeed, they often become classics:

- ◆ *Titanic* (Maury Yeston). Maury Yeston's musical depicts the 1912 tragedy of an "unsinkable" ocean liner.

- *Cabaret* (John Kander and Fred Ebb). A bitingly harsh, realistic musical drama about pre-Hitler Germany, with its decadence and let's-live-as-though-there's-no-tomorrow attitudes.

- *Miss Saigon* (Claude-Michel Schönberg, Richard Maltby Jr., and Alain Boublil). This show reworks Puccini's *Madame Butterfly* as a Vietnam War drama.

- *Les Misérables* (Claude-Michel Schönberg and Alain Boublil). Utilizing the French Revolution as background, *Les Misérables* (*Les Miz* for short), which was based on the classic novel by Victor Hugo, told the tale of escaped prisoner Jean Valjean and the mercilessly moral policeman Javert who pursues him. *Les Miz* and *Miss Saigon* were two of the leading musicals to be *through-sung* and use *recitative* and *leitmotif* in a brilliant and commercially successful manner.

Lyrical Lingo

Through-sung means sung in its entirety, without dialogue. **Recitative** is a talking style of singing. **Leitmotif** is a musical theme that recurs throughout a show to refer to a specific event, idea, or character.

The Musical Fantasy

Musical fantasies appeal to almost everyone, from children to all but the most jaded adults. Other genres come and go, but the commercial appeal of fantasies remains undiminished. If you're a writer with a rich imagination and a love of make-believe, this musical arena could be right for you. Musical fantasies take on a wide variety of topics, as the following list demonstrates:

- *The Lion King* (Elton John and Tim Rice). A combination of wizardly stage-craft and puppetry, this adaptation of the Disney film featured an Oscar-winning score by Elton John and Tim Rice.

- *The Little Shop of Horrors* (Howard Ashman and Alan Menken). Based on the 1960 low-budget film of the same name, this show pitted a nerdy hero against a man-eating plant and became the fifth-longest running off-Broadway musical in history.

- *Starlight Express* (Andrew Lloyd Webber and Richard Stilgoe). This show anthropomorphized trains on a cross-country race that made unlikely but effective subjects for Andrew Lloyd Webber's offbeat musical.

- *Nine* (Maury Yeston). Fellini's film *8½* furnishes the source material for Yeston's musical about a film director's fantasies.

The Musical Biography

True-life heroes and heroines always make fascinating musical material. If you want to musicalize a colorful personality (and can obtain the rights), it often results in box office gold:

- ◆ *Gypsy* (Stephen Sondheim). In a daring, innovative approach typical of Sondheim, this show concentrated on a vicious, conniving stage mother named Rose who shoved her daughter (stripper Gypsy Rose Lee) into the limelight and then felt abandoned after Gypsy's success. In this case, the main character wasn't famous, although her children were. (Rose's other daughter evolved into actress June Havoc.)

- ◆ *Barnum* (Cy Coleman and Michael Stewart). This play about master showman Phineas Taylor Barnum featured juggling, tightrope walking, and trampoline feats by Jim Dale.

- ◆ *The Will Rogers Follies* (Cy Coleman, Betty Comden, and Adolph Green). Beloved humorist Will Rogers provided the centerpiece for a lavish revue/biography with razzle-dazzle choreography by Tommy Tune and a glitzy production worthy of Florenz Ziegfeld himself.

- ◆ *Dreamgirls* (Henry Krieger and Tom Eyen). The Krieger/Eyen score didn't actually say the three heroines were the Supremes, but Supreme Mary Wilson has confirmed that director Michael Bennett based his play on Motown's most popular trio. The composers cleverly located the drama of this story by focusing on Florence Ballard, the tragic Supreme who died young after being ousted from the group. It's always preferable when you can take a known story and present it with a fresh twist, as composers Henry Krieger and Tom Eyen did here.

- ◆ *Evita* (Andrew Lloyd Webber and Tim Rice). Audiences love glamour, and *Evita* is one of the most glamorous of modern heroines. She's a woman who rose from poverty to become Juan Peron's wife and a powerful Argentinian figure in her own right. Her elegance and magnetism are emphasized when she tells a dress designer, "Christian Dior me, Lauren Bacall me."

Novel Adaptations

Shows based on classic novels are a Broadway staple. Al Kasha and I were nominated for a Best Score Tony for *Copperfield*, our Broadway version of Charles Dickens's *David Copperfield*. Lionel Bart turned another Dickens classic, *Oliver Twist*, into the show

Oliver! Rupert Holmes was inspired by an incomplete Dickens work to create *The Mystery of Edwin Drood.*

These great musicals all stem from classic books:

- *Big River* by Roger Miller

- *Ragtime* by Lynn Ahrens and Stephen Flaherty

- *The Scarlet Pimpernel* by Frank Wildhorn and Nan Knight

- *Jekyll and Hyde* by Frank Wildhorn and Leslie Bricusse

- *Phantom of the Opera* by Andrew Lloyd Webber, Charles Hart, and Richard Stilgoe

Play Adaptations

Dramatic plays or comedies are often changed into musicals:

- *Sweeney Todd* by Stephen Sondheim is based on Christopher Bond's *The Demon Barber of Fleet Street.*

- *Hello, Dolly!* by Jerry Herman is an adaptation of Thornton Wilder's *The Matchmaker.*

- *Do I Hear a Waltz?* by Stephen Sondheim and Richard Rodgers is based on *Time of the Cuckoo* by Arthur Laurents.

- Jerry Herman's *Mame* comes from *Auntie Mame* by Patrick Dennis.

- *110 in the Shade* by Harvey Schmidt and Tom Jones is a musical version of Richard Nash's play *The Rainmaker.*

Movie Adaptations

Movies have long been popular source material for composers, but now the trend is stronger than ever. For example, John Kander and Fred Ebb have created several shows from movies: *Woman of the Year* and *Kiss of the Spider Woman* are based on the movies of the same names, *Zorba* comes from the movie *Zorba the Greek,* and *Chicago* is based on the film *Roxie Hart.*

These musicals are also examples of movie adaptations:

- The film *Sunset Boulevard* inspired Andrew Lloyd Webber and Don Black to create the musical *Sunset Boulevard.*

- The film *Grand Hotel* became the musical *Grand Hotel* by Robert Wright and George Forrest, with additional music and lyrics by Maury Yeston.

- Frank Loesser's *The Most Happy Fella* is adapted from the film *They Knew What They Wanted*.

- *Promises, Promises* by Burt Bacharach and Hal David is based on the film *The Apartment*.

- *Applause* by Charles Strouse and Lee Adams is based on the film *All About Eve*.

Offbeat Adaptations

Ideas for musicals come from places as unexpected and diverse as cartoons, famous art, and opera. *Annie* was a comic strip called *Little Orphan Annie*. The Stephen Sondheim musical *Sunday in the Park with George* was based on the pointillist art masterpiece *Sunday Afternoon on the Island of La Grande Jatte*. The rock musical *Rent* by Jonathan Larsen came from the opera *La Bohème*. *The Producers* was transformed from Mel Brooks's 1965 film comedy of the same name.

> **Backstage Banter**
>
> Sarah Jessica Parker of *Sex and the City* once played the lead in *Annie*.

Shakespeare and the Bible

Shakespeare's plots are models of melodrama, action, and comedy, and songwriters have been turning to them for years:

- *Two Gentlemen from Verona* by Galt MacDermot and John Guare is a musical version of the Shakespearean play of the same name.

- *Your Own Thing* by Hal Hester and Danny Apolinar is their version of *Twelfth Night*.

- *The Boys from Syracuse* by Richard Rodgers and Lorenz Hart is an adaptation of *The Comedy of Errors*.

Nothing beats the Bible for musical adaptation. Stephen Schwartz launched his career with *Godspell*. Andrew Lloyd Webber and Tim Rice have had much success with both *Jesus Christ Superstar* and *Joseph and the Amazing Technicolor Dreamcoat*.

Originals

Many composers would rather do musicals based on original stories than adapt proven properties. This approach is riskier, because producers usually seek protection from tried-and-true materials. Still, brilliant originals have achieved great success:

- *Falsettos* by William Finn
- *I'm Getting My Act Together* and *Taking It on the Road* by Gretchen Cryer and Nancy Ford
- *The Magic Show* and *Pippin* by Stephen Schwartz
- *Bells Are Ringing* by Jule Styne, Betty Comden, and Adolph Green

Get It on the Stage

Those who devote themselves to theater can't get enough of it. Theater people rush to see every possible production they can, musical or not. So should you. Don't attend just the highly publicized, expensive productions; see shows presented in 99-seat houses as well. College theater, community theater, high school and dinner theater can all provide exposure to a fine performance, an unusual orchestration, or a score you're not familiar with.

Once you've written a musical, you must get it on stage to analyze its virtues and weaknesses. Never mind where: a living room, a roof, or a restaurant will do. Only when you observe actors singing your words and music can you deepen your comprehension of lighting, costumes, scenery, and choreography. You'll then be able to rewrite without big money pressures and without temperamental stars to derail you.

Show Me the Money

It's one thing to write a show, another to pay for its production. Backing can come from anywhere—producers, publishers, businessmen, or even relatives. When a score is completed, composers seek out backers. Often the money comes from one or two deep-pocketed sources. More often it comes from several. Throughout theatrical history, composers have hired singers (or sung the material themselves) for backer's auditions, auditions in which investors are invited with the idea of convincing them to contribute financial backing to the show. Sometimes studios or auditoriums are rented; other times the material is performed in a living room.

Hirschhorn's Hints

On the occasions when you attend a bad performance, try to learn from the mistakes and avoid them in your own work. Pinpoint what the problems are—ask what songs don't work and whether certain lyrics slow down the action.

As a rule, however, you should hire a few other singers. The variety of voices makes everything much clearer to your listeners, all of whom are unfamiliar with your show.

Be sure you can explain the plot clearly and how your numbers fit into it, but don't interrupt the songs with overly lengthy explanations. Rehearse the presentation until it becomes second nature to avoid stuttering or stumbling. Finally, don't apologize for the lack of scenery or lighting. No one expects a full physical production. People can imagine a great deal, especially if your performance is simple, concise, clear, and to the point.

Do a Local Production

It's a mistake to think that local theater is consistently inferior to the highly budgeted productions. If you missed *Dreamgirls* the first time around, you'll still hear the songs and enjoy Michael Bennett's original concept in a converted garage. *A Chorus Line* in a relatively miniature format might gain intimacy that it lacked on Broadway.

Trouble Clef

Never make the mistake of thinking that great talent is only on the Broadway stage. In doing a local production, you may discover a future star, someone who will excite high-level producers and turn your show into an appealing package.

Local theater is overflowing with talent. Exposure to it will inspire you as a composer, and also give you a sense of how many modest avenues there are that provide launching pads for your own work.

Talk to theater companies in your area and present your material. Find out if they're willing to put on a production of your show. If they will, you'll have access to a cast, musicians, director, and producer. Colleges, drama clubs, high schools, church groups, and dinner theaters are other outlets, and some of the shows they present are extraordinary.

Be a Talent Scout

Try your songs at parties and clubs. Work with singers who appear talented but haven't landed their first booking yet.

When John Kander and Fred Ebb discovered Liza Minnelli, she was a novice, despite having Judy Garland and Vincente Minnelli as parents. Kander and Ebb created special songs for her, studied carefully what she did best, and helped her to spotlight her individuality and move out from the long shadows of her mother and father. With increasing fame, Oscars, and Tonys, Minnelli stayed with the composers who had seen her potential in the beginning.

> ### Trouble Clef
>
> When a song doesn't fit, don't try to force it. Irving Berlin wrote a song called "Mr. Monotony" for the movie *Easter Parade*. It slowed down the story. Then he put it in *Call Me Madam* and had to take it out when the show went on the road. Finally, it showed up in a compilation film, *That's Entertainment III,* and didn't work there either.

Hold a Workshop

Organize a workshop. Gather actors together and develop your musical. Recently I workshopped a new show and was reminded again of how effective the process is. You can't get an accurate impression of the way the script plays or whether the songs and script are cohesively integrated until you watch it unfold before a live audience. Once you invite people to see the workshop production, you'll start to see what scores a bull's-eye and what needs correcting.

When you produce a workshop, watch for these common problems:

- Be alert for slow stretches when the audience begins to cough or squirm.

- Watch out for songs that sound beautiful on their own, but bring the story to a halt.

- Study your characters for flaws. Is one character too dominant, another too passive? Is a supporting player knocking out the audience with the best song, and your lead losing ground because he has the weaker numbers?

- Make sure your ending feels right. Is it too happy or too optimistic for the story that precedes it? Or is it too sad, leaving audiences depressed when they'd rather be elated? If you're honest with yourself, you'll feel those vibes.

- Check to see whether the show is song-heavy. Or is it too "talky," in desperate need of a song or a dance sequence? Whatever the problem is, don't rationalize. Don't blame it on the actors or on a "bad" audience. Be open to problems and willing to fix them.

- Watch for second-act trouble. It usually means that the first act has failed to set up interesting plotlines that need resolving, or the second act may simply go on too long. Audiences grow more impatient as the evening wears on. Wind up the act fast.

Trouble Clef

Make sure your singers can act, so they can convincingly represent the characters they're playing. It's not enough, especially in theater, for singers to just breeze through the melody technically. They have to bring the show's characters alive, whether in person or on a CD.

Take It on the Road

If your show attracts interest, be willing to take it to other towns and cities. In this video age, you should videotape all, or most of, the performances. Keep that video camera going, much the same way you keep your cassette recorder going when you compose. You might accidentally catch magic when one of your singers is practicing a number. Magic can't be predicted, so be ready to preserve it when it happens.

Cut a CD

Ideally, a well-produced CD of the musical's material will convey even more than live performance. You can do every song, but sometimes just recording the highlights is better. Include your big ballad, a couple of songs that establish your main characters, the opening of your show, and the closer. Make sure that your selections cover enough territory to make the basic story clear.

As in your commercial demos, be mercilessly strict with yourself about the choice of singers. This is not a time to let your friends participate (unless, of course, they're on a par with Audra McDonald or Brian Stokes Mitchell).

Hirschhorn's Hints

Contact the Dramatist's Guild in New York for a list of important producers. Many of them will want your work to arrive through an agent, so focus your agent search with the same intensity. Two excellent sourcebooks to consult are *The New York Agent Book* and *The Los Angeles Agent Book*, both by K. Callan.

Find Available Theaters

Theater Directory, published by Theater Communications Group, Inc., lists 335 not-for-profit professional theaters across the country. The listing includes contact information, performance season, and key personnel names (such as artists, management, and board members). The directory also describes the kind of plays the theaters concentrate on. Target those theaters that specialize in the type of show you've written and send them your music and synopsis.

The Producer's Viewpoint

Rob O'Neill, who has produced award-winning versions of *Sweeney Todd*, *A Little Night Music*, and *Fiddler on the Roof*, looks for certain criteria when choosing a show to produce:

> "When I produced *A Little Night Music*, it was relatively easy to sell tickets, because the show had a specifically targeted audience, women who were going to see Dale Kristien and Amanda McBroom in the roles. I produced *Fiddler on the Roof*, because most people know it and I could attract the whole family. I look for broad appeal, what the consumer is going to want in terms of tickets. The show doesn't always have to reach everyone, but it should appeal to one complete segment of the public."

Here is Marvin Hamlisch's opinion about the trend of today's theater:

> "Very family-oriented shows. A child will go to see *Beauty and the Beast* and want to see it again and again. So you're talking about two tickets and repeat business. But there's also room, and there's always been, for moving, important theater as well."

Hirschhorn's Hints

The road to Broadway is never easy, but the rewards are worth it. Marvin Hamlisch says, "There's a lot of money to be made from a hit show. In terms of a composer, tons more than a hit film. You get a percentage of the gross each and every week, in every town and country. You rarely, if ever, get percentages from movies."

Hits from Shows

Broadway shows used to be a prime source of hit songs. *West Side Story* featured "Maria" and "Tonight." Shows like *Guys and Dolls* ("I've Never Been in Love Before"), *Funny Girl* ("People"), *Gypsy* ("Small World"), and *Oliver* ("As Long As He Needs Me") and dozens of other productions could be counted on to produce at least two or three Top 40 records.

Rock and roll changed the scene, because rock music wasn't included in most Broadway musicals until "Jesus Christ, Superstar" and "Tommy." But hit songs still come from musical theater, and Broadway is much more open to rock than it was in the past.

Cats gave us "Memory." *Dreamgirls* produced the R&B hit "And I Am Telling You I'm Not Going." The Latin-flavored hit "Don't Cry for Me Argentina" came from *Evita*.

"What I Did for Love" was the showstopper in *A Chorus Line*. *A Little Night Music* introduced "Send in the Clowns," Stephen Sondheim's biggest hit as a solo composer/lyricist.

If you're writing a musical, try to create excitement about the score well in advance by releasing singles or a soundtrack before the musical is produced. The score for *Les Misérables* was first released as a best-selling double album. Andrew Lloyd Webber and Tim Rice offer an excellent example of using hit songs to garner interest in a musical. "Don't Cry for Me Argentina" and "High Flying Adored," two songs that later appeared in *Evita*, topped the charts before Webber and Rice approached Harold Prince to direct the musical. When the show opened in London and New York, the popularity of the songs helped *Evita* to become a hit.

Singles are only a small part of royalties a successful Broadway show can offer you. Hit soundtracks represent a lifetime annuity. Some recent hit soundtracks from Broadway shows include *Rent*, *The Phantom of the Opera*, *Les Misérables*, and *Big River*.

Special Material

Writing for popular in-person performers offers top training for the theater. Al Kasha's and my theatrical development was aided by writing special musical material for Zero Mostel, Charles Aznavour (including eight songs for Aznavour's one-man Broadway show), Ginger Rogers, Valerie Harper, and Liza Minnelli.

When you write such material, you'll quickly learn that you can't just string together a lot of tunes; your job is to develop an act that will capitalize attractively on every facet of the performer's personality. In other words, you're creating a character. You'll have to highlight their funny side, show their humanity, and give them numbers that express their emotional depth. You'll be forced to come up with specific, meticulously tailored lyrics and wean yourself of any tendency to turn out generalities.

Hirschhorn's Hints

When you see stars in person or on television, get past the normal response of being dazzled by their personalities. Listen to what they're singing. Make note of the subject matter. Practice by writing tailored tunes and words for them.

You need cleverness and wit. Once you've honed your ability to write humor, you're more than halfway home as far as theater is concerned. Sheldon Harnick of *Fiorello* and *Fiddler on the Roof* fame was told as a struggling young lyricist, "Don't worry about love songs or ballads. Anybody can write those. Write the special material, the comedy stuff, because that's hard to come by." Harnick heeded the advice, searching for offbeat ideas, and by the time he wrote his first Broadway musical, *The Body Beautiful*, he was a seasoned theatrical lyricist.

If you know any local acts, submit your work. Up-and-coming performers desperately need good material, and they need an image. Maybe you can supply it.

The Least You Need to Know

- Songs for the stage have to create the illusion of reality, whereas songs for the screen have realistic settings.

- Musicals fall into 10 major categories.

- Showcase your musical at a local theater.

- Organize a workshop to learn where your musical needs improvement.

- Promote your musical with a CD, and take it on the road.

Part 4

The Business of Songwriting

Agents, managers, and publishers are the people who will help you gain exposure as a writer and, if you aspire to be a singer/songwriter, a performer. But you should only work with people if you have complete faith in their ability to handle your song catalogue and career. Equally as important as finding the right people is learning how to make the right demo. In the following chapters I'll show you how to make the best possible business choices and avoid the most common mistakes.

In addition, you'll learn the mysteries of producing your own record, whether in someone else's studio or in your own. The experience you gain from learning to produce your own recordings will be invaluable as you build your career.

Chapter **16**

Agents, Managers, and Labels for Singer-Songwriters

In This Chapter

- ◆ What to look for in an agent, manager, and entertainment lawyer
- ◆ A legendary record executive's view of what makes a successful singer/songwriter
- ◆ Ways to get the media behind you
- ◆ Major and minor record labels
- ◆ A career in cabaret

Do you have singing talent along with a gift for writing? If so, it's worth developing. Freelance songwriters, even writers as prolific and successful as Diane Warren, always have to depend on others to cut their material.

The Elton Johns and Billy Joels of the world have the luxury of writing and enjoying a guaranteed outlet for the work—themselves! Even though their labels or their producers might voice objections from time to time, singer/ songwriters basically hold the power to immediately put their new songs on CDs, thereby guaranteeing that they will be released.

If you're convinced that you can be a successful singer/songwriter, and you're ready to dedicate yourself to a recording career, start lining up a support system that will help you reach the top. You may not find the right agent or manager immediately. While searching, book yourself as many gigs as you can. It will give you a chance to work out the kinks in your act, polish your presentation, and find out which songs work best with an audience. By the time agents or managers see you, you just might be the kind of total professional they're eager to sign.

What Makes a Good Agent?

An agent's prime responsibility is arranging for live appearances. When you sign with an agent, be sure that his or her commitment to your career is total. A half-hearted representative who pushes you only when others have already expressed excitement is no asset.

Until you know if your agent is an ideal representative, it's best to keep the contract length as short as possible. It's typical for an agent to ask for three to five years, an untenable time if things don't work out and you're trapped in a dead-end deal. Try to negotiate a shorter commitment.

Trouble Clef _____

If you suspect that your singing talent is minimal, don't push yourself as an artist simply because you want an outlet for your songs. Be committed to singing for its own sake. Not all songwriters are star vocalists. Observe with as much objectivity as possible the reactions of those around you. Ask yourself: Do I have what it takes to be a singing star? Am I willing to make the required sacrifices?

There's a cliché that says "Don't depend on an agent to get you a job." I don't buy that. Nor do I buy the old bromide "Agents don't get you work, but they can negotiate a deal for you." When you're starting out, you need someone to hustle and land you gigs. You can help, of course, and you should help. But you shouldn't have to do it alone, not if you're shelling out 10 percent of your earnings. After you've gained recognition, there will always be people who can negotiate contracts. You can be sure that Marty Erlichman, Barbra Streisand's representative of over 35 years, didn't get that position without working up a sweat to help his client. Nor did he sit back after she made it.

Whether you go with a small or a big agent, make sure your agent won't be insecure and undersell you so that you're knocking yourself out for practically nothing. If the agent accepts jobs that pay too little, there should be a specific reason. Possibly the exposure is important, and people who count will see you. You also want somebody who knows how to pace your career without burning you out by overbooking you. Your agent has to view you as a human being, not a machine he or she can use to make a few extra bucks.

Speaking of bucks, agents shouldn't ask for—or be granted—a share of your recording or songwriting royalties. They should only be compensated a percentage of the income you earn for your public appearances.

Small Agencies

The advantage in signing with a small agency is that its client list is not so extensive that you get lost in the shuffle. If you're heckling your agent and so is Will Smith, who will be listened to first? Your agent might be just as new and hungry as you are, and even though he or she hasn't established all the contacts in the world, a powerful desire to promote you will compensate.

The Big Enchiladas

The major agencies have more contacts, more money, and more power. Major agencies represent artists in every field: films, television, commercials, concerts, and records. They have close relationships with record labels, and a single call from them can get you the attention you need.

Managers

People outside of the entertainment industry often don't know the difference between managers and agents, but they serve very different roles. Unlike the agent who books you, a manager isn't expected or legally permitted to get you jobs. Only your agent can do that. But the manager handles just about everything else: contracts and promotion, the shopping of CDs

Hirschhorn's Hints

Try to find a manager who you think will be good at discovering your various other gifts and will help to develop them. Many singers and writers can also act, write scripts, produce, or direct. A manager should never be shortsighted. You want a person who pulls talents out of you that you never even knew were there.

and cassettes, and a marketing strategy. Above all, a good manager should supply an overall approach to your career. Nothing prohibits you from lining up work for yourself, and many enterprising singer-songwriters do that, but the help of agents and managers makes things easier. Agents and managers are experienced in strategizing, and you can work with them to conceive and act on a workable plan.

Mutual Obsession

If a manager has sufficient belief in you, you could literally become his or her life's project. Good manager-client relationships are a combination of friendship, desire, and a dedication. A manager who makes you such a top priority will attend performances he or she considers crucial to the building of your reputation. Count yourself lucky if you find someone with a drive that matches your own, a drive that centers on you.

I Just Want to Be Your Everything

Daylle Deanna Schwartz, author of *The Real Deal*, quotes an excellent definition of managerial participation by Peter Ciaccia (PC Management):

> A manager winds up being everything to the acts … the A&R person, the publicist. A manager has to make good judgment calls for the band. He is the liaison between the artist and the record company. When a band is unsigned, he works with them from the beginning to find a home for them. He's out there selling the band, selling the image and music of the band. He has to have a good sense of what the market calls for, what would interest people, and how to get to the people. He creates a realistic buzz about the band … he has to be tied to the street.

> **Backstage Banter**
>
> For total involvement in advancing your career, managers usually earn between 15 and 25 percent. Contracts are often for 3 years, but they may run for as long as 5 or even 10.

The Business Manager

The business manager concentrates on the very details that most creative people struggle to avoid: taxes, and the money that must be set aside to pay them; paying bills; and suggesting investments. Fees ranging from $1,000 to $3,000 are common, and it can range considerably higher for hot, established stars.

A Lawyer You Can Trust

Although the multitudes of lawyer jokes would have you believe otherwise, there are many hardworking, honest, effective attorneys. Just don't jump for the first one you meet. We need attorneys because they have more information and experience in the law than people who haven't passed a bar exam do. The old saw "A man who represents himself has a fool for a client" is all too true.

You Gotta Shop Around

Even if you meet an attorney who impresses you and whose expertise is in entertainment law, check him or her out (just as you would a doctor). Find out how much the attorney knows about the following areas:

- Publishing
- Performance rights, foreign rights, and recording
- Current copyright laws

Don't Be Frightened by Fees

When I started in the music business, I met an attorney who quoted me fees that almost provoked cardiac arrest. But the attorney saw potential in me. I had just signed a contract with RCA as a recording artist, and four of my songs were about to be recorded. Although the situation was no guarantee of success, it indicated the possibility of an enduring future.

We agreed that he would get paid a percentage of future earnings. My records sold minimally at first. Yes, I could have made 10 million and given away a huge chunk of income, but it was just as likely (or more so) that I wouldn't even get on the charts at all. Settling on a percentage was a gamble, but it removed my initial anxieties about costs and made it possible for me to have good representation when I needed it. He also had strong industry contacts and arranged introductions that furthered my career.

Do You Have What It Takes?

Do you have a target audience? A certain style? Charisma? Enough songs to attract a top record label?

Who Are Your future fans?

Are your targeted audiences made up of 13-year-olds? Do you covet the college crowd? Or is your music tailored to 30-somethings? It's not enough to say, "I want to appeal to everyone." Dr. Dre has his public, just as Clint Black, Christina Aguilera, and the Dixie Chicks have theirs. And those audiences are not the same.

You may have a clear, fully formed concept of how you want to be perceived. If not, you have to invent yourself. Bruce Springsteen was a more passive, folk-oriented performer before he became a forceful, physical, sexual "boss."

Hirschhorn's Hints

When you make a video, think it through carefully. You must come across as colorful, fascinating, and idiosyncratic. If you're an excellent dancer, work that in. Find a unifying theme, rather than just going through a bunch of unrelated images.

What Do You Look Like?

In today's visually oriented music world, appearances count. You don't have to be handsome or beautiful in the classic movie star sense, but you do need an individual look, an offbeat style of dressing. Depending on the audience you hope to attract, you might want to wear big hats or suspenders. Or you might wear dark glasses, green eye shadow, or a nose ring. Regardless of how conservative or far-out your garb is, you need a look to distinguish you from your competitors.

Russ Regan's Rules

Producer/record label president Russ Regan discovered and promoted Elton John, Neil Diamond, and The Beach Boys to superstardom. Regan has the following to say about the careers of singers/songwriters:

> Singers/songwriters have to have charisma. And intelligence! I love an artist who has charisma and is smart, because if he's smart, he can handle success. Those qualities were obvious in Elton John. He was electrifying on stage, a combination of great songs and a fantastic stage presence.

> When you're just a songwriter and you go to a publisher, you don't want to overwhelm him with songs. You're selling the music, not yourself. But a singer/songwriter is different, because you're being judged as a potential album artist. When a singer/songwriter comes to me, I want to hear at least five songs. You can't really judge an artist on one or two anymore, you've got to hear five.

> And the other thing is, the more you write—if you have talent in the first place—the better you become. As for demos, I personally don't mind piano-voice. I can hear a song, because I'm a song person. But a lot of people like

full-blown demos. I'm an exception. It would be wiser and safer for a new singer/songwriter to do a demo that gives a complete idea of what the record will be like.

Feed the Media Monster

Certain singers/songwriters have an innate sense of how to handle the press. They know when to be outrageous, when to be humble, and when to be controversial. Madonna went from sexual shock tactics to spirituality, authorhood, and motherhood. Elvis was a master in his day, doing raunchy bumps and grinds on stage and talking offstage about his beloved mom and his ties to the church.

Until you become the next Elvis or Madonna, though, you'll have to continually feed the media. Keep the following tips in mind to make your time with the media as meaningful as possible:

- **Do interviews.** Prior to any performance, advance pieces should be set up to tout club or concert appearances. These pieces are often more effective than reviews at drawing public interest, especially if the reviews don't turn out to be raves. Meeting journalists face to face is preferable, but most of the time you'll be doing *phoners*, telephone interviews that rarely last more than 15 minutes. As you grow more adept at phoners, you'll become skilled at packing in details about your specialty, your musical style, your overall image, and the various ways you differ from your competitors. Pertinent facts will roll off the tip of your tongue.

- **Use exclusives.** Depending on how far along you are in your career, you might land an exclusive, a highly visible spot in *The New York Times*, for example, or one of the other major newspapers. Press conferences also have value, although they generally only allow for sound bites and provide sketches of a performer's personality, rather than a full portrait.

 Hirschhorn's Hints

Make your press releases and press kits lively. Include demos, videotapes, articles, reviews, and pictures. All newspapers and magazines, as well as deejays and heads of radio programming, expect these materials.

- **Hire a publicist.** Good publicists are expensive and hard to find, but there are some who will get behind new singer-songwriters and promote them because they believe in their future. Beyond contacts, publicists must have imagination and fresh ideas about promoting the individual qualities that make performers and writers unique. It's no achievement when a publicist gains tremendous coverage for Justin Timberlake. A publicist once proudly told me (with a straight face) that he had gotten layouts all over the country for Paul McCartney, an accomplishment that would have happened automatically. When publicists are able to take relative unknowns (or just-rising singers) and get them impressive spreads, it shows that they have clout with the press.

- **Go regional.** Small papers and television stations are valuable when starting out, and publicists can concentrate on making performers local stars. Once singer-songwriters acquire a regional following, their reputations begin to spread. Word of mouth has a way of traveling beyond local gigs, and at that time, your publicist can work on breaking you nationally.

- **Try for top billing.** Your manager will always fight for better billing, and should. People do raise their estimation of your worth as your billing escalates. But don't insist on being a headliner right away; being an opening act for a major star also reflects favorably on you.

Backstage Banter

Elvis Presley was asked to do *A Star Is Born* and he refused because he couldn't bear to be billed second to Barbra Streisand. At the time, his film career was foundering. As the burnt-out rock star, he would have been superb and would have given the picture a hot, gritty realism. Always ask yourself: How good is the gig, how big is the booking, how instrumental will it be to your career?

Signing with a Label

There's no doubt that a singer/songwriter gets less personal attention from a major label than from a minor one. The major label compensates by having more resources at its disposal, including more money to spend on promotion, more powerful distributors, larger staffs, and bigger video and production budgets.

Hirschhorn's Hints

Make extensive use of the Internet by visiting websites and getting information about the labels you're interested in signing with. Be sure you know the names of the A&R people responsible for acquiring new artists.

The Majors

A major-league label has many advantages to offer, including the following:

- **Marketing department.** Publicity, promotional videos, in-store displays, and album cover artwork are the responsibilities of this department.

- **A&R department.** This group decides which artists to sign after listening to their demos or seeing them in person. They supervise record projects and suggest or select producers for their acts.

- **Sales department.** This department's job is to get records into stores.

- **Promotion department.** This department follows the record when it's released and makes sure that it has maximum airplay.

- **Business affairs.** Their priority is contracts between the singer/songwriter and record label, but also with record clubs and foreign distributors.

Even if you prefer to sign with a large company, that company might not be as eager to sign you before they see early signs of success. It's difficult to win a contract until the majors have evidence of your local success and impact on audiences. If the impact is strong enough, or promoted with sufficient strength and vigor by a publicist, you just might be able to attract them.

Hirschhorn's Hints

A comprehensive list of major and independent labels can be found on BANDGURU.com.

The Independent Labels

An independent label will see you as more of an individual human being. The purse strings will be tighter, but it's entirely possible that the financial output, though more selective, can accomplish just as much.

Suppose your manager gets an offer from one of the independents and tries to talk you into signing. Receiving the offer might thrill you so much that you want to sign that afternoon. Investigate the company, and see the artists they've promoted. Small independent labels have competed credibly in the marketplace: Bloodshoot to Sub Pop (Nirvana), Stiff (Elvis Costello), Chess (Muddy Waters), Epitaph (Offspring), along with Motown and Stax.

Come to the Cabaret

When we think of singer/songwriters, rockers are generally the images that come to mind. But other singer/songwriters represent a fast-growing and hugely popular genre. They don't get mentioned in *Billboard*, but they have die-hard fans in small clubs around the country. They are cabaret artists.

Cabaret performers appeal to the more sophisticated segment of the population. They do Cole Porter, Lorenz Hart, Noel Coward, and Stephen Sondheim. Very often they write their own witty and brilliant material.

Amanda McBroom, who wrote the million-selling standard and Golden Globe winner "The Rose" for Bette Midler, has become one of the key cabaret performers of the new millennium. She starred in *Jacques Brel Is Alive and Well and Living in Paris* at New York's Village Gate and has seen her songs recorded by Judy Collins, Anne Murray, Harry Belafonte, The Manhattan Transfer, and Betty Buckley. McBroom's CD *Portraits* contains such beautiful and definitive cabaret songs as "Best Friend," "Errol Flynn," "Whoever You Are," and "Ship in a Bottle."

The progression of McBroom's career is a textbook example of a cabaret singer's/songwriter's climb to fame, as you'll see by the following interview I did with her:

Q. How did you become a cabaret artist?

A. I had been a theater singer, done a lot of musicals, folk singing throughout high school and college. I wanted to do songs that would express my personal feelings and have them performed. A friend of mine who had an act at the Bla Bla Café sang some of my material, and I got it into my head to do a nightclub act.

Q. How would you define a cabaret singer?

A. There are two different kinds. One is a preserver of the tradition, which is the people who sing Jerome Kern, George Gershwin, people like Julie Wilson. Then there are the others, like me, those that write for the theater, or intend to, and find the cabaret a perfect forum for their work. The modern sophisticated balladeers are cabaret songwriters.

Q. How do you feel about rock and roll?

A. I love it, but I feel cabaret suits me better. Cabaret material is what I write best.

Q. Do you play an instrument?

A. I play three: piano, drums, and guitar.

Q. What's the advantage of being a cabaret singer/songwriter?

A. It's very spiritually rewarding. If you're a cabaret singer, my advice is, "Don't put a label on yourself." Write what your heart believes. It will find its niche, whether cabaret, rock, garage metal.

Q. What's your writing process?

A. Carry around a pencil and a piece of paper. Write down what comes to you at any time. Don't ignore things and wait for them to come back to you later.

Q. Does your work have a theme?

A. My life is my theme. I write about all my feelings. And remember, there are many places open to a cabaret performer. There's the Cinegrill in Los Angeles, Davenports in Chicago, Arci's Place in New York.

Hirschhorn's Hints

In addition to McBroom, listen to the highly regarded team of Karen Benjamin and Alan Chapman's hilarious satire *Everybody Wants to Be Sondheim (But Me)*, which is cabaret at its best. Anyone interested in learning how to write humor will gain immeasurably from exposure to McBroom, Benjamin, and Chapman.

Cabaret writing is show writing, and it's an ideal way to improve your skills and eventually arrive on Broadway. The form has also made current inroads in pop culture through films such as *Chicago* and *Moulin Rouge*. At their best, cabaret lyrics are clever and witty. But they also have tremendous emotional depth.

The Least You Need to Know

◆ Agents, managers, and lawyers are necessities for becoming successful as a singer/songwriter.

◆ You must have, or develop, an audience concept and a look to advance your singing career.

◆ A carefully orchestrated publicity campaign helps build your audience and attract the best professional support.

◆ It's not the size of your record label that counts; it's the promotion they do for your album.

◆ A cabaret career can take you to Broadway.

Chapter **17**

Working with Publishers and Agents

In This Chapter

- ◆ Know what a good publisher does
- ◆ The pros and cons of signing with a publisher or publishing your own work
- ◆ Write for attainable artists
- ◆ Understand the artist's personality

In the music business, publishers are firms or individuals whom songwriters enlist to promote their song or song catalogues to record producers and artists. The publisher also handles synchronization licensing, which includes placing material in films, on television, or in commercials. Publishers collect the money for songs they license and split the royalties with their writers. The split is generally 50-50.

In addition to acquiring outside material from freelance writers, publishers often employ their own staff of composers and lyricists. Sometimes these staff writers are simply composer/lyricists; other times they're singer/songwriters.

The Benefits of Working with a Publisher

An experienced and gifted publisher can provide financial support through weekly advances (which they recoup when and if your songs are recorded and released). Beyond that, they have a finely honed understanding of what successful performers and producers need, and the connections to get that material to these people.

Whether composers are freelance writers or singer-songwriters, they can benefit from having their work handled by skilled publishers. Although songs by recording artists are generally a larger part of a publisher's overall catalogue today, freelance writers are gaining ground. To a great extent, this gain is due to the amazing efforts of one woman, Diane Warren. Warren is not a singer and has no interest in becoming one. She simply wants to have her material recorded. A 2001 inductee into the Songwriter's Hall of Fame, she has blazed a trail for freelancers everywhere.

A publisher who believes in you and has a passion for your music is worth his or her weight in gold. Whether you're freelance or a singer/songwriter, the fact that the publisher takes care of the business leaves you with time to do what you enjoy most: create.

The Right Publisher

Just because publishers are listed in books or trade publications, don't assume they can get songs recorded easily. Some publishers are extremely active in approaching artists and securing recordings, but many just acquire catalogues and let performers or film companies come to them for the use of the material. Before signing on with a publisher, check to see what it is doing with current songs written by others and whether any well-known composers and lyricists are on staff.

Staid, older, wealthier firms are unlikely to hustle the way that hungry new firms do. There's no point in allying yourself with a publisher who won't promote your work.

> **Backstage Banter**
>
> Promoting work by freelance writers used to be a publisher's only priority. Today publishers handle many artists who write and record their own material, and they're expected to get songs from these CDs covered by other performers.

Good publishers always know what's going on. Naturally, they're aware of when Shania Twain plans to record, but they also know about lesser-known artists' upcoming recording sessions—and these performers are the ones you might not notice in your zeal to get a cut by Enrique Iglesias. Remember, hit groups and artists were once beginners, too, and they smashed through with talent, dedication, promotion, and good songs.

Publishers who get things done are tireless. They have a list of contacts, and they phone them constantly.

When they're not shopping songs, they're having lunch with producers and forging relationships. They attend recording dates even when their own songs are not being cut, and they develop a feel for what producers want.

A good music publisher will work nonstop to make sure his or her songs are recorded, including the following:

♦ **Pick the song.** The publisher's role, first and foremost, is to choose songs he or she feels can be recorded and turned into hits. You'll know fairly quickly if the individual you're meeting with has a particular enthusiasm for your material. If he or she says, "This stuff isn't for me, but bring me more," look upon that as a highly promising sign. Keep submitting. Listen to the publisher's viewpoints. Find out the type of material he or she prefers to promote. Keep your ear open for the kind of demos he or she considers effective. Good publishers meet with their staff at least once a week, go over the material in their catalogue, decide which songs are to be pushed, and then concentrate on those particular tunes.

Hirschhorn's Hints

Treat everyone who works with the publisher with respect, including the general professional manager and others on staff. They might be the ones who cover the street and service your songs.

♦ **Follow up on holds.** When artists and producers like a song, they ask for a *hold*. Publishers generally grant this request, but the hold has to be reasonable. After a few weeks or a month (or longer when the artist is exceptionally hot), publishers have to keep checking to see whether the song is going to be recorded. If no definite plans have been made, a publisher will ask for the tune back in order to send it to other singers. You want someone who will keep on top of the song and not drop the ball until all enthusiasm for the material has waned.

Lyrical Lingo

A **hold** is a period of time requested by the producer to consider the song, with the understanding that it will not be shown to anybody else during that period.

♦ **Nurture contacts.** To be effective, publishers need a list of contacts, a list they're constantly adding names to. The best ones know that there are hundreds of outlets for songs beyond those that seem obvious. Contacts are generated through years of bonding with producers, artists, and arrangers. Hustling publishers will fly to Philadelphia or Miami or Rome on a moment's notice to hear an artist perform, if that artist has done the publisher's material in the past.

They nurture relationships with artists and go out of their way to make successful singers happy.

◆ **Promote covers.** Good publishers don't forget songs once they've been recorded. If Justin Timberlake's recording of your song doesn't make it a hit, your publisher will take the song to another artist, and if that cut doesn't score, and he or she truly believes in the song, the publisher will shop it to a third artist. Some publishers get a dozen recordings of a tune before the right record catapults it to the top.

◆ **Handle subpublishing.** Rarely does a writer think beyond the United States, but good publishers do. They have subpublishing deals with other firms in England, France, Germany, and Japan. They'll work a song until cuts start showing up in other languages. Their efforts will lead to printed editions of your work where the sheet music is released individually or as part of a songbook.

Lyrical Lingo

Mechanicals are royalties that come from the record company and are for record sales only, not for performances logged by BMI, ASCAP or SESAC.

◆ **Show you the money!** Through contacts and experience, publishers are able to collect the *mechanicals* due you (and them). This collections expertise is an important consideration, because record companies would always rather pay later than right away; a good publisher has the clout to speed up the process. The current standardized mechanical rate is 8.5¢ per unit sold, whether album or single. In January 2006, the rate is scheduled to go up to 9.1¢.

Record labels pay mechanicals to the publisher, and the publisher distributes these payments every three or six months, depending on your contract. Quarterly is more standard and far preferable if the publisher agrees. Sometimes the record company will request a reduced rate (usually), and if the record is important enough and the artist sufficiently hot, publishers will go along with it rather than lose the cut completely.

If you've signed a song over to a publisher, don't sit back and decide that it's the publisher's job to sell the song and there's no need for you to pitch in. Writers have to help themselves. There's never a time when you should place total responsibility on someone else so long as you have the energy and resources to push your material. Try to imagine the assertive and prolific Diane Warren taking a backseat and giving all the power to someone else. Publishers, in general, appreciate your help, but you should be in constant touch with them so you don't see the same people they do and create confusion.

Big and Small

Publishers come in all shapes and sizes. The big ones, like Sony/ATV and Warner/Chappell, are tied to film or record companies. Small independent organizations aren't tied to anyone and function separately, often assigning their administration to one of their large-scale counterparts. Administration duties include issuing songs, paying writers, and registering copyrights.

Publishers with Production Companies

Publishers who also produce records have a quicker, more direct route to getting songs recorded. Early in my career, I was a staff writer for Bob Crewe, producer of such Four Seasons hits as "Rag Doll," "Let's Hang On," and "Dawn." We wrote with him, and he had the power, as producer and publisher, to put the songs immediately on a recording date. Most nonproducing publishers don't have that instant, direct access, so whenever you can write with a producer/publisher, you are better off in terms of recordings.

Working Exclusively with One Publisher

If you become a successful songwriter and a publisher offers to sign you to an exclusive contract, you might be tempted to grab it. "Just think," you might say to yourself, "with no money worries I'll be able to create in a relaxed, pressure-free atmosphere." The following sections give you the information you need to make an informed decision.

Signing with a publisher sounds good, but before you put your name on the dotted line, examine the long-range implications of the arrangement, good and not-so-good:

- ◆ **R-E-S-P-E-C-T.** You don't have to love your publisher, but you do have to respect him or her. Is the person in tune with the current tastes and trends of the market? Someone who says, "Give me Sinatra," when the popular singers of the day are Linkin Park, Matchbox Twenty, or Jagged Edge, isn't someone you want to tie up with.

- ◆ **Your own headquarters.** Being signed gets you off the street. You have an office

Trouble Clef _____

In what area has your publisher had success? If most of his or her contacts are with adult contemporary artists and you're interested in country, it won't make sense to sign with that publisher. Make certain your priorities are the same.

of your own and access to musical instruments, computers, stationery, phones, fax machines, and e-mail. That's a tremendous advantage, if it doesn't offer so much structure that you lose your cutting edge. If you do accept such a setup, be sure you get out where your fellow writers are. When you're building a career, stability isn't your prime goal.

♦ **Musical siblings.** Back when songwriters Carole King, Gerry Goffin, Barry Mann, Cynthia Weil, Howie Greenfield, and Neil Sedaka were signed to Don Kirshner at Screen Gems Music in the early 1960s, they created an atmosphere of friendly rivalry. It was a rivalry Kirshner did nothing to discourage. The competition drove everyone in the office to greater heights. The presence of other songwriters pursuing the same artists will give you extra incentive.

♦ **Make sure you fully understand what exclusivity means.** If a producer offers you a job composing his or her film, that producer is more than likely going to want to keep the copyright, and the same goes for television. The publisher who pays your salary certainly isn't going to let you do a project that doesn't bring the firm any revenue. So you'll very likely be forced to turn down the opportunity. Factor this potential conflict into your decision before signing any exclusive agreement.

♦ **Typical deals.** Publishing companies typically pay new writers a $300 to $500 weekly stipend. Hit songwriters earn a good deal more. This money is not a salary, but an advance against future earnings. If you do write a hit record while you're signed with a firm, the advances will be subtracted from record sales (not BMI or ASCAP airplay), and you'll be paid the remainder.

Doing Your Own Publishing

If you're a good promoter, with a talent for casting and pitching, you may not need a publisher. Many songwriters find they have the ability to get records on their own steam. If that's the case, you're in a far stronger financial position than songwriters who are signed to publishers.

As your own publisher, you have a perfect right to show your song to as many people as you choose to. You also get to keep your publishing rights, which doubles your income. It places you in a far more flexible position. A major artist usually wants a piece of the publishing, and if you own it yourself, you're in a position to give it to the artist or at least negotiate a split that's mutually agreeable.

If you decide to be your own publisher, affiliate with music logging organizations such as BMI, ASCAP or SESAC. Make sure you register your material with the Copyright Office at: Information and Publications, Section LM-455, Copyright Office, Library of Congress, Washington, D.C. 20559 (see Chapter 24 for more on the guilds and registering your copyright).

Selling Your Songs to Singers

Finding an artist to record your work can be complicated. Here's an obvious tip: Don't pick someone who records his or her own songs exclusively.

Your best chance is with an artist who takes outside material on a regular basis. Search *Billboard*'s Hot 100, and you'll come up with something like this entry:

> Lesson in Leavin'
> Jo Dee Messina
> Producers: B. Gallimore, T. McGraw
> Writers: R. Goodrum, B. Maher

You can see from the entry that Messina didn't write her own song, so you know there's a chance she'll consider recording one of your songs.

Make sure any material you send artists is appropriate for their style. If you want country superstar Tim McGraw to record one of your songs, for example, you wouldn't send him a rap song more suitable for Eminem. Seems obvious, doesn't it? But new writers send material to wildly inappropriate people. Half the time, they just ship it out to a dozen artists without regard to the artists' specific needs. Send the song to your first choice, and if the artist you've chosen doesn't ask to hold it for further evaluation or possible recording commitment within a reasonable time period, send it to the next in line.

Trouble Clef

Do your homework and study available performers and the kinds of songs they're recording, or you're asking for rejection. Worse, once a producer sees that you've submitted illogical material to his or her artist, you can expect a pass on what you send later, even when it's ideal.

Hilary Duff Is on Tour

There's no point in writing for Hilary Duff if she's just finished an album and won't be cutting a new one for the next eight months. Ideally, the material should be sent a few months in advance of when the artist will be recording an album. Check, however, to see if there's a cut-off date, so you don't submit songs after the selections have all been made. You have to investigate who's coming up for a date and needs material immediately by calling record companies and checking out tip sheets such as the following that announce this information:

♦ *New on the Charts*
1501 Broadway
New York, NY 10036
212-921-0165

Hirschhorn's Hints

Do a search for "music tip sheets for songwriters" on Google for a wealth of other information. Jeff Mallett's Songwriting Site (www.lyricist.com) is a detailed, exhaustively researched, and noteworthy site worth checking out.

Trouble Clef

Stars aren't everything. Don't think you can succeed only with stars. My own career proves the opposite. Two of our biggest hits were with unknowns: The Peppermint Rainbow ("Will You Be Staying After Sunday?") and Maureen McGovern ("The Morning After").

♦ *Parade of Stars*
The Chellman Bldg.
1201 16th Avenue South
Nashville, TN 37212
615-320-7270

♦ *Song Connection*
12390 Chandler Blvd. #C
N. Hollywood, CA 91607
818-763-1039

♦ *Song Placement Guide*
Marcia Singer
PO Box 189
Pacific Palisades, CA 90272
213-850-3606

♦ *Songwriter's Market*, published annually and available in bookstores

♦ *Billboard Talent & Touring*
www.billboard.com

♦ Nashville Songwriter's Association International
1701 West End Avenue, Third Floor
Nashville, TN 37203
1-800-321-6008

Combing *Billboard* with care will also give you a good idea of the artists' schedules. Keep producers in mind when pitching your songs; they frequently write for their artists and often collaborate.

Listen to the Artists' Records

Once you've identified a few potential artists, listen to at least three of their CDs and all of their singles. Try to find common denominators in their material. Are there intervals they always seem to favor? Octave leaps? Blues notes such as flatted thirds? What rhythms seem to predominate? Do their tastes run mostly to ballads?

As for personality, are they victims, or do they take over? Is the theme of their songs more often heartbreak, or are the songs about free spirits who don't get tied down? Once you make these determinations, you don't have to follow them with clinical precision, but they will give you a sense of what the artists are like, what they try to express, and what their musical capabilities are.

When you first listen to their songs, don't study them. Listen a second time and then a third. At that point, start your analysis. Without a single fact about an artist, without knowing where he or she was born or went to school or whether he or she has any sisters, you'll discover the essence of that person through his or her music. Music reveals just as much about individuals as facts do.

Whether you sign with a publisher or freelance, if you believe in a song, keep pitching it. When Wilco submitted their 2002 album, *Yankee Hotel Foxtrot*, to their record label and were turned down, they took it to another label, got it out, and garnered major critical acclaim.

The Least You Need to Know

- ◆ Target artists who are available.
- ◆ Study every facet of the artist's records.
- ◆ You must respect the publisher you sign with.
- ◆ Choose a publisher with wide and varied contacts.
- ◆ Self-publishing is fine if you're a good promoter.

Chapter 18

Making the Best Demo

- ◆ Piano-voice, guitar-voice, and other demo approaches
- ◆ Ways to locate the best vocalists and musicians
- ◆ How to make the most of your time in the studio
- ◆ The demo package and presentation

Writing a song isn't enough. You have to get others excited about it, and the only way to do that is by producing a strong demonstration record, or demo. A few composers still fight the idea of demos. They harbor the mistaken notion that they can present their songs in person to a publisher, producer, or artist. Unless you happen to be at a party or a social event and you have the opportunity to sit down at a piano and spontaneously showcase the material, in-person presentations won't yield desired results.

Even if an artist or producer listens to a personal performance of a song, that person will probably say, "I like it. Now do a demo so I can *really* hear it." In past decades, people trusted their ears. They had the imagination to envision a final record without every bit of musical and rhythmic detail spelled out. Few people have that sense of security anymore.

In addition, publishers don't want the psychological discomfort of facing an eager songwriter and having to express their opinions directly. With a demo, they can play and replay the material, soaking it in and mentally working up production possibilities. From your point of view, a demo can also be a positive. You can embellish on your work in the studio and paint in the musical colors it needs.

Choosing Your Musical Approach

On the off chance that you *do* get to perform your songs in person, be well rehearsed. Don't stumble, say you have a cold, or clear your throat incessantly. Make sure the publisher, producer, or artist has a clear copy of the lyrics to read. Don't do more than three songs, preferably two. Don't try to force reactions before they're offered, and don't get defensive if the verdict is negative.

Hirschhorn's Hints

Remember, all responses are simply opinions, although some are more educated than others. Al Kasha and I performed a song called "Will You Be Staying After Sunday?" for a major publisher and he said, "I'm sorry. It's definitely not a hit." After the song became a Top Ten record and sold a million copies, we ran into him on the street. He just shrugged and said, "We all make mistakes."

Piano-Voice Demos

If you've written a beautiful ballad and hired a superb singer to perform it, sometimes a recording of a singer with piano accompaniment—called the piano-voice demo— will be enough. In a song of this kind, people want to hear the melody and words with complete clarity. Remember, though, the piano has to be the whole orchestra. Whether you're doing the playing or you've recruited a studio pianist, the keyboard work must have as much body and dimension as possible.

Guitar-Voice Demos

Another simple demo approach is the guitar-voice demo. Again, this approach is best when you feel you've written an outstanding tune or lyric, and you want it to be strongly spotlighted. Guitars are naturally funkier than pianos; they convey a rhythm and blues or country feel more effectively than keyboards.

Voice with Piano, Guitar, Bass, and Drums

A guitarist, bassist, drummer, and pianist with a powerful lead vocalist and expert background singers are ideal for many demos. A setup of this kind offers clean, simple strength and will give you any groove you need.

Live Combinations or Synthesizer

Beyond the basics just discussed, there are no rules. You can utilize synthesizers alone or in combination with live instruments. Your imagination is your guide, determining how spare or full you want the presentation to be.

Cover Your Bases

When you cut a demo, you want to be certain it has the broadest possible appeal. Yes, your main goal is to persuade Jennifer Lopez to do your tune, but Lopez receives thousands of tunes and your chances are slim. Why not open up new vistas in case she turns you down? One way to do that is to write a lyric that can be sung by either a man or a woman. You can also use a solo singer for one version of the demo and a group of singers for another version.

Trouble Clef

A tastefully produced demo is preferable to an over-produced one. Don't get so caught up in the icing that you forget the cake. Your first priority is to show off the song, not to cloud it with too many instrumental figures and vocal parts.

Choosing the Singer

Writers are remarkably careless when it comes to selecting singers for their demos. Half the time they're considered as an afterthought. Don't make that mistake.

Don't pick a singer on the basis of hearing him or her live. The visual impact of a singer's presentation may deafen you to how his or her voice sounds. Physical impact, expansive gestures, and personal charm can misguide you, no matter how keen an ear you have. Someone who prides himself or herself on holding big notes probably doesn't know how to let the microphone do the work. Insist on getting a tape or CD of your potential vocalist's voice.

Hirschhorn's Hints

Every singer excels in certain categories. A demo singer who specializes in country might not be able to rap or sing Latin-oriented rock with the authenticity of a Shakira or Marc Anthony.

Picking the Right Musicians

The care you take in choosing a demo singer must be extended to musicians as well. As with vocalists, everyone has a specialty. Some musicians play brilliantly, but they can't read music. Others read parts at a glance, but they lack creative ideas and the ability to improvise. Some musicians want full lead sheets. The majority of musicians are content with just chords.

When possible, pick players who have worked together in the past. You'll benefit immeasurably, both creatively and in terms of time saved, from their rapport.

Locating the Best Players

If you're new to making demos and you need to connect with superior musicians, check out these places:

♦ **Your local musician's union.** The union will be more than happy to suggest people. In an era when live players are being supplanted by electronic music, the union is eager to get its members booked as often as possible.

♦ **Recording studios.** Get in touch with recording studios around town and ask the people who work there for recommendations. As you develop relationships with producers, studio owners, and engineers, ask them if you can sit in on their sessions. Not only will you become familiar with the finest players, you'll absorb invaluable studio procedure.

♦ **Visit clubs.** Speak to musicians and get their tapes.

♦ **Study CDs.** Comb the backs of CDs for musicians' names. All the players are listed there, with detailed information about their particular specialties. Look at the acknowledgements. In these sections, recording artists cite further information about guitarists, synth players, drummers, or other individuals who have made a significant contribution to the record.

> **Backstage Banter**
>
> The key element to a hit song isn't getting a known star (although that can shorten the journey to chart status); it's having a great record to promote. And the route to a great record is a great demo that isn't so meticulously specific that any other performer is shut out.

When You're the Artist

Many composers have no interest in becoming recording artists. Their main priority is writing the best possible songs with the greatest hit potential. But if you have singer-songwriter aspirations, demos are an excellent place to hone your skills and assemble a tape for presentation to a label.

Figuring Costs

A few publishers exist who might like your work and be willing to foot the demo bill, but chances are more likely that you'll have to cover the cost of the demo yourself (unless you're already established and signed as a staff writer to a firm).

If demo costs are coming out of your own pocket, you'll probably be keeping close watch on what you spend. But even if you're cutting a demo for a publisher who's paying for it, you need to watch costs. When you exceed the allotted budget the publisher has given you, the additional money you spend will be subtracted from your royalties if the song is eventually recorded.

> **Trouble Clef** _____
>
> I once worked with someone who felt that we should split the demo costs 30-70 in his favor because he had more experience in the business. Our collaboration didn't last long. Be wary of suggestions like these. When you're writing a song together, 50-50 should be the split if the contributions are equal.

Prepare Now or Pay Later

Recording studios aren't cheap. Even at the low end of the scale, expect to pay anywhere from $75.00 to $100.00 an hour. Live musicians add greatly to the expense, so that a demo with four or five musicians easily can add up to $1,000 or even more. If a synthesizer is doing most of the instrumental work, it can cut the cost in half, and if you're the one playing the synthesizer, that reduces the costs further.

Many writers prefer to "wing it," letting the creative process guide them when they get into the studio. Naturally, you'll fall upon fresh ideas and try new approaches when the session gets underway. But certain basics should be handled in advance to keep in-studio costs down:

> **Hirschhorn's Hints** _____
>
> It pays to shop around and find the most competitive studio rates. Some will work with you and be extremely reasonable (in the $50 an hour range).

- ◆ **The singer's key.** A surprising number of songwriters base the performer's key on his or her previous recordings, rather than making sure the key is absolutely perfect in the specific piece of material. Don't be satisfied if a singer tells you, before the date, "I'm always fine in the key of C." Test the key out and make sure it's exactly right. Trying songs out in various keys once the session has started becomes time-consuming and prohibitively expensive.

Sometimes, when the key isn't quite right, writers ask musicians to *transpose* the key. Many musicians are skilled at transposition, but others can do a good job only if the right chords are written out. That forces you, as the writer, to scribble a new lead sheet with the altered key, and this process eats up studio time, which means money.

Lyrical Lingo

To **transpose** is to take a key and change it to another one: to take a song written in the key of C, for example, and write or play it in D.

- **Avoid nonprofessional vocalists.** When you have a limited budget, you may be tempted to compromise by using a friend or family member to sing your demos, but you have to be tough-minded. Certain demo singers are repeatedly hired by successful songwriters because these singers have studio savvy. They're quick, adaptable, and thoroughly professional, and they save time. Any money you save by hiring a nonprofessional will be swallowed up by their lack of recording experience.

Making the Demo

After you've planned the music for the demo, found the vocalist and musicians you'll be using, and figured your costs, you're ready to record your demo at home or in a studio.

Hirschhorn's Hints

A tiny studio without any reputation might give you exactly what you need. Ask for recommendations from friends and fellow songwriters.

Choosing a Studio

Before picking a studio you haven't used before, ask for samples of other albums it has recorded. Analyze the sounds it gets on its vocals. Sometimes, demos produced by the most highly praised studios sound surprisingly thin or simply not right for the concept you have in mind.

Enlisting Creative Support

When you get the right musicians, you want to enlist their creative support. Never rule with an iron hand. Encourage a free, easygoing atmosphere. The record business is studded with instances in which a spontaneous solo turned the song into a smash.

As nervous or impatient as you might become, don't be overly critical. If someone makes a mistake, treat it lightly. Never go on the attack. If someone does a competent take that could still be improved, simply say, "That's terrific, but I'd like to give it one more try." When talented people are appreciated in the studio, they rise to unexpected heights. If they feel attacked or unappreciated, resentment will set in, and the results will be mediocre.

Staying Creatively Focused

In addition to being warm and open about suggestions, keep sharply focused on your own artistic vision. If you're new to making demos (and sometimes even when you're not), you can be swayed by experts into abandoning your original concept.

Remember that even experts are just volunteering opinions; nothing is written in stone. Even if you're recording your first demo, you might be on to something others don't grasp.

Holding Your Ground on Tempo

Never settle for a tolerably satisfying tempo. Don't accept a rhythmic pulse or groove because the engineer, the background singers, or even your own partner says it's okay. If you have that uneasy feeling in the pit of your stomach, pay attention to it. Otherwise, you'll find yourself at home a day later in a state of despair because the rhythm lacks excitement and drive.

Handling Studio Disasters

Creative leadership in the studio means more than making proper artistic decisions. It means keeping your cool when problems arise.

Occasionally a musician you've hired won't show up. Stay calm. If it's a missing guitarist, the piano player might be able to fill in the part. A livelier bass line could compensate for the missing drums.

In this era of synthesizers, the absence of a musician is less serious, unless you're determined to do all the parts live. If you want that live sound, lay down a temporary track of the part until you can book someone to come in and duplicate it on a live instrument. If you maintain a calm state of mind, the difficulty will resolve itself. And as you gain experience creating demos, you'll be surprised how capably you handle crises when they arise.

Demos at Home

More and more, writers are purchasing their own equipment and recording songs at home. Obvious creative advantages include the luxury of working out parts by yourself by testing drum fills, guitar licks, or a piano line. You also have innumerable instruments at your disposal.

Suppose you're doing a rock record but it suddenly occurs to you that a bassoon might lend something fresh and interesting. If you have a synthesizer at home, a lush woodwind section is one button away. Even if you decide to do the demo in a large studio later on (or finish it after recording basic tracks in your garage), you'll have a great head start, and you can test ideas without being stressed out by a ticking clock and escalating studio costs.

> ### Backstage Banter
>
> It's not unheard of for demos to be turned into masters—final recorded versions ready for release. This happened in the 1960s with Carole King's demo-turned-master version of "It Might As Well Rain Until September," and later on when Bruce Springsteen and Pete Townshend of the Who each put out demos as albums that earned critical acclaim for being more "raw."

Hirschhorn's Hints

Don't think that because a synth isn't new it's not good. If you've done great things with your M-1, you don't have to give it away because something new is on the market. I still use a lot of my early equipment.

Upgrade Slowly

The trick with a home studio is to keep a sense of financial proportion, at least in the beginning. Once you enter the seductive world of home recording, you'll want to continually upgrade your equipment. Remind yourself that you don't need every state-of-the-art piece of equipment to turn out a good demo.

Equipment changes with dizzying speed. To determine what technology to invest in, attend seminars, browse through stores, and ask questions of other musicians. Study the equipment you see in studios or at the home studios of your friends.

Submitting Your Song

Once you have a demo ready to send, you can't just slide the CD in an envelope and send it off to publishers. You need to prepare an entire demo package. Keep reading to find out how.

My feeling is that the more information you can send, the better off you'll be. Therefore, I recommend sending a lyric sheet (typewritten lyrics with contact information and a copyright notice), a recording of the song, and a lead sheet (handwritten sheet music with melody, chords, and lyric) whenever you submit a song.

Preparing a Lead Sheet

For all those who can't read music, dozens can, and if they like the song, they'll probably want to follow the music as they listen in order to familiarize themselves with every aspect of it. If you aren't sufficiently skilled to notate the music and chords yourself, ask a musician, fellow writer, or arranger to do it for you.

To prepare a lead sheet, follow these steps:

1. Define the style. Here are some examples:

   Moderate gospel rock

   With a heavy beat

   Moderately bright

   Slowly

   Swing feel

   Lighthearted rock

   Folk-ballad style

   Moderately slow with a double-time feel

   Medium rock beat

   Heavy backbeat

2. Put in the treble clef.

Trouble Clef _____

Above everything, be neat. Many composers labor to make their songs perfect and then present them in a sloppy fashion. Nothing screams "amateur" more than messy lead sheets.

3. Don't forget the key signature, whether it's G, D, F-sharp, B-flat, or any other key you choose. If you don't specify the number of sharps and flats your key contains, the person who plays the music will hear only a senseless cacophony.

4. Specify the time signature: Is it 3/4, 4/4, 2/4?

5. No crooked bar lines. Again, use a ruler.

6. Don't cram notes unevenly into each measure. Keep the spacing even.

7. Write lyrics under the correct notes. Many beginners (and even those who should know better) dash off words and don't align them exactly with the proper notes. When artists, producers, or publishers see this kind of sloppiness, they usually throw the song into the discard pile.

8. Use chord symbols properly. Like lyrics, they should be placed over the notes they belong to. Although there's more than one way to indicate a chord, the following notations are widely accepted:

   C major = C

   C minor = Cm

   C augmented = C+

   C diminished = Co

   C major 6th = C6

   C major 7th = Cmaj7

   C major 9th = Cmaj9

   C minor 6th = Cm6

   C minor 7th = Cm7

   C minor 9th = Cm9

   Dominant 7th = C7

   Dominant 9th = C9

   Dominant 11th = C11

   Dominant 13th = C13

   Diminished 7th = Co7

9. Take advantage of technology. Software that notates music is becoming increasingly popular, whether the goal is to write parts for a small band or for a large orchestra. Some of the alternatives include:

Musitek's Smart Score, which features music scoring, MIDI sequencing, and music scanning.

Sibelius's G7 was designed by guitarists for guitarists and is one of the fastest way to create signature riffs.

Geniesoft's Overture 3 is a simple to use notation software strong enough to satisfy professional composers.

Finale 2004 PC offers complete notation with audio export capabilities.

Hirschhorn's Hints

A songwriter doesn't have to be an arranger. When you notate music, it's best to keep it simple. A complicated, overly detailed lead sheet will frighten off artists and producers, most of whom can't read music. The melody line and chord symbols are usually enough.

10. When you've completed the lead sheet, play it as written and check for mistakes. Go over it two or three times, because the eye frequently misses errors the first time.

11. Don't send out your only copy. Always keep one for yourself.

Remember, even if you never become an expert at music notation, it's enough if you capture the basic chords and melody for your own convenience, so each idea is preserved. When showing your demo to a publisher, producer, or artist, use these basic tips:

◆ If you're presenting the demo in person, be quiet while the demo is playing. Don't attempt to point out the song's virtues during the song.

◆ If you're mailing the demo package, make sure you're sending the material to the right person at the company. Enclose a cover letter describing the songs. In the letter, let the producer or A&R person know your background, especially if you've had songs recorded.

◆ Label everything in the demo package, including the CD and lead sheet, with your name and contact information (including e-mail address), the name of the song, and copyright information.

◆ Target your material. Don't send the head of A&R a selection of your best work without including the singers the songs are for. Find out in advance which performers are heading to the studio and send them the songs prior to their sessions. It does no good to send a hit to Norah Jones if she completed her album two weeks earlier and doesn't intend to record for another year.

◆ Make sure you enclose a stamped, self-addressed envelope. Otherwise, the songs won't be returned.

- If financially feasible, put the songs on CD rather than on cassette.

- Don't leave too much *leader* between songs, or your listener might get restless.

Lyrical Lingo

The empty stretches between songs on a recording are called **leaders**.

- In choosing the songs to spotlight, pick the ones you feel are the most powerful. Your first song should be the one you believe in most. It's no good if the third song is a hit; your listener won't get that far. Never include something you feel others *might* like. You must be passionately convinced that each tune is the next big Grammy winner.

- Don't pressure your listener for an answer.

- Don't submit the only demo you have. CDs are frequently misplaced or lost. Producers and artists expect you to have backup copies.

- Wait a few weeks before following up. If you don't get an answer, wait two or three weeks more and then call again.

In the past, songwriters turned the responsibility of creating a demo over to an arranger. Today, songwriters have to take on the role of the arranger and even the producer. It's up to you to create the whole musical canvas. Because you'll want to show off your song, you'll become more aware of rhythms, figures, vocal parts, and arrangements, and you'll learn more and more about how to put a song together. The exciting creative dividend of the modern music business is that it ensures that you'll continue to grow as a composer and lyricist.

The Least You Need to Know

- Piano-voice and guitar-voice demos are often enough when the song is sufficiently strong.

- Budgeting carefully and preparing for studio time will save you heartache later.

- The best demos are made when a producer invites creative output from all participants.

- Making demos at home will give you extra time and will save you money.

Chapter **19**

Producing Your Own Songs

In This Chapter

- ◆ Learn about producing
- ◆ Choose the right material
- ◆ Cut the best track
- ◆ Try a different musical approach
- ◆ Have a productive attitude in the studio

Songwriters might enjoy the triumph of having their work recorded by major artists, but they rarely retain artistic control over the final product. As a producer, you are able to make certain that the record turns out the way you envision it.

From the time you make your first few demos, you'll have a sense of whether you have the talent for record production. You won't be satisfied with a merely acceptable demo—you'll keep reworking it, making sure it competes favorably with records you hear on the air. If you feel you have the gift, my advice is to pursue it. You'll enjoy increased financial rewards as well as the satisfaction of hearing your songs exactly as you conceived them.

A Producer's Job

A record producer, along with the label and artist, finds the material, supervises the recording, and mixes the final product.

Techno or No?

Some producers are comfortable with every facet of technology and engineer, or co-engineer, their sessions. Others, though creative in the areas of performance and musical arranging, let their engineers do the majority of the technological work. Either approach is fine if it works for you. All that matters is the result, no matter how it's accomplished.

Hirschhorn's Hints

Record producing isn't something you generally learn in school. You learn it only by watching and doing. Go to every session you possibly can and study producers in action. Absorb everything. You'll decide by observation what you want to emulate or avoid. Listen to records of every kind. Set aside your personal tastes and prejudices. No one ever learned a craft selectively. Many high-power movie directors had to work on low-budget films before they created high-budget epics. The same goes for record producers.

How Involved Will You Be?

People sometimes look critically at creators who want to assume huge responsibility. The assumption is, "He's an egotist ... he's taking too much on ... it'll never work." Only you know how much responsibility you're capable of assuming. In movies, Woody Allen tackles all phases of his films. On records, Walter Afanasieff (Mariah Carey, Celine Dion) does the same. Afanasieff creates the arrangements, writes the songs, and records all the backing tracks.

Be a Director

When you produce, be decisive, but don't try to do everyone else's job. Don Cook (Brooks & Dunn, Lonestar) claims he wouldn't "dare touch a knob" of the engineer's, although he makes suggestions about mixes. "He's so good I wouldn't tell him how to do what he does any more than he would tell me how to do what I do."

On the other hand, you must express yourself with clarity. You've chosen to handle three or four roles, and your personnel will look to you for final answers. Even if you're not absolutely positive about something, don't seem nervous and doubtful. You don't necessarily have to run a "totalitarian dictatorship," as Snuff Garrett—who produced "Gypsies, Tramps and Thieves" and "Half Breed" for Cher—defines it, but you should always be perceived as a leader.

You need to be able to see the whole picture and visualize the end result. But don't become impatient with details. As Michael Cuscuna (Dave Brubeck, Dexter Gordon) says, "Most of the fun is in the details, whether it's horn obbligatos, a very tasteful slide guitar part, or a wonderful organ chord."

Planning a Recording Date

Whether you're recording a solo singer, a group, or yourself, you need to follow certain organizational steps. Most vital is picking the right material.

What Are the Songs?

Even when the songs to be recorded are yours, you need to be ruthless about your choices. Unless you feel the song is one of your masterpieces, don't include it in the session. Of course, objectivity is harder to achieve when you're assuming the multiple responsibilities of writing, producing, and possibly singing.

Consider everything from the record company's point of view (the people who have to promote the record) as well as your own. Yet if the record company expresses a preference for some of your songs, and you feel that you've written better material, fight for your point of view. You won't always win, but if you feel passionate about it, you have to try.

Backstage Banter

Andy Johns (Bon Jovi, Van Halen) has this to say about studios:

The room where the instruments are has to sound good. The mixer is not important as long as it's not horrible and doesn't break down. The monitors have to be good. Tape machines can be analog or digital. As years go by, I find that stuff is less and less important. I don't use drum machines or samplers. I get the sound from the room. If the sound isn't right, the guy's got the wrong gear—wrong guitar, wrong amps, wrong drums.

—Anastasia Pantsios, *The Encyclopedia of Record Producers*

Try Different Studios

Each studio offers uniquely different sounds. David Z. (Prince, Sheila E., and Jody Watley) favors recording in different studios because you work a lot harder. There are a lot of records out there that sound the same because they're done in the same room. David likes to stretch a little by using closets, bathrooms, and hallways.

Finding the Right Engineer

Engineers (also called audio mixers) supervise the console, handle all the various tracks, and mix these tracks into a cohesive whole along with the producer and artist. They usually come with the studio. Sometimes the artist or producer brings in an engineer not specifically affiliated with the studio.

Hirschhorn's Hints

Try to know as much about engineering as the engineer does, even if you don't do the engineering yourself. Ask questions. That way, you'll have a stronger grasp of the overall process.

Make sure your engineer sees things the way you do. Sometimes engineers are aspiring record producers, and they can have a strong sense of the final artistic goal that might clash with yours. The engineer you work with is a crucial ally. Be sure you communicate well with the engineer, both artistically and personally. Above all, make certain the engineer excels at mixing.

Hirschhorn's Hints

Everything is negotiable, but a typical royalty rate for producers is 2 to 4 points (percentages of retail). Superstar producers have a good chance of getting a higher percentage—5 to 10 percent of retail sales.

Up-Front Budgeting

When you're working in your own studio on an independent master—a production you hope to sell to a company after it's completed—you can afford more freedom with time. But if you've been hired by a record label to produce, work out your budget carefully right from the beginning and adhere to it. Your budget will include prices for the amount of session time needed, musicians, your engineer, an arranger, and background vocalists.

Rehearsal

To save time during the recording session, rehearse your material as thoroughly as possible beforehand. Make sure the singers' keys are perfect and try out several, rather than taking your artist's word for it. Even if you're the artist, don't pick the first key that seems comfortable. Often, comfortable keys don't offer the maximum impact. Stretching for a high note, pushing, or wailing might be more effective. When deciding on that final key, the depth and power of emotion should be your overriding priority.

Get Organized

I've assumed many times that my equipment was fine, and have been shocked to discover in the middle of a recording session that one thing or another wasn't working properly. Check your equipment incessantly, even neurotically. You don't want mishaps during a session, especially if you've hired other people.

In the Studio

Before you spend a lot of time concentrating on the vocal performance, pay attention to the *tracks*. Zero in on the track with percussion, or the one with guitar. Work on your drum sound until it's just right; the main goal is to find a drum sound that matches up well with the other instruments.

Be sure your groove falls right in the pocket—not too fast, not too slow. Keep in mind that excessive speed doesn't guarantee excitement. Don't work out a tempo by intellectual means. Just because another, similar hit with a similar groove uses a certain metronome beat doesn't mean that same beat will work perfectly on your tune. Each number has highly individual rhythmic requirements.

Lyrical Lingo

Tracks are individual channels of recorded sound, which are then blended together to create a multitrack recording—16 track, 24 track, 32 track, or any other combination desired.

Examining Alternatives

The Beatles recorded *Sgt. Pepper's Lonely Hearts Club Band* on four tracks, with no loss of artistic quality. Today, you can easily work with 100 tracks. Even though you're confronted with so many possibilities, try to decide what you want to feature in the beginning. You can test other alternatives after you do the basics, but be aware that the number of available tracks can be a trap. Some producers become so overwhelmed by choices that they can't make a final decision and don't finish the record on time. And when they do, they're still not sure they made the right choices after the mix (the final combining and balancing of every element in a recording). Try to work out a vision and a plan beforehand to avoid this confusion.

Engineer Jeffrey Norman recalls that Creedence Clearwater Revival's John Fogerty knew where every part was going to be. For example, in the thirteenth bar on the seventh eighth note, he knew there was going to be a little "yeah" on one of the tracks, and it sounded completely spontaneous, but it was all planned.

Work with Your Creative Team, Not Against Them

If your singer starts to flub notes and lyrics and looks exhausted during the recording session, don't come on like a tyrant. The same goes for your engineer and any other personnel. If you drive people too hard, you'll get diminishing results. Curb your anxiety and all-consuming desire to get things finished. When the personnel you're working with get the breaks they need, they'll give you much better work.

Musical Approaches

There are as many musical approaches as there are producers, but they all have the same object: to capture the attention and imagination of the audience.

Trouble Clef

Dave Bascombe (Depeche Mode, Tears for Fears) advises against mixing a track so much that you lose perspective. He feels that it's hard to mix your own work if you've lived with it a long time and you've pushed the fader up every day, over and over again. Retaining freshness is vitally important.

Maybe you're interested in capturing the spirit of the performance, maybe you'll do anything to record an emotional, exciting vocal. No matter what style you aspire to master, try not to let technical precision outshine a great performance.

When analyzing takes of a performance, you may find that one take is technically astonishing and another is flawed but more dramatically affecting. Go with the one that moves you and the other people listening. Dozens of singers have expressed regret that they went for technical perfection at the expense of a certain feeling. Some performances tap into emotions and can't be duplicated; they're just one-time miracles. Don't let any of those get away.

Go with the Good Goofs

Musicians and singers are human, and they make mistakes. I can't tell you how many times a guitarist or a singer hit a supposedly wrong note and started rushing to correct it when I called out, "Wait! That's terrific. Can you do it again?" Turns out their goof was much better than what I'd originally written. Don't be so focused on your original concept that your mind is closed. It could cost you a hit.

Experiment

In pre-synth days, when acoustic orchestras and bands reigned supreme, experimenting and coming up with new, offbeat sounds was a minor priority for artists, writers, and musicians. Today, with electronic access to so many sounds, noises, and instrumental combinations, experimentation is a key factor in hit recording.

> ### Backstage Banter
>
> The theory was to do anything we needed to sound different. We even talked about putting guitars under water at one point, just to see what it would sound like. We just did all kinds of weird things—multiple source recordings, which I still do a lot of—especially with guitars. I take it from one amp and split it into another one; that way you can basically make sandwiches of sound.
>
> —David Z., quoted in *The Encyclopedia of Record Producers*

Play with the Atmosphere

Kurt Bloch (Fastbacks, Mudhoney) likes to set up, as he calls it, an "artistic vibe":

> Sometimes it might be appropriate to have incense and candles burning and the lights down. Sometimes it works better to have all the lights on and have everybody going "eahhrrgghh" and drink a lot of coffee and be screaming at each other and all revved up so they rip through their songs or whatever. Everybody is different. Every session is different (quoted in *The Encyclopedia of Record Producers*).

Vary Your Themes

When you're in the studio and you want to sell yourself as a songwriter and producer, make sure the songs you pick are highly varied. Utilize different rhythms. Follow a ballad with something up-tempo. Lenny Kaye, legendary punk-rock guitarist, likes to have many different styles within an album because that gives an artist a chance to move into whatever his or her next album will be, and it will make sense. He doesn't believe in monochromatic records. He will, for example, place a song with a little

Trouble Clef

Songwriters frequently feel the need to change the demo that got everybody excited in the first place. They tinker and embellish to a point where the charm and specialness of the original is lost. If the demo worked beautifully without a mass of strings, keep the strings out. If it was magical with acoustic guitar, don't substitute an electric one. Maintain that original magic.

string quartet next to a piece of avant-garde noise. Kaye has never been one for pure music. He likes mongrel music, "where styles copulate with each other and form some weird child that sounds different."

Start with Whatever Works for You

Never mind how other record producers do things. We all have a unique way of hearing.

Jack Clement (Johnny Cash, Charley Pride) views his role of producer as orchestrator. He finds a voice, and then finds out what works with that voice, what instrumentation. "Sometimes it's heavy with piano, sometimes it's heavy with guitars, and sometimes it's heavy with fiddles and steel guitars" (quoted in *The Encyclopedia of Record Producers*).

Trouble Clef _____

You can labor over a production until it becomes overcrowded. Too many ideas cancel each other out. Hearing a superb guitar solo, a brilliant piano lick, and a wonderful vocal note simultaneously is a waste. Choose your spots and feature them so that they stand out and count for something.

Trouble Clef _____

LaRocque also warns not to favor one's own instrument at the expense of others. If you're a drummer, your temptation in the mix will be to feature drums. If you're a pianist, you'll often get keyboard-heavy. Keep an overall perspective, and concentrate on what's best for the overall mood and song.

You Have to Love It, Too

When you're getting close to the end of a recording date, you may tell yourself, "I don't love it, but the people will." Such an attitude is a recipe for disaster. If you don't love the record, why should the public? Try to figure out what dissatisfies you. Is there something in the lead performance or the arrangement that seems lacking? Have you talked yourself into something that you don't really feel? Search for clues. Ask those around you, but don't let people hear your work unless you're 100 percent certain of its worth.

Mixing

Mixing involves blending a song's tracks together and highlighting the important elements. It can involve featuring a guitar solo or a piano figure, or highlighting the vocals while downplaying the band. Roger LaRocque, who has produced tracks for such varied artists as Julian Lennon, James Ingram, Frankie Valli, Billy Preston, Sheena Easton, Quincy Jones, and ZZ Top, offers this basic advice on mixing:

> If you don't experiment with simple gear, you won't have a basis for what comes later. The

important priority is learning how instruments work together, how rhythm sections blend. In mixing, you have to be able to divide your frequency so everything doesn't land in the extreme low end, high end, or mid range. Some of this information you're taught, but much of it is the result of moving faders, trying things out.

LaRocque continues ...

Trusting the first mix you hear in your headphones is a mistake. Mixes always sound better in headphones, but the only true way to evaluate them is to hear the music on your speakers.

Hirschhorn's Hints

Let a day or two go by and listen to your mixes again minus the emotion of immediate recording. You'll know clearly at that time what needs to be subtracted or built up.

Top Producers

The following producers are among the best in their field. This list provides a small sample of their records as a guideline to expert producing talent.

◆ **Walter Afanasieff**

Michael Bolton: *Time, Love, and Tenderness* (Columbia, 1991)

Mariah Carey: *Emotions* (Columbia, 1991), *Hero* (Columbia, 1993)

Natalie Cole: *A Smile Like Yours* (Elektra, 1997)

Barbra Streisand: *Higher Ground* (Sony, 1997)

◆ **Brian Ahern**

Johnny Cash: *Ghost Riders in the Sky* (Columbia, 1979), *The Essential Johnny Cash (1955–1983)* (Legacy, 1992)

Emmylou Harris: *Portraits* (Warner Bros., 1996)

Anne Murray: *The Best ... So Far* (EMI, 1994)

◆ **Rod Argent**

Nanci Griffith: *MCA Years: A Retrospective* (MCA, 1993)

The Zombies: *Time of the Season* (Date, 1969)

◆ **Burt Bacharach**

Patti LaBelle: *On My Own* (MCA, 1986)

Dionne Warwick: *Greatest Hits—1979–1990* (Arista, 1989)

Dionne Warwick: *Golden Hits Part 1* (Scepter, 1967)

◆ **Dave Bascombe**

Depeche Mode: *Music for the Masses* (Sire, 1987)

Erasure: *Pop, the First 20 Hits* (Sire, 1992)

◆ **Howard Benson**

Blue Meanies: *Pave the World* (Beach, 1996)

Pretty Boy Floyd: *Leather Boyz with Electric Toyz* (MCA, 1990)

◆ **Joe Chiccarelli**

Lone Justice: *Shelter* (Geffen, 1986)

Oingo Boingo: *Nothing to Fear* (A&M, 1982)

◆ **Robert Clivilles and David Cole**

James Brown: *Universal James* (Scotti Brothers, 1992)

Aretha Franklin: *Greatest Hits, 1980–1984* (Arista, 1994)

◆ **Michael Cuscuna**

Luther Allison: *The Motown Years—1972–1976* (Motown, 1996)

Dave Brubeck: *Time Signatures: A Career Retrospective* (Columbia, 1992)

◆ **David Z.**

Fine Young Cannibals: *Finest* (MCA, 1996)

Jody Watley: *Greatest Hits* (MCA 1996)

Hirschhorn's Hints

Ask for help, especially at the beginning. Don't be ashamed of not knowing something. Many producers have a mentor side to their personality and are glad to answer your questions.

◆ **Rhett Davies**

Legend Soundtrack (MCA, 1986)

King Crimson: *Three of a Perfect Pair* (EG, 1984)

◆ **John Fogerty**

John Fogerty: *Willy and the Poor Boys* (Fantasy, 1969)

John Fogerty: *Blue Moon Swamp* (Warner Bros., 1997)

- **Snuff Garrett**

  Cher: *Gypsies, Tramps, and Thieves* (MCA, 1971)

  The Brill Building Sound: Singers and Songwriters Who Rocked the Sixties (Era, 1993)

- **Andy Johns**

  Van Halen: *Best Of—Volume 1* (Warner Bros., 1996)

  Rod Stewart: *Storyteller: The Complete Anthology* (Warner Bros., 1989)

- **Quincy Jones**

  Michael Jackson: *Thriller* (Epic, 1982)

  Michael Jackson: *Bad* (Epic, 1987)

- **Lenny Kaye**

  Patti Smith: *Masters* (Arista, 1996)

  Suzanne Vega: *Solitude Standing* (A&M, 1987)

- **Robert John "Mutt" Lange**

  Shania Twain: *The Woman in Me* (Mercury, 1995)

  Billy Ocean: *Greatest Hits* (Jive, 1989)

> **Backstage Banter**
>
> Producer Mike Clink (Guns N' Roses, Sammy Hagar) says, "I used to spend all my money on records. I'd read the backs of album covers, listen to the music, and try to figure out how they were made."
>
> —*The Encyclopedia of Record Producers*

> **Hirschhorn's Hints**
>
> Other producers worth checking out are the Neptunes (Britney Spears, Justin Timberlake, Madonna), Dr. Dre (Eminem), Steve Albini (Big Black, Nirvana), Bob Rock (Metallica), T. Bone Burnett (Counting Crows, *O Brother, Where Art Thou* soundtrack), and Brian Eno (Roxy Music, Talking Heads, U2).

Even the songwriters today who aren't officially record producers think like producers when composing. When conceiving a song, it's important to go beyond the basics and concentrate on how the song can be heightened by sound, mixing, and instrumentation.

The Least You Need to Know

- The way to learn producing is to study every hit record.
- Record only the songs you truly believe in.
- Figure out which instruments you want to feature.
- Be confident about learning new technology.
- Always experiment.

Part 5

Finishing Touches

Everyone has their own work habits, and the more you go with what works best for you, the better your results will be. In this part you'll find out about the most popular songwriting techniques and why rewriting is so essential. If you work with a partner, I'll help you figure out how to adapt to your collaborator's creative rhythms.

And remember—if you do a good job, you're entitled to be paid properly for your work. BMI, ASCAP, SESAC, and the Songwriter's Guild of America will help you collect every dollar you've earned. You'll also want to utilize the vast resources of the Internet. Finally, study the lists of top songs and performers in Chapter 25. Once you've listened carefully to the material, your writing will automatically improve and touch audiences.

Chapter 20

Different Creative Styles

In This Chapter

- ◆ The importance of flexibility
- ◆ Words vs. music for Rodgers, Rice, David, and Newman
- ◆ Writing for an artist

Should music or lyrics come first? As someone who has worked as both a composer and lyricist, I can answer this question from both sides of the fence. There are no fixed rules, despite the insistence of songwriters on all sides that one method is superior to the other. The only rules you should worry about are the ones that work for you and, if you have one, your collaborator.

Follow Your Instincts

My first encounter with the big what-comes-first question came when I was a teenager and RCA signed me as a writer/recording artist. After being told to buy collegiate sweaters, wear dark glasses, and get a crewcut, I sat down to write songs for my first record session.

I had written some material, but I'd never given the process much thought. Now I was told by an executive, "Your song will only work if you write the music first." He seemed knowledgeable, so I tried it his way on a song called "Will You Stay in Love?" I found myself bursting to finish the lyric, but I repressed the desire and nearly drove myself crazy laboring on a tune instead of following my instincts. I missed my first deadline, and arranger Norman Paris, who was set to do my recording session, asked what the trouble was. I told him, and he said, "Write the lyric. That's the way your mind works. It's like forcing yourself to be a right-handed pitcher when you're left-handed."

Hirschhorn's Hints

Newscaster Ted Koppel became a stutterer because he was forced to write with his right hand when he was a leftie. The problem was solved when he did what his brain demanded and started writing with his left hand. Forcing your thoughts along one channel when they ache to go in a different direction can be equally destructive for songwriters. Be open-minded and receptive, especially if the person giving advice has years of experience. But if the advice feels wrong, and you've weighed it as objectively as possible, then don't go along with it just because of your adviser's seniority. Trust your instincts and remember that no one, no matter how confident he or she may sound, has all the answers.

Major Songwriters Weigh In

Examining the way skilled composers and lyricists handle the what-comes-first problem is the best way to clarify your own ideas on the subject. The following examples describe how different songwriters work.

Tim Rice

Tim Rice, lyricist for *The Lion King*, *Aida*, and *Jesus Christ Superstar*, recalls that while working with Andrew Lloyd Webber, "We had the tune first every time. He'd play it for me and I'd pick it up. If I couldn't pick it up quickly, obviously it wasn't a very good tune. I'd tape it on a recorder … or if not, I'd just have it in my skull" (quoted in *In Their Own Words* by Bruce Pollock).

Hal David

Hal David always felt comfort and freedom in his daily writing routine with Burt Bacharach, a routine that resulted in such classics as "Don't Make Me Over," "Close to You," and "Raindrops Keep Falling on My Head." In the Bacharach/David relationship, neither words nor music came first; it was a constantly evolving, change-able mode of working. David describes it this way:

> On occasion, I just think in lines, but most of the time the idea comes to me with a title. And often it occurs in two lines. I see things in hunks, rather than specific sentences. I'll think of an eight-bar phrase. Burt and I would meet in one room, and I was very hardworking, as he was. I was always writing lyrics; he was always writing melodies. The question most repeatedly asked was, "What do you think of this? What do you think of that?" Either my lyric would set him off to write a melody or vice versa.

Randy Newman

Randy Newman, composer of the scores for *A Bug's Life*, *The Natural*, and *Toy Story*, and the hit singles, "Mama Told Me Not to Come" by Three Dog Night and "Short People" for himself, says that an inspiration might come to him in the middle of the night, but more often it takes place while he sits at a piano.

Bob Dylan writes alone, and he starts out with melody before words. So do Stevie Wonder and Paul Simon. Charlie Fox has done just fine writing music to Norman Gimbel's lyrics ("Killing Me Softly with His Song," "Ready to Take a Chance Again," and "I Got a Name").

> **Backstage Banter**
>
> Many legendary composers from the pre-rock era, including Jerome Kern, Harry Warren, Harold Arlen, and Arthur Schwartz, believed that having lyrics first stifles creativity.

Practice Wearing Both Hats

Although most composers and lyricists have a preference about whether music or words come first, others easily slide back and forth, relaxed with any order the process takes. Some writers, particularly those who handle all the music and lyrics, do things only one way, but would prefer to be more flexible. My advice is to take a musical track, either from an instrumental or a hit song, and write words to it. Then try it the other way around, taking a famous lyric and providing your own tune. Regardless of whether you wind up favoring one method over the other, you'll expand your musical perceptions, and the results will reflect that creative testing and freedom.

The Rhythm in Your Mind

If you're a lyricist, hearing a tune before you begin can make things easier. The leaps in the melody direct your emotional approach. The rhythm is also spelled out. In any case, lyricists, even those who don't write tunes, are generally musical. They hear tempos in their heads. If they have dramatic thoughts, they can imagine a melody swooping up or dropping down as they write.

No Borders

Without a melody to give a lyricist defined borders, he or she may occasionally wander. The lyricist doesn't need the entire tune; a verse is enough to provide structure. It doesn't matter what the structure is, as long as the lyricist is given the basic foundation.

Backstage Banter

Stephen Schwartz, winner of two Oscars for Best Song, says, "I always get down as much of the lyric idea as possible. I think music is much easier than lyrics, because lyrics are craft, and music is an emotional response to a situation or a particular feeling. So I handle the lyric first. It's important that I get as much of the lyric done as possible, because once the music is done, that's it for me. I'm trapped in that form."

The same goes for melody writers, who might need words to help organize their thoughts. In that case, lyrics, whether in fragments or fully conceived, can help to bring out the melody writer's best work.

Take This Song and Shove It

Sometimes the lyricist's words limit the direction that the tune writer can take with the song. David Allan Coe's "Take This Job and Shove It" could never (let's hope) be turned into a Celine Dion ballad. The words compel a tune writer to provide pulsating, angry music. Similarly, Sarah McLachlan's "I Will Remember You" suggests a mood of nostalgia and sadness and would be inappropriate if paired with a pulsating rap or dance melody.

If a tune writer plays lush, jazz-oriented chords, those chords will lead a lyricist in a different direction than if the chords are harsh and dissonant. Throbbing hip-hop rhythms are emotional explosions; a slow ballad pace cries for sensitivity.

Hooked on a Feeling

In today's rhythm-oriented world, the inspiration for a hit song can be simply a "feel" or rhythmic pulse. Once the tune writer supplies the beat, the song is set in motion.

Backstage Banter

Each project follows a different path. When Al Kasha and I wrote our Oscar-winning song "The Morning After," for the 1972 movie *The Poseidon Adventure*, we knew that a unifying concept was mandatory before a single note or word was written. The producer told us, "A ship is turning over. People are drowning. The boiler room is exploding. So make it positive!" In other words, we had to convey a message of hope in the midst of devastating catastrophe.

Once we landed on "The Morning After" as a title and followed that line with "if we can make it through the night," our overall concept was nailed. Then we worked together, line by line, testing out alternatives on each other. We also created the melody using this line-by-line approach.

For "The Old-Fashioned Way," which became a worldwide standard with Charles Aznavour, Al and I received a melody from Aznavour. He made it abundantly clear that "not *one* note, *one* rhythm, *one* phrase was to be touched." Our job was to do lyrics only. Fortunately, the tune was so beautiful that we had no desire to change anything.

The all-important feel or groove is the key to pop songwriting today. The tune writer can play it on an instrument or tap it out; a lyricist can come up with a *dummy line* that conveys the needed syncopations and tempo.

Steven Tyler of Aerosmith also emphasizes the value of an instrumental riff in launching hits. According to Tyler, "Walk This Way" started out as a Joe Perry guitar riff. After that, Tyler added his rhythm licks on top. The Rolling Stones' "Start Me Up" also began as a Keith Richards riff. With that as a basis, Mick Jagger wrote the rest.

Lyrical Lingo

A **dummy line** is one that uses words to get the writer started, to give him or her a sense of rhythmic or musical pattern. These words are throwaways and rarely, if ever, make it to the final draft.

Feel Your Way to Creativity

Rules are meant to guide, not to strangle. Thousands of composers and lyricists torture themselves in their efforts to do the "right" thing. Any composing system that produces quality material is the right one. For composers such as Randy Newman and Billy Joel, who work alone, the right system is the one that feels the most comfortable at the time. For people who write with partners, the right system is the one that can be mutually agreed upon by two or three collaborators or even, as in the case of "Say

My Name" by Destiny's Child, seven collaborators (R. Jerkins, F. Jerkins III, L. Daniels, B. Knowles, L. Luckett, K. Rowland, and L. Robertson)!

Lindsey Buckingham of Fleetwood Mac makes another point worth remembering. A writer should exert a certain amount of craftsmanship and conscious control, but not so much that a sense of spontaneity and inspiration are eliminated. Buckingham says:

> You may start off with a certain intent, and you start putting strokes on the canvas, but because it's so intuitive and one on one, the colors will lead you in a direction you didn't expect to go, or you may have a preconception of what the song is going to be, melodically and otherwise, and you may end up in a totally different place. And that is probably more the norm than the exception (quoted in *Songwriters on Songwriting*, by Paul Zollo).

Preparing to Create Songs for Artists

If you're creating material for artists who record *outside* songs, you'll want to do an analysis of their previous work before you make a what-comes-first decision.

As a Composer

Study former hits of those artists for the following elements:

- **Chords they particularly favor.** It helps to buy sheet music and listen to records until you become familiar with their signature chords.

Lyrical Lingo

When an artist is willing to record songs composed by other writers, those songs are known as **outside** songs.

- **Chord progressions.** Does this particular artist like songs that frequently use C Am F G7 or G Bm C C/D? If you study the catalogue of any particular artist with care, you'll begin to notice that certain progressions keep resurfacing.

- **Rhythm.** Does the artist like waltzes? Bossa novas? Bo Diddley rhythms?

As a Lyricist

Look for these lyrical elements:

- **Recurring themes.** Determining that the artist cuts love stories is not enough. What kind of love stories? Does he or she lean toward the optimistic or the tragic? Is the artist's approach cheerful or cynical?

◆ **Attitude.** Does the artist lean toward middle-of-the-road conservatism or is he or she rebellious?

◆ **Style.** Does the artist prefer flowery lyrics or straightforward descriptions?

After doing this pre-work, you can move to the writing. You'll have a sense of that individual artist, both personally and artistically.

The Least You Need to Know

◆ When it comes to writing songs, there are no hard-and-fast rules about whether the lyrics or the melody should come first.

◆ If you're a lyricist, have a rhythm in mind when you write.

◆ If you're a tune writer, imagine words that correspond to the mood of your melody.

◆ Learn the craft, but don't get so locked into it that you sacrifice spontaneity.

Chapter **21**

How Collaborators Work

In This Chapter

- ◆ The trials and rewards of partnership
- ◆ Work habits that need work
- ◆ Ways to find a partner
- ◆ International songwriting collaborations

One of the most remarkable partnerships in music history is the team of Jerry Leiber and Mike Stoller. Their collaboration began in the early 1950s, and now, nearly half a century later, they're still together. Leiber and Stoller wrote Elvis Presley's biggest hits, as well as "Charlie Brown" for the Coasters and "Is That All There Is" for Peggy Lee. Another long-term partnership is that of Barry Mann and Cynthia Weil, who have written successfully since the mid '60s, with songs that include "You've Lost That Lovin' Feeling" and "Soul and Inspiration."

These collaborators are heartening proof that a songwriting partnership can endure, surviving all the inevitable stresses that arise in the course of day-to-day creativity.

Making a Partnership Work

Partnerships don't just coast along blissfully without traumas and trials. Even the best of them take dedication, work, and compromise. But if you're willing to put forth that effort, the rewards are often emotionally and financially satisfying.

Songwriting partnerships are like marriages. They involve much more than the ability to turn out hit songs. New writers are usually bewildered when they see such a team as John Lennon and Paul McCartney go their separate ways. But temperament, philosophy, and long-range goals are as crucial to a partnership as creative ability. If the divisions are too wide on these issues, the relationship comes apart.

Hirschhorn's Hints

Some people look upon writing as a grim, back-breaking chore. Compatible partners don't see it that way. As John Kander says, "Writing is never hard, even if it takes a long time. Freddy [Fred Ebb] and I never don't have a good time when we're writing." His positive approach is part of an overall attitude that sustains collaborations.

When partners are compatible, they're totally open to input from each other. The process begins with a single line, and then addresses issues of range, altered lyrics, and rhythm. No one is saying, "That's *my* area; stick to your own," whether subtly or directly.

A lyricist might write four verses that make perfect sense, yet the words lack emotional build. At that point, an astute partner might realize that the first and second verses, if switched around, would make the song far more powerful. Or the lyricist will see that the ending should rise for more impact.

Dividing the Labor

Sometimes the collaborative songwriting process is extremely simple and friction-free: The lyricist comes up with a complete set of words, and the tune writer hands his or her partner a finished melody. Whether the words or music come first or second is irrelevant. The division of labor in such cases can be clear to the point where each partner accepts the other's contribution without any suggestions.

Trouble Clef

If at all possible, heed producer Lynda Obst's words when you sense that a partnership of value is threatened: "Resist all impulse to turn incident into drama." Search for areas of compromise. You'll be glad you did.

More often, though, writing roles vary. Even if the lyricist doesn't contribute a specific note of music, he or she may have some strong ideas about how to strengthen the tune. The melody writer might notice a cliché and suggest word substitutions that would make the line fresher and more original. Both people must remain open to the other's viewpoint.

Backstage Banter

An example of a clash between lyric and melody occurred when Carole Bayer Sager and the late Peter Allen were writing a song called "Ah My Sister." Carole had her own definite ideas about it, as did Peter. Peter was talking about his actual sister, and she was talking about a kind of sisterhood for women. The result disappointed her, and she referred to it as a mixture of thoughts that sounded schizophrenic.

Finding a Mutually Acceptable Working Time

Suppose you're a night person and your collaborator is only able to think clearly during the day. You have to ask yourself if you can adjust to a different time schedule. How about if you work together evenings for three days a week and early mornings for the other four?

Dealing With Lateness

A common collaborator complaint is that one of the partners is habitually late. The best you can do is try to convince your partner how much his or her tardiness disturbs you. Keep emphasizing it, without letting your feelings flare into open hostility. After a while, if nothing changes, you have two choices: Break up the relationship or live with it. Remember this fact: In any relationship, individuals rarely change when someone else pushes them. They have to make the decision to change on their own.

Keep in mind that no partnership flows evenly without some bumps and bruises. You probably have traits that annoy your collaborator, who also has to repress his or her emotions for the greater good of your creativity.

Handling Deadlines

Another common conflict between partners is the attitude toward deadlines. When a team is given three weeks to complete a song, one person may want to work slowly and methodically every day, analyzing and discarding dozens of different alternatives. The other person might let two and a half weeks slide by, and then rush frantically to complete the song.

Frequently you'll hear the cry, "That's the only way I can work!" Again, compromise is called for. The person who functions only at the last minute is probably perfectly capable of working on the music and lyrics throughout the allotted time given. Or the more methodical person could provide the last-minute person with a list of ideas to review closer to the deadline.

Trouble Clef _____

> Cy Coleman, the composer of Broadway's _Sweet Charity, Seesaw,_ and _I Love My Wife,_ worked with a lyricist named Joe McCarthy. Together they wrote a Frank Sinatra standard, "Why Try to Change Me Now?" But the work process, as Coleman admitted, caused him constant frustration. "It took Joe days and days, and I hated it because you had to sit with Joe. I didn't want to sit with him while he contemplated." Remember that excessive dependency and emotional neediness can undermine a partnership. Be independent.

Blending Personality Types

In most songwriting partnerships, one person is more extroverted, and the other is more retiring. If your partner wants to seize the limelight, are you content to let him or her dominate, or do you need equal appreciation? Two people who want dominant, highly public positions rarely maintain their creative connection for long.

Trouble Clef _____

> If you begin collaborating with a partner who demands that you stick strictly to his or her style of working, you should cut off the relationship immediately and search for someone else to work with. You both have to function in a way that's natural to your basic style and personality.

If you're the introvert, you have to decide whether you're capable of or willing to subordinate your personality to your partner's. If you're outgoing and your partner is shy and subdued, you might want him or her to pitch in more and get more involved rather than linger in the background. Ideally, your two personality types can blend, but many teams shatter because one feels neglected or deprived of proper credit, and resentments quietly escalate.

Avoiding Competition

The key element of a writing partnership is the song! Don't get too caught up in competition with your partner, or you'll lose focus on the main issue. Competition, left unchecked, poisons everything. If the song is successful, there's plenty of glory to go around.

Handling Criticism

Sammy Cahn once told me that he never directly criticized a melody brought to him or bluntly said he disliked it. Sammy was wise. If you criticize a collaborator, you should suggest alternatives and say something diplomatic, but you should never be cruel and harsh. Your lack of tact will be resented and will undermine the partnership.

At the same time, you shouldn't write lyrics to a melody you don't care for or a tune to words that fall short of your standard. Eventually a language evolves between co-writers, and their true feelings are clearly communicated by a word, a gesture, or a joke. These tactful ways of expressing reservations don't ever come across as attacks.

> **CAUTION**
>
> **Trouble Clef** _____
>
> Alan Jay Lerner, lyricist for _My Fair Lady_ and _Camelot_, once told me, "If you tell your partner you don't like something, be prepared to say why. Don't just say, 'It doesn't appeal to me.' If you're putting thumbs down on something, have good reasons and be able to express them."

Defending Your Vision

Be open to the opinions of your partner, but also be willing to fight for a tune or lyric you passionately believe in. Listen without being defensive if your collaborator doesn't seem as enthusiastic as you expected him or her to be. In the end, if you reach an impasse and your collaborator is dead set against a particular product, you have to capitulate. But try to defend your point of view if it's a strong one. Otherwise, you'll hate yourself for giving in too easily.

> **Backstage Banter**
>
> People often say, "Don't get too professionally involved with your partner, and above all, don't live with him (or her)." Like all dogmatic, black-and-white statements, this one fails to account for differences in individuals. Barry Mann and Cynthia Weil are together after nearly 40 years. Jeff Barry and Ellie Greenwich divorced, but Alan and Marilyn Bergman are still married and are more professionally active than ever.
>
> Songwriting spouses can find life wonderfully satisfying and productive if they both have the same goal. In a situation like this, work usually continues after the sun goes down. Writing is the cornerstone of a composing partnership between husbands and wives.
>
> If you live and breathe work 24 hours a day, marriage to a partner will be ideal. If you want to escape and tune out your musical career for large chunks of time, major adjustments will have to be made. There is, however, great, unmatchable satisfaction in creating a bond that means so much to you both.

Partnering Up Part-Time

Some partners choose to work exclusively with one another. Others mix things up a bit, picking different partners for different projects. Whatever the structure of the partnership, it's vital to agree on the terms up front. Your co-writer can feel threatened if you decide to write "just one song" with another collaborator. His or her security may rest in keeping your pact exclusive.

Certain composers and lyricists like to work primarily with one person while having the freedom to occasionally partner with someone else. This arrangement is often an ideal way to avoid the sense of being confined.

Carole Bayer Sager composed frequently with her ex-husband Burt Bacharach ("That's What Friends Are For," "On My Own") while providing lyrics for Peter Allen, Albert Hammond, and Melissa Manchester. Tim Armstrong writes mostly with Lars Fredericksen in their band, Rancid, but lately Armstrong has collaborated with Pink.

You might prefer to write rock with one person, country with another, rap with a third, and a motion picture theme song with a fourth.

How to Find Your Partner

You might be the kind of person who expects a partner to be a psychotherapist, a mother/father confessor, or a pal. Or you might prefer a collaborator who's all business. Hooking up with a songwriting partner is very similar to finding a lover or a friend. The right partner is out there if you keep searching.

Don't wander around, praying that an elusive, ideal co-writer will magically appear. If you choose to write with someone else, rather than alone, you have to conduct your search in a thoroughly organized fashion.

Start Locally

Potential partners are everywhere. The logical place to start is your immediate vicinity. Consider members of local bands. Chances are that some of them have songwriting ambitions. Go to clubs in your area and form friendships with performers. If they write, fine. If they don't, they might put you in touch with people who do. The musician's union, an organization that works on behalf of musicians for their rights, benefits, and salaries, is another rich source of potential partners.

Don't be afraid to look beyond local opportunities. Go where the action is in the main music circles of Los Angeles, Nashville, New York, San Francisco, Chicago, and London. Write to every publisher you can and set up appointments well in advance of your arrival. Find out who reviews material in each firm and establish a running dialogue with him or her, so you won't be a complete stranger when you show up. Be prepared with lead sheets and recordings of your songs when you walk in. Once you present your work, let the publisher know you're looking for a partner. Publishers know all the best writers and frequently arrange collaborations. I met my lifelong writing partner, Al Kasha, through a publisher's introduction.

Advertise

If you're a student, run an ad in your school newspaper. State your desire to team up with someone and spell out your specific needs. Or do the same thing on a national level, by buying ad space in *Musician Connection* magazine. Many rewarding collaborations have materialized through this fine publication. Put up notices in music stores, churches, synagogues, and music clubs, and check local papers and websites. And if you start getting frustrated, keep in mind that Elton John and Bernie Taupin met through the classifieds.

Your ads can be as simple as the following:

> Young composer looking for lyricist in the Chicago area. Ron Garvey, 124 Rosemont Drive, Chicago, Illinois 00000

> Lyricist seeks composer of Latin/rock music for collaboration in Enrique Iglesias/Marc Anthony style. 619 N. Kingsbridge Road, Bronx, New York 00000

 Hirschhorn's Hints

Making contacts can be difficult at first. A shortcut, if it's creatively feasible, is to work with someone who has more connections. It's also an asset if your collaborator has a studio setup, which will save you a fortune in recording fees.

A good source for help in locating a partner is the Songwriter's Guild of America (see Chapter 24 for more on this organization). Mention the type of music you specialize in (pop, R&B, rap, country), specify whether you're interested in a tune writer or lyricist, and include information about how interested parties can reach you.

Establish Industry Contacts

Everybody in the industry is a possible contact, a possible lead, a possible partner. Talk to background singers, arrangers, and copyists. Start a favorable buzz going.

Never forget: One introduction leads to another. Chat with a gatekeeper, a secretary, or an assistant. They might be forbidding and cold, but not always. Some are sympathetic, friendly, and helpful. They might mention your name directly to the boss, but they can also tell the vice president and the office manager. Eventually, your name might filter upward to the person in charge.

Getting to top people in the recording industry isn't easy. You can't just stride into the office of a record company president or *Billboard*'s number-one producer of the year. To establish a link, you need middlemen.

Backstage Banter

Sometimes just being on the proper turf is enough.

When I was 17, a famous songwriter named Charlie Singleton saw me wandering in the hall of Manhattan's Brill Building and took me to a well-known publisher, Robert Mellin Music. Charlie's compassion for a lost-looking newcomer brought me my first record, "All About Love," sung by Clyde McPhatter. After I was armed with an important cut, other, better-known songwriters wanted to write with me, and I started collaborating with a host of talented composers and lyricists.

Contact ASCAP, BMI, and SESAC

ASCAP (American Society of Composers, Authors, and Publishers), BMI (Broadcast Music, Inc.), and SESAC (Society of European Stage Authors and Composers), the three societies that log music around the world and pay writers for accrued airplay, are supportive and helpful in putting songwriters in touch with one another (see Chapter 23 for more on ASCAP, BMI, and SESAC). Put together a tape of your material and take it to these societies to evaluate. In addition, these organizations host workshops and seminars that provide opportunities to meet other writers searching for a partner.

Backstage Banter

Al Stillman wrote dozens of hits for Johnny Mathis, including "Chances Are." My mother remembered that she had dated Stillman in high school, so I called him and reminded him of their friendship. This call led to our working together, and it gave me a start in the industry.

Go for a Lucky Long Shot

Billboard lists the national hits weekly in all categories, along with names of their songwriters and producers. Make careful note of these names and study the styles they compose in. Armed with this information, you can try to get in touch with those you particularly admire. When you do eventually connect, you'll be sufficiently well informed about them to see if a partnership is possible.

If entertainment attorneys feel you have talent, they can offer direct access to their illustrious clients. Agents might also be coaxed into arranging valuable introductions.

Work with Those in Control

On a practical level, collaborating with producers and artists, instead of with publishers, increases the chance of getting records. Producers and artists have total control, and unlike publishers, they automatically supply the recordings. Working with an artist (such as Bernie Taupin's collaboration with Elton John) can guarantee entire albums of your music or lyrics.

Cold, Hard Business

As I mentioned, getting a partnership's emotional ground rules worked out from the beginning is vital. Just as important are the business decisions. Here are some questions that must be answered before you start working with a partner:

♦ Will you each get 50 percent of the royalties, or will one of you get a higher percentage? Will the partner who accepts the smaller share feel resentful later on if the song is a hit?

♦ Will you both co-own the song's publishing? Again, there's fuel for rage if one person owns the entire copyright and has the power to sell it later on and collect the profits.

♦ If a song doesn't succeed, will one writer or the other have the power to take his or her lyric or melody back and find another writer to put fresh words or music to it?

I've had writers say to me, "We began with a 50-50 split, but I wrote more. Don't you think it's fair that the percentages be amended to 60-40 or 75-25?" My answer is a thunderous *no!* In an ideal partnership, there should be no list-making or toting up of scores of who did less or more. In the long run, the contributions even out, and a you-did-this, I-did-that attitude is the death knell for the partnership.

Trouble Clef _____

Never pay a collaborator to put words or music to your material. True collaborators share royalties and operate on an equal basis.

Inspiration from Across the Sea

Collaborators can be as close to home as the next room. But sometimes they can be on another continent.

Long-Distance Gold

Paul Anka probably didn't suspect what an impact "My Way" would have on the world when he co-wrote the lyrics with collaborators from overseas (with C. François, J. Revaux, and G. Thibault). Other Euro-American classics include: "Volare" (F. Migliacci, D. Modugno, and M. Parish), "You're My World" (C. Sigman, U. Bindi, and G. Paoli), "Yesterday When I Was Young" (C. Aznavour and H. Kretzmer), and "More" (N. Newell, N. Oliviero, and R. Ortolani).

Hirschhorn's Hints

Be prepared for strange ways of collaborating. Al and I discovered that when an opportunity came to write with Charles Aznavour, who gave us a melody and asked us to write English lyrics. When we completed it, we had to sing it for him via a long-distance phone call. From his den in Paris, he made the decision to cut the song, which ultimately became "The Old-Fashioned Way," a song which has had more than 300 recordings to date.

Certain lyricists have practically based their entire careers on long-distance collaborations. The name Carl Sigman ("Losing You," a hit for Brenda Lee in 1964; "You're My World"; and "What Now My Love") is synonymous with long-distance composing. Juliana Hatfield and Freda Love sent cassette tapes back and forth to collaborate on "Feel It," their 2003 song for new band Some Girls. Stephin Merritt (of the Magnetic Fields, and a great songwriter) and Claudia Gonson frequently write long-distance for their band Future Bible Heroes.

Starting Out with a Hit

Collaborating with international artists to rework hits in their country of origin is often a good idea. The past success of the song in another country increases its chances of the *cover record's* success in the United States.

Lyrical Lingo

A **cover record** is a new recording of an already existing cut. Cover records are valuable, because the more a song is covered, the better chance it has of lasting permanently.

Sometimes international material comes to an American lyricist with words already written in a different language. Two things might happen:

◆ The American writer might be asked to adhere, verse by verse, to the ideas in that lyric.

◆ The American writer might be granted the freedom to conceive entirely new ideas of his or her own.

Give Collaboration a Try!

When writers start out, they often oppose the idea of partnership and insist on writing alone. If you find that your work is being rejected, don't close your mind to the idea of working with other people. Sometimes an individual who does words and music lacks objectivity. That second pair of ears will hear flaws and correct them so that a competent song evolves into a fine one.

Certain writers, even those who can do words and music on their own, prefer the feedback of a partner. Solitary composing can be lonely, and partnerships provide the joy of sharing, as well as the comfort of having a permanent support system when you're forced to deal with disappointment.

The Least You Need to Know

- ◆ Try not to let the stress of conflicts pull apart a productive partnership.

- ◆ Organize a mutually acceptable work schedule and stick to it; don't leave assignments until the last minute.

- ◆ Increase your opportunities by writing with producers and artists.

- ◆ Decide on your royalty split with your partner in advance.

- ◆ Collaborate with international writers to increase your visibility.

Rewriting Melodies and Lyrics

In This Chapter

- ◆ Overcoming your resistance to rewriting
- ◆ Becoming a better songwriter through rewriting
- ◆ Choosing the right rewriting place and time
- ◆ Dealing with writing disappointments

Every songwriter wants to nail his or her music and words on the first try. Although on rare occasions songwriters might sit down and churn out a near-perfect song in a single sitting, ordinarily a first draft is just that: an early assemblage of ideas and lines that only suggest a final, polished product. To turn those rough lyrics and melodies into successful songs they have to be put through the rewriting process.

Rewriting is just as much an emotional process as it is a creative one. Songwriters recognize how important it is, but they resist it. Refusal to rewrite is more than a mistake; it's a catastrophic blunder that could keep you from "making it" in the music business.

Rewriting Rules

Songwriters use all kinds of weak reasons to resist rewriting songs that they know need it. To help you overcome almost any excuse you can think of for tackling the all-important rewrite, I've outlined several rewriting rules for you. Hopefully, by the time you finish reading this chapter, you'll have a whole new attitude about rewriting.

Trust Your Intuition

When you complete a song, you always have special affection for particular notes or lyrics. So you say to yourself, "I'll work around these. I'll correct other places and try to match them up with the lines I like best." That's not total rewriting because it restricts creative freedom. If new ideas necessitate discarding old ones, don't be afraid to throw out the old stuff.

> **Backstage Banter**
>
> Norman Gimbel, who wrote the lyrics to "Killing Me Softly with His Song," has said, "Very rarely do I get lucky and does it really explode. I usually have to work my ass off. Even after all the things I've written, I have a lot of problems to be looser ... to be freer. And yet I think it's valuable that I go through all that struggle. My songs aren't as much written as they're rewritten."

A big mistake is to come up with a sensational line and say, "I can't use it, because it will mean tossing something else out." If the old line or tune has to go, send it on its way without regret.

The danger of throwing good stuff away during a rewrite is greatly overestimated. You're in the driver's seat. You have total control over what's kept and what gets discarded. Examine everything carefully, methodically, and slowly. If a line or a musical phrase feels comfortable, keep it. Trust your intuition. If something isn't working, you'll sense it.

Above all, believe you can make it better. Writers, new ones in particular, throw up their hands and cry out, "I can't do any better." It's a perfectly normal reaction. You have to remind yourself that you can improve your song immeasurably.

Rhyme and Rhythm Both Matter

Suppose the song is basically there, but a few rhymes feel like compromises. Don't tell yourself, "People won't notice them. They'll just react to the overall feeling." Even if nobody notices a specific compromise, listeners may know that you settled for a less-than-perfect rhyme. Lots of things work, but is adequate enough for you? It's worth it to find a rhyme word with more color, more cleverness. Don't say, "It's the feel that counts today. Rhythm is the main thing, and words don't matter." Everything matters.

Let rhymes flow. As the late Harry Chapin said …

> Don't force it. Don't submit to what Robert Frost called "the tyranny of rhyme." I know when I write a bad line or a bad rhyme, I've got to throw the damn thing away. I've time and time again come up with a great line and I can't find another line that rhymes with it. So you try to change it around, you do something else. You've got to work with practical realities and be tough with yourself. I edit, I struggle, I throw away, and I resurrect.

Second Verses Matter, Too

Just because people have a strongly positive initial reaction to a melody or lyric doesn't mean they won't notice if the second verse is comparatively boring. Discounting the value of a second verse means that the lyricist doesn't know how to develop the story of the song. Melodically, the second verse usually repeats what the first verse does, so it's less of a concern for the tune writer.

The Bridge Is a Big Deal

I'm a big believer in bridges—the mid-section of a song, which features an entirely different tune than the verse or hook, and adds a welcome flavor to the overall tune. By adding a bridge, you can launch into an entirely new rhythm and a fresh chord progression. Sometimes you can just talk the bridge rather than utilize music at all. Even if you think you might not use a bridge, write one and then decide during the revision process whether you want to keep it.

Hirschhorn's Hints

If you write both words and music, and your first priority is words at the expense of movement, listen to records and concentrate only on the bass and drum parts. One of my earliest publishers said it best: "Lyrics will get a publisher interested, but only a great track and feel will make it a hit."

Don't Plagiarize

It's one thing to use a common chord progression. You can hardly avoid it. But if you discover in the revision process that three or four measures of your tune are exactly or almost exactly like the latest Beyoncé single, change them! In this case, reluctance to rewrite can get you into big trouble. You don't want to find yourself in court like George Harrison, forking over a fortune because you duplicated someone else's work. (Harrison's "My Sweet Lord" ended up being the same tune as the 1963 hit "He's So

246 Part 5: Finishing Touches

Fine" by The Chiffons, written by Ronnie Mack.) Led Zeppelin had to pay Willie Dixon a huge settlement for adapting his work. Sometimes these things are unfortunate accidents, but if you're aware of the similarity, it would be madness to take a chance that "no one will find out."

Balancing Rhythm and Lyric

Rhythm is the key to today's music, but it has to be the right rhythm. Is your melody written so that the backbeat (emphasizing beats 2 and 4 of the bar) is emphasized? Without that emphasis, the tune won't be danceable.

Is your lyric wordy? Too many words hold down the rhythm. When I started, I was too verbose and too concerned with an excess of poetic imagery, and publishers would tell me, "It's nice, but it doesn't swing!" You can sacrifice words to preserve the rhythm, but you can't sacrifice rhythm to preserve the words. Keep the lyrics simple and uncluttered; if they're not, you'd be wise to rewrite them.

When you're playing the song, do you find your body moving automatically? If you're playing it on piano or guitar, you won't be able to keep still if the beat is right.

Don't Fix It in the Studio

The problem with rewriting in the studio is that you don't have enough time, and the financial and emotional pressure is on. Yes, great ideas do sometimes spring up during the recording process. But is it worth taking a chance on this possibility when you can work out the kinks at your leisure?

Saying you'll fix it in the studio is just another way of avoiding what seems like an arduous and boring task. It's like an actor saying, "If the audience doesn't respond properly, I'll make up new lines," because he or she doesn't want to learn the scripted dialogue.

> **Backstage Banter**
>
> Two-time Oscar winner Richard Sherman, who, with his brother Robert, composed the songs for *Mary Poppins*, says, "The key to our success is that we both have to feel 100 percent about every word, every note, every concept, before we show it to a third party."

Don't Settle for First Drafts

Some songwriters say their best work is "spontaneous." Spontaneity is fine at the beginning, and a few first-draft melodies (though rarely lyrics) wind up being the final product. But this occurrence is so rare that it's not worth considering. There's always a chord that can be improved or a lyric line that can be phrased better.

Don't Rush

"I want it finished now," say many songwriters, as though speed were synonymous with artistic achievement. Unless you've been given a difficult deadline, there's no reason to rush. Everyone likes immediate satisfaction, but how about total satisfaction? No one is pointing a gun to your head. When you have the luxury of extra time, take advantage of it. Strive for perfection.

Make Sure the Title Is Right

Suppose the song works and you're satisfied with the title. Yet that little voice is buzzing in your mind: "It's too ordinary ... It's good, but it's not a grabber ... I think people will like it ..." If those inner thoughts keep returning, I can assure you that you'll never be satisfied with that title. Weeks, months, or even years later, you'll still be asking yourself why you didn't change it.

Backstage Banter

While you're writing and rewriting, something mystical can happen. Barry Gibb of The Bee Gees says, "We can't think of something, and it just comes. We just leave it to the open spaces ... we play along and when it's time to do that line, it's not just a good line, it's an amazing line, and Robin and I look at each other and say, 'Where did that come from?' And we'll sit there looking at each other numbly, especially when we find out that that line connects all the lines before it, which wasn't planned."

Do you write down titles when they occur to you? Do you keep a title list? If you don't, you should. Even if you look over the list and nothing seems right, it will spark dozens of other title ideas. Rewriting titles might seem like a threatening process, especially when the song is completed. You can't help worrying, "What if a title change forces other changes? What if it changes the whole meaning of the song, and leads to massive rewrites from top to bottom?" These changes mean only that the song wasn't quite finished—that changes are needed.

Avoid Weak Endings

Composers and lyricists frequently rush their endings, wanting nothing more than to be done with the song. Even if it's not quite as exciting as it should be, even if it doesn't put a powerful button on the production, they resist tinkering with it. Here are just some of the rationalizations about endings:

- When the singer hits a big note at the end, it'll be exciting.

- A dynamite drum fill will give it the impact it needs.

- All that's needed are background singers in that section.

Nothing is more important than the right ending. The beauty of the song construction doesn't matter if the proper payoff is missing.

Save Rejected Material

Suppose you show the song to a producer and he's not enthusiastic. Do you automatically toss the song into the wastebasket? No! If you believe in it, if you think it has something of value, re-examine and rewrite it. Granted, rewriting something when you don't get a positive response is hard. The temptation is to start something new. But who is to say that the person who rejected the song is right? If you, as a writer, felt the song had something special, you might be more on the mark than the person you played it for.

A star might turn to you and say, "I don't feel this; it's not me." This comment doesn't mean that there's anything wrong with your work. Stars have an image they want to project. They sing certain notes more effectively than others. You might have written some notes that are out of their range, that would force them into uncomfortable registers that don't do their singing justice. Singers have their own needs and their own prejudices. A song that's wrong for Mariah Carey might be just right for Christina Aguilera. Matchbox Twenty's Rob Thomas and the Stones' Mick Jagger collaborated on "Disease" for Jagger's solo record *Goddess in the Doorway*. But Jagger decided against using it. Thomas decided to use it and it became a Top 40 hit for Matchbox Twenty in 2002.

Ignore Compliments

Who doesn't love the sound of "Bravo!" when he or she completes an artistic work? But don't let compliments convince you that rewriting is unnecessary. As a songwriter, your objectivity has to be ruthless. It's not enough that your mom thinks the song deserves an Oscar or that your girlfriend feels Garth Brooks is an amateur by comparison to you. Do you love the song you've written? Do you feel that it's in such perfect shape that no rewriting is required?

Keep an Open Mind

You might not want to rewrite, but your partner does. Don't throw up your hands and say, "Go ahead, then." If your partner doesn't feel you've nailed it completely, he or she is probably right. Even if you think your partner is nitpicking, that no rewriting is required, go along with his or her request. Respect the person's desire to improve the song, unless you feel that his or her perfectionism is too extreme.

Of course, you always run the risk of rewriting until you've completely altered the product and removed the qualities that made it special in the first place. Unless you feel that your revisions are hurting the song, don't fight your partner. Your resistance to rewriting could backfire when the song is rejected or when people pick up on the weaknesses in the record that you were too lazy to correct. At that point, your partner is likely to resent you for not rewriting. He or she might say so straight out or smolder inside; either way, unnecessary tension is created.

Starting the Process

If you have a partner, you might prefer to begin the rewriting process alone, and then show him or her what you've come up with. Or your partner might want to come up with changes and then show them to you. Find a rewriting approach that suits you both best. It doesn't matter how you accomplish it; it only matters that it gets done.

Take It from the Top

The best way to approach rewriting (especially if you're fighting it) is to think of your composition as a brand-new song. Look at it as though you've never seen it before.

Write from Someone Else's Point of View

Another method for maintaining emotional objectivity is to pretend someone else wrote the song. Tell yourself you're rewriting the material for a friend. That way, you won't have such a violent need to defend it or to personalize the process so much that you lose your grasp of the overall picture.

Tell Yourself It's Fun

Part of the reason songwriters dread rewriting is the fear that they won't be able to solve the problems, no matter how hard they try. Comedic as it sounds, just tell yourself over and over again that the rewriting process is fun. View it as an enjoyable challenge rather than a grim, deadly strain. Visualize the rewards that will come to you as the song gets into tighter shape. Visualize higher royalties with each chord and Grammies with each lyric change.

Create Your Own Time Patterns

If you're like many composers and lyricists who fight the rewriting process, it's best to work on rewrites when your mind is clear. If working at night is a trial for you, don't start your corrections at 10 or 11 P.M. Doing so will only add to your reluctance. You can often work through less-than-ideal hours when you're hatching your first draft, but when you rewrite, pick times when you know you're absolutely at your best.

When you sit down to rewrite, you don't have to keep going until all the changes have been made. Stop if you want to. Have a soda. Walk around the block. Call a friend. Or maybe even put your music away and start fresh the next morning. You can direct your mind, but you can't exert tyrannical control over it. When you feel your rewrites aren't top-notch, that's the time to quit for a while. Sometimes, even with all the motivation and dedication in the world, the well runs dry. At other times, creative ideas pour out in a monumental flow, and you can't get them down fast enough.

Trouble Clef

The only danger of rewriting is that you might use it as an excuse to avoid showing your work altogether. At a certain point, you just have to jump into the deep end of the pool and let the world evaluate what you've done. Don't be like a composer friend of mine who's been rewriting a song for three years and feels it's "almost done"!

Choose the Right Environment

An office can become claustrophobic. Your room at home might seem too routine and familiar to inspire creativity. Worse, some environments dampen initiative. If you're anywhere near a television set, you might use that as an excuse to slack off and watch *Survivor* or a *Seinfeld* rerun. When the environment interferes with your work, change it quickly. My first recorded song was written on a park bench. You can sit in the car with a notebook and finish a lyric. I know writers who operate best while having coffee in a restaurant. A writer friend of mine has done some of his most successful work on a rooftop.

Rewriting, in particular, demands a new way of seeing, a different point of view from what you've already composed. New backgrounds and new sights encourage that fresh perspective.

It's No One's Fault

Jerry Bock once said, "Songs aren't written. They're rewritten." The initial burst of inspiration is an emotional state; rewriting is the objective phase. Don't resent people who push you to improve your work. It's better to perfect something than to have a publisher say, "This sounds like a first draft."

Take Old Material from the Trunk

You've written a song, a major artist has recorded it, and it gets on the charts. It starts at number 100, and moves to 89—83—81—and then off! You can't believe it. In your despair and disappointment, you might want to throw the song into the trash. Don't. It was recorded and made the *Billboard* charts, so it has something special.

Let a little time go by and then take another look at the song. Maybe it didn't reach the Top 20 because of a weak line or lyric, or a bridge that went on too long—or not long enough. Rewrite the song, fixing all weak areas that you've identified, then try to get it recorded by someone else. Whatever attracted the first artist to it will inevitably attract a second one.

If you've rewritten a lyric and left the melody alone, you can bring a singer back (or get a new one) and do another pass at the vocals. If the tune has been changed, however, you'll have to do another recording altogether. The thought of that might make you groan (whether for artistic or financial reasons), but it will be worth it if the song is vastly improved.

Hirschhorn's Hints

Rewriting isn't always a pen-and-paper process. Suppose you do a recording of the song, and it doesn't capture the feeling you had in mind. If the song is strong enough, it's worth recording it again. Maybe it's a question of overdubbing a few lines or adding a background part. Possibly the singer is wrong, even if the track is great. Studio stitching and pasting can bring the recording up to par in some cases.

Don't Take Anything Personally

Writers are sensitive, and they frequently see critical response in a personal light. Such thoughts flood in as, "He has something against me," "She doesn't like young writers," "He doesn't like old writers," "She's old-fashioned and doesn't like the fact that I'm experimental," and on and on.

The music business is just that—a business. Most of the time, those evaluating your work are not judging you as a person. They just want to know if you're showing them something that will earn them money. If they suggest a rewrite, it's not because of the color of your shirt or where you went to school. They want a commercial product. The fact that they're asking you to rewrite at all is a positive sign. It means they think your work has possibilities. If they didn't like it, they would quickly dismiss you.

Try a Different Instrument

If your rewriting isn't flowing as well as you'd like, you can trick your creative mind into submission. Suppose you play both piano and guitar. If you're having difficulty working the song out on the piano, try guitar instead. If neither feels comfortable, sing without any accompaniment.

You might also stimulate creative rewriting by turning on the radio or a favorite CD. Soak in the music without trying to relate it to what you're writing. Richard Rodgers was famous for listening to classical music for at least an hour before starting to compose.

Don't Rewrite Too Much

When you're rewriting, you want the song to be as tight and professional as possible. But you don't want to rewrite the character out of a song. If you see the chords becoming too complex and lush, the lyrics too self-consciously clever or slick, catch yourself. Above all, no matter how much rewriting you do, you want to retain that sense of honesty and naturalness.

Check Early Drafts

When you rewrite, there are times when you realize your early stuff was better than the corrections that came afterward. Be grateful when this occurs; it doesn't happen often. All it means is that you examined every alternative, analyzed it, tested new tunes and lyrics, and discovered that you'd hit the bull's-eye right at the start. You won't be any worse off for carrying the whole process through. Rewriting is a wonderful creative practice and a fine way to flex your musical muscles.

The Least You Need to Know

- Don't rationalize your way out of rewriting a song that needs it.
- Overcome your resistance to rewriting by remembering that it can make you a better songwriter.
- Take a positive approach and choose the most supportive environment and time periods for rewriting.
- Don't let disappointing results keep you from finding creative solutions.
- Look upon rewriting as a pleasure, not a chore.

Chapter 23

Protecting Your Songs: Royalties and Guilds

In This Chapter

- ◆ The history of ASCAP, BMI, and SESAC
- ◆ Royalties and payment procedures
- ◆ How guilds log performances
- ◆ Copyright basics and caveats
- ◆ The Songwriter's Guild of America

Songs are an art form, but sooner or later, you'll want to get paid for your art. Royalties, which are semi-annual or quarterly payments to writers and publishers for record sales or airplay, are aptly named because it can be a royal pain if you don't receive them, or you can feel like financial royalty when they show up in your mailbox. The beauty of royalties can be summed up in the words of a dancer friend of mine: "When songwriters get old, they have an annuity whether they work or not. I don't."

Radio stations, television stations, and all other venues (such as theaters and hotels) in which copyrighted music is performed or broadcast must pay to use that music. Because it would be extremely difficult for songwriters to track down every venue in which their music is played and obtain money from those places, organizations have been created that handle this process. These organizations track the performance of their members' works, ensure that all venues pay for those performances, and pass a portion of that money on to the songwriters.

Assuming you've built a songwriting catalogue that contains compositions that are continually replayed, you'll be able to live (moderately or handsomely, depending on the case) on royalty checks you receive every three months. This is a goal well worth striving for. In this chapter I'll tell you about the organizations whose purpose is to assist songwriters get their fair share.

The Big Three: ASCAP, BMI, and SESAC

From the point of view of any songwriter who has had hit songs or songs recorded by important artists, ASCAP (the American Society of Composers, Authors, and Publishers), BMI (Broadcast Music, Inc.), and SESAC (Society of European Stage Authors and Composers) are the most important organizations in the music business. BMI, ASCAP, and SESAC track media play of songs, collect the money, and send a percentage of that money to members every three months.

Hirschhorn's Hints

New writers who feel alone or who haven't quite found their bearings should know that the societies are their second homes. All three are endlessly helpful in making calls for writers, pairing them up with collaborators, or suggesting them for projects.

Hirschhorn's Hints

In addition to emotional support and career advice, BMI and ASCAP offer loans to member artists.

BMI, ASCAP, and SESAC are sympathetic and supportive of songwriters and publishers. I can state quite simply, as a longtime insider, that I might not have had the satisfying career I've experienced without the assistance of BMI. Friends of mine who are members of ASCAP are equally grateful for their ASCAP affiliation.

You can only belong to one of the three organizations at a time, and songwriters are divided about the relative merits of each one. If you are dissatisfied with one organization, you can join a different one when your contract expires.

Basic Functions

BMI, ASCAP (the two largest, with the majority of songwriter membership), and SESAC license songs for performance on radio, television (broadcasting networks as well as cable), and the Internet. Nonbroadcast sources of revenue include restaurants, colleges, orchestras, airlines, skating rinks, theme and amusement parks, arenas, and anywhere music is publicly performed or played.

The greatest amount of performance income stems from radio and television, with approximately 15 percent coming from hotels, clubs, and arenas.

> **Backstage Banter**
>
> *Esquire* magazine singled out BMI president Frances Preston as "the most influential and powerful person in the country music business." *Ladies' Home Journal* cited her as one of the 50 most powerful women in America.

ASCAP

A small group of writers, including Irving Berlin, Victor Herbert, John Philip Sousa, and James Weldon Johnson, formed ASCAP in 1914 with the intent of collecting public performance fees and dispersing these payments as royalties to the society's members. The nonprofit organization made it clear that musical works were copyrighted and owned, and anyone who wanted to use the songs had to obtain the owner's permission.

 Trouble Clef _____

> It has become increasingly common for writers who are members of different societies to collaborate. If you do this, be prepared for you and your partner's royalty amounts to differ. Because the organizations' logging systems are different and they sample different songs and scores, the amounts received quarterly by writer and publisher members of the societies can vary significantly.

Music users objected violently in the beginning, and there is, even today, reluctance by some clubs, hotels, and restaurants to pay for use of music. That they do is a tribute to Frances Preston, president of BMI; Marilyn Bergman, president of ASCAP; former presidents Ed Cramer (BMI) and Hal David (ASCAP); BMI senior vice president Thea Zavin, and a host of others who preceded them.

Approximately 25 percent of ASCAP's income comes from agreements with foreign licensing societies. Roughly one half is the result of performances from networks and television stations. Radio accounts for 25 percent of total royalty collections.

ASCAP collects from these organizations:

ABC, CBS, and NBC television networks

PBS (public television)

Cable television

Other commercial television networks: Warner Brothers (WB), Fox, and Paramount (UPN)

Background music services (Muzak, airlines)

Local commercial radio stations

NPR (National Public Radio) and college stations

More than 2,000 colleges and universities

More than 1,000 symphony orchestras

Nearly 6,000 concert presenters

Theme parks, Internet service providers, restaurants, hotels, bars, skating rinks, and circuses

Membership

Until the 1940s, ASCAP's members were principally Broadway, film, and pop composers. Today, members are accepted on the basis of one published song or a song that has been commercially recorded. The society has a board of 12 writers and 12 publishers, which is voted in by its membership. There are presently 130,000 members.

Hirschhorn's Hints

Annual dues of $10 for writers and $50 for publishers were established in 1914 and remain the same to this day. You can obtain membership applications, sample contracts, and other information by writing or phoning any of the ASCAP offices listed at the end of this section or visiting the website at www.ascap.com.

Showcases and Awards

In addition to collecting and distributing royalties, ASCAP offers to members film-scoring workshops and workshops in R&B, pop, country, musical theater, jazz, Latin, and concert music. The organization also sponsors showcases in which members can perform before important industry people. The ASCAP Foundation offers scholarships, awards, and grants to composers.

Payment Procedure

To determine what musical works are performed, ASCAP, as well as BMI and SESAC, utilize *cue sheets* furnished to them by broadcasters or directors of programming. The guilds then analyze the cue sheets for their royalty value. In addition, they take computer-based program schedules and network or station logs into account. The royalty amount is based on a number of factors, including the programming time, the size of station (prime-time, local, cable), and the type of outlet (radio, TV, concerts, restaurants).

The major television networks submit program logs, as well as cue sheets. For non-network stations, ASCAP surveys *TV Guide* and cue sheets and information provided by *TV Data* and Tribune Media Services. Cable television's performance data is derived from program guides and contributed to by cue sheets and cable services.

Lyrical Lingo

A music **cue sheet** includes the title of the musical composition, when and how it was used, the name of the songwriters or background scorers, and the publisher.

ASCAP also prepares its own surveys, which consist of a random sampling of local commercial television airplay; a sample of local commercial radio airplay; a complete count of performances on the major television networks; a sample of performances on airlines, ice skating shows, and some circuses; and a sample of performances on wired music performances (Muzak).

Payments are sent to members every three months. Writer royalties are sent out in October, January, April, and July. Publishers receive their checks in September, December, March, and June.

ASCAP Locations

ASCAP has offices in the following locations:

Los Angeles
7920 W. Sunset Boulevard,
Third Floor
Los Angeles, CA 90046
Phone: 323-883-1000
Fax: 323-883-1049

London
8 Cork Street
London W1X1PB
Phone: 011-44-207-439-0909
Fax: 011-44-207-434-0073

New York
One Lincoln Plaza
New York, NY 10023
Phone: 212-621-6000
Fax: 212-724-9064

Chicago
1608 West Belmont Avenue,
Suite 200
Chicago, IL 60657
Phone: 773-472-1157
Fax: 773-472-1158

Nashville
Two Music Square West
Nashville, TN 37203
Phone: 615-742-5000
Fax: 615-742-5020

Puerto Rico
510 Royal Bank Center
255 Ponce de Leon Avenue
Hato Rey, PR 00917
Phone: 787-281-0782
Fax: 787-767-2805

Miami
844 Alton Road, Suite 1
Miami Beach, FL 33139
Phone: 305-673-3446
Fax: 305-673-2446

BMI

BMI was formed in 1940 by 480 broadcasters in reaction to ASCAP's closed-door policy against composers who wrote R&B, country, gospel, jazz, and folk music. Today, no such prejudice exists, and ASCAP is welcoming of all genres, as is BMI. BMI represents more than 300,000 writers and publishers.

> **Backstage Banter**
>
> BMI's stockholders comprise its board of directors. The company's president and executive committee devise company strategy and handle daily decisions. Stockholders receive no dividends.

> **Hirschhorn's Hints**
>
> After you get a song recorded, it's vital that you join one of the societies. Tracking airplay on your own is virtually impossible and you'll lose income if you don't affiliate.

Like ASCAP, BMI utilizes a blanket license system. It collects license fees from each user of music that BMI licenses and distributes to its writers and publishers. Through cue sheets and computerized data, BMI pays its members for all performances on network, syndicated, and cable television on a true census basis, keeping track of over 6,000,000 hours of programming annually. Just like ASCAP, BMI operates on a nonprofit basis, and so aside from operating expenses, every penny is sent directly to its writers and publishers.

Membership

You are eligible to join BMI if you have completed songs or recorded demos, or if you've written a song posted on a website.

For information on becoming a member of BMI, to view sample contracts, or to download a membership application, go to their website, www.BMI.com, or write or phone one of the BMI offices listed at the end of this section.

Seminars, Workshops, and Showcases

BMI hosts many seminars and workshops around the country to help songwriters, including the following:

>   The BMI-Lehman Engel Musical Theater Workshop
>
>   Sundance Composer's Lab
>
>   BMI TV/Film Composer's Conducting Workshop
>
>   Film and Television Composer's Workshop
>
>   BMI Jazz Composer's Workshop

To check locations, dates, and times for each of the above events, refer to bmi.com.

Payment Procedure

Monitored stations send BMI all the information about the music they broadcast. BMI then enters this information into an elaborate computer system that multiplies each performance listed by a factor that reflects the ratio of the number of stations logged to the number licensed. BMI monitors approximately 500,000 hours of commercial radio programming annually.

In addition, BMI tracks 50,000 hours of non-commercial college radio programming and generates separate payments for these performances. Feature, theme, and cue music performed on television networks, cable television stations, and local television stations are reported to BMI on music cue sheets. In addition, performances are logged using such sources as *TV Data*, cable program guides, and local television station logging reports.

> **Backstage Banter**
>
> BMI has constructed a sampling procedure in which once a year individual stations are sampled for three days. This technique adds up to 440,000 sample hours from commercial stations and 50,000 sample hours from college stations annually. The stations are not told when they're being logged.

Networks send BMI cue sheets of all the music they use. All works that have had more than 25,000 logged U.S. feature performances are paid at bonus rates, which range from 25 to 100 percent.

Hirschhorn's Hints

Keep in mind how valuable it is to aim for motion pictures and television. A "film work" written for a full-length motion picture or a made-for-television movie receives BMI's Upper-Level Bonus Payment rate if it's utilized as a featured work of not less than 45 consecutive seconds or as the main title theme or closing credits work.

BMI royalty payments are sent out in January, April, July, and October. Live concert royalties are distributed every six months in April and October for pop concerts and annually in July for classical concerts.

BMI Locations

BMI has offices in the following locations:

Los Angeles
8730 Sunset Boulevard,
3rd Floor West
West Hollywood, CA 90069-2211
Phone: 310-659-9109

Nashville
10 Music Square East
Nashville, TN 37203-4399
Phone: 615-401-2000

New York
320 West 57th Street
New York, NY 10019-3790
Phone: 212-586-2000

London
84 Harley House
Marylebone Road
London NW1 5HN, England
Phone: 011-44-171-486-2036

Miami
5201 Blue Lagoon Drive,
Suite 310
Miami, FL 33126
Phone: 305-266-3636

Atlanta
PO Box 19199
Atlanta, GA 31126
Phone: 404-261-5151

Puerto Rico
255 Ponce de Leon
East Wing, Suite A-262
Royal Bank Center
Hato Rey, PR 00917
Phone: 787-754-6490

SESAC

The Society of European Stage Authors and Composers (SESAC) was founded by Paul Heinecke in 1930. SESAC, unlike BMI and ASCAP, is a for-profit organization.

It provides international representation for publishers and songwriters. Unlike ASCAP and BMI, SESAC membership is selective. The company's creative staff works with songwriters to develop and perfect their talents. The corporation's owners, Freddie Gershon, Ira Smith, Stephen Swid, and the merchant banking house of Allen and Company, distribute 50 percent of the firm's income and retain the other half.

> **Backstage Banter**
>
> When people thought of SESAC's catalogue in the past, they thought of gospel and Christian music only. It now includes Latin, new age, television and film themes, jazz, and pop.

SESAC consults music trade publications, such as *Billboard, Radio and Records, The Gavin Report*, and *College Music Journal*, to determine how much music is being played. It also gathers information from affiliates. Its major sources of information are radio playlists, the *Billboard* information network, network and cable programming service logs, regional editions of *TV Guide*, program syndicators, and a census of movie performances from *TV Data*.

SESAC has offices in two locations:

New York
421 West 54th Street
New York, NY 10019
Phone: 212-586-3450

Nashville
55 Music Square East
Nashville, TN 37203
Phone: 615-320-0055

Copyright Basics

In the United States a work is protected by copyright for the life of the author (or the oldest living co-author) plus 70 years. Lyrics and melody are covered by copyright law; rhythm and harmony by themselves are not.

The owner of the copyright has control over the particular song or work, and is the only one permitted to produce or reproduce his or her composition or allow others to do so. Copyright protection gives composers, lyricists, and publishers the right to sue infringers and collect damages if their material is illegally used. Once the copyright expires (70 years after the author has died), the song lapses into the public domain. When material enters the public domain, it is no longer protected by copyright and may be used by anyone.

> **Backstage Banter**
>
> When two or more songwriters collaborate, all the writers own the copyright equally unless specific contractual stipulations are made to the contrary. In states with community property laws, rights to the song are divided between the writer and his or her spouse.

Copyright Act of 1976

Known as the "author's bill," the Copyright Act of 1976 offered writers the following:

♦ **Term of copyright.** Unlike the old act, which required songwriters to obtain copyright renewal after an initial term of 28 years in order to get a second 28 years of protection, this one offers a single term: the author's lifetime plus 70 years. The writer of any song composed after January 1, 1978, can rest assured that his or her work will not fall into the public domain until the copyright expires.

♦ **Contract termination.** A songwriting contract can now be terminated as to United States rights after a specific period of years (usually 35).

♦ **Statutory mechanical rate.** The rate structure is as follows:

January 1, 2004   8.5¢ per unit sold

January 1, 2006   9.1¢ per unit sold

Copyright Registration

A composer and/or lyricist should obtain the proper form from the Copyright Office in Washington, D.C., and then submit the completed form with the filing fee ($30) and a copy of the work for registration. If the song is unpublished, one copy is sufficient; if the song is published, two copies are expected. Although the Copyright Office doesn't demand them, it's a good security measure to send lead sheets and cassettes or CDs.

For information and forms, contact the Copyright Office:

Copyright Office, Library of Congress
Washington, DC 20559-6000
Phone: 202-707-3000
www.copyright.gov

Watch Out!

When you make a deal with a publisher to assign copyright ownership of a song, the following guidelines will help protect you and your song:

♦ Make sure there's a reversion clause. Possibly you'll be willing to grant a publisher two, three, or even five years of ownership, but somewhere down the line, the song should revert back to you if no records have been attained.

◆ Don't accept a contract that doesn't have an organized royalty payment schedule, preferably payment every three months. Six months is maximum.

◆ Don't leave the issue of "future advances" up in the air. A publisher once told me, "I believe in a handshake arrangement. Don't you trust me?" Questions like that are pure intimidation. Business is business. The publisher might seem like the most honest person in the world, but if so, why should he or she be reluctant to verify specific terms by signing an agreement?

◆ Ask for 50 percent of the publisher's income on all licenses the company issues.

> **Trouble Clef** _____
>
> When I first started taking my songs around the Brill Building, one publisher made an offer to publish a song of mine for $200. In my anxiety to be a professional and get my career going, I almost agreed. This arrangement is not acceptable under any circumstances. You don't pay a publisher to take your song.

The Songwriter's Guild of America

The Songwriter's Guild was formed in 1931 by writers Billy Rose, George M. Meyer, and Edgar Leslie to rectify a system of payment that often omitted royalties or paid them on only 1 percent of sheet music sold. At the time, the rate for *mechanical royalty rights* was equally unjust.

Today, the Songwriter's Guild of America (SGA) continues to protect the interests of its members. It does so by offering a completely fair writer's contract, reviewing the publishing contracts of its members, providing a copyright renewal service, helping writers to find collaborators, and campaigning in Washington, D.C., for its members' rights.

> **Lyrical Lingo** _____
>
> **Mechanical royalty rights** (those pertaining to sales rather than royalties for airplay) allow usage of any material on records or CDs, as long as they give notice to the copyright owners and pay them.

The Popular Songwriter's Contract

The Guild's contract provides maximum protection for songwriters assigning copyrights to publishers, and it is not necessary to be a member of the SGA to use it. If you're signing any publishing contract other than the one supplied by the Songwriter's

Guild of America, take it to an attorney. Granted, the fee might be a rough pill to swallow, but if your song goes Top 10 and you find yourself with barely enough money for lunch, you'll regret not having an expert look the papers over in advance.

To obtain an SGA membership application, sample contract, or other information, contact one of the following offices:

New York
1560 Broadway, Suite 1306
New York, NY 10036
Phone: 212-786-7902

Hollywood
6430 Sunset Boulevard, Suite 705
Hollywood, CA 90028
Phone: 323-462-1108

The Least You Need to Know

- ASCAP, BMI, and SESAC collect royalties for your airplay performances.

- ASCAP and BMI have showcases and other services for their writers.

- ASCAP and BMI pay songwriters four times a year.

- If you don't use the SGA's contract, be sure to get legal advice before you make a deal with a publisher.

- Publisher contracts should provide for payment every three months, six months maximum.

Chapter **24**

Songwriting and the Internet

In This Chapter

◆ How illegal file sharing is cutting into songwriters' profits

◆ Using the Internet to further your songwriting career

◆ Finding the right online resources

◆ Creating your own website

After rock entered the music scene, many pop songwriters dropped out. When synthesizers and sequencers made their initial impact, nervous devotees of the acoustic world let their careers fall apart. Now that music has entered the Internet age, songwriters must once again make the necessary adjustments if they want to keep making music.

Don't be part of the group that retreats at the first sign of change; there are always those who protest, "It's a fad." In motion pictures, "talkies" (movies with sound) were pronounced a passing fad, too. History keeps proving that some fads have a way of sticking around. If you look at the web in a positive light, you'll find an amazing new world that you can use to further your career.

The Good New Days

Songwriting communities are being created all over the Internet on websites, chat rooms, e-mail lists, and newsgroups. The Internet is a communication device that gives the songwriter more power than ever before in history.

Hirschhorn's Hints

Get a laptop and immediately adopt it as a friend, your writing alter ego. You can write in the car, in an airplane, or on vacation. Carry a spare battery.

If you're uncomfortable with computer technology or have lingering doubts about whether the web is a good thing, try to put your feelings aside and read on. This chapter is full of information about the many ways the web can help songwriters, beginning with how it changed composer Steve Schalchlin's life.

Steve Schalchlin's Internet Miracle

Perhaps the most inspiring and instructive story the web has ever produced centers on composer Steve Schalchlin. In 1996, Schalchlin was diagnosed with AIDS and told he had very little time to live. He began an online diary as a good-bye letter to the world, and he adapted the emotions and material from the diary into a musical, *The Last Session*, which he co-wrote with life partner Jim Brochu. It told the tale of a songwriter who plans to cut his final album and then commit suicide. This story reflected Steve's mindset, but he defied all medical authorities and began to recover, aided by experimental medicines and the surging creative drive to share his dramatic experiences with the world.

Backstage Banter

In 2000, another show, *Bare*, gained a lot of publicity through e-mail and chat groups. Some of the show's songs were available on the web at www. barethemusical.com.

Steve named his online diary site www.bonusround. com. Before long, people began to read the diary and become interested in the show based on it. The website unexpectedly evolved into a huge promotional tool, proving the power of online promotion and exposure and turning *The Last Session* into a critically acclaimed hit show. It remains one of the most impressive demonstrations that shows and songs can gain be promoted through the Internet and gain worldwide exposure.

Downloading Music

Steve Schalchlin's story demonstrates the positive power of the Internet, but for songwriters, it also has a dark side: illegal music downloads. Songwriters are sustained by royalties, and every composer and lyricist I know is deeply concerned that millions of people are downloading songs for free—without giving the artists their financial due—via illegal file-sharing services.

In 1999 the Recording Industry Association of America (RIAA) filed a well-publicized lawsuit alleging that Napster—a website that provided free software that made it possible for people to share music files without paying for them—for copyright infringement. The suit shut Napster down, but other free, unauthorized services emerged in their place, and millions of people still continue to download songs without paying for them.

A seemingly positive result of the suit that eliminated early Napster is its return in a legal form, offering more than 500,000 tracks at 99¢ each. It claims to have the world's largest collection of digital music. Other legal services are proliferating. Apple's iTunes, which opened in early 2003, has sold several million downloaded songs at 99¢ apiece.

> **Backstage Banter**
>
> Leiber and Stoller, Elvis Presley's most famous songwriting team, were the top names on many of the lawsuits against Napster and its equivalents.

Yet another positive side to the Napster story is that access to the huge online music libraries offers exposure to multiple musical genres, and songwriters can benefit from studying material in all genres. However, to satisfy the public's growing appetite for downloaded music, while at the same time protecting songwriter earnings, companies will have to continue to compete with the illegal services and establish high-quality sites that give creators a fair share of the income.

Valuable Online Sites and Resources

A wealth of material exists online, providing songwriters with creative and business tips. The following are worth checking out:

♦ **TAXI (www.taxi.com)**   TAXI has a 150-member team of specialists trained to evaluate and critique songs.

♦ **Jeff Mallett's Songwriter Page (www.lyricist.com)**   Excellent resource site for tips, useful articles, legal advice, lyric critiques, videos, songwriter organizations, and national and international music instruction.

♦ **Songwriting Educational Resource (www.craftofsongwriting.com)** Songwriting contests, courses, Nashville contacts for country writers.

♦ **Cat Cohen Songwriter's Website (www.cat@CatCohen.com)**   Hit song analysis, workshops, classes, and private instruction.

◆ **www.Berkleemusic.com**   Online extension school of Berklee College of Music, appropriate for beginning and experienced songwriters. Helps writers to master elements of style and structure, search for ideas, and to also master programs like Finale and Pro Tools to notate songs.

◆ **www.SongwriterUniverse.com**   Includes such features as song and CD evaluation, individual consultations, song of the month contest, and music business information.

◆ **Music & Recording Contracts for Musicians (www.internetpagecreations. com)**   A guide to record contracts, indie labels, publishers, and copyrights.

Hirschhorn's Hints

By making note of the Top 100 songs, the kind of songs they are, and the labels that are releasing them, you can get a good idea of what each label is looking for. *Billboard*'s website, www.billboard.com is the ideal place to begin this study, as it lists the hit songs and their labels.

Hirschhorn's Hints

Through the Internet, you have a better chance to understand and market your material than songwriters ever did in the past. Armed with this information, you won't make the kind of mistake I did as a newcomer by sending a Bobby Vinton-type ballad to R&B-oriented Atlantic Records— not exactly their type of thing.

Record Labels Online

Every record label has different guidelines for the type of songs it requires, and you can study these requirements on the web. Here are some major label's websites:

◆ **A&M**   www.amrecords.com

◆ **Arista**   www.arista.com

◆ **Atlantic**   www.atlantic-records.com

◆ **Capitol Records**   www.hollywoodandvine.com

◆ **Columbia**   www.columbiarecords.com

◆ **Curb**   www.curb.com

◆ **Elektra**   www.elektra.com

◆ **Geffen**   www.geffen.com

◆ **J**   www.jrecords.com

◆ **MCA**   www.mcarecords.com

◆ **Motown**   www.motown.com

◆ **RCA**   www.rcarecords.com

◆ **Warner Brothers**   www.wbr.com

Other Websites of Interest

♦ **CMJ New Music Report (www.cmj.com)**   Weekly magazine covering current radio airplay information.

♦ **The Internet Music Pages (www.musicpages.com)**   Furnishes links to music industry resources.

♦ **The Ultimate Band List (www.ubl.com)**   Site featuring links to radios stations, record labels, and record stores.

Creating Your Own Website

If you want to alert the music world to your material, creating your own website is vital. You'll want to let everybody know, via pictures, biographies, and personal background, what your image is and the kind of songs you write.

You might be skilled enough to craft your own site, but if not, it pays to call in an expert. Unless the site has an offbeat, creative look, you won't stand out and establish your own individuality. Just as importantly, you must publicize the site. Make sure all of your correspondence—your letters, faxes, and e-mails—mention the site. Register it with search engines. Create links with other sites.

Keep the site updated. If you're a band, fill people in on where you're playing. If someone has recorded one of your songs, let the world know where they can get it.

Make Your Songs Available on Your Site

Making some of your songs available for download own your website is a great way to establish yourself on the Net and let the world know about you and your music.

Philip Walker of Songwriter's Resource Network explains:

The most common way of getting your music heard is to make your music downloadable to another person's computer from your website. From there they just play it back from their Internet browser on their PC to speakers or save it as a file and play it later. A second method is to contact a service provider who allows audio streaming. Using this method you do not actually download the music, but it is played in real time directly to your computer. This allows

Trouble Clef

Before you make your songs available for downloading, make sure you copyright them.

you to almost immediately listen to various parts of a song without having to wait for it to all download.

Walker cautions …

It's important to remain focused on exactly what you do and why you want someone to know about you. Surfers who are looking for music don't want to spend a lot of time reading details about an artist they do not know. They are looking for music or pictures that they can quickly find and download.

Working the Internet

Making cold calls, especially to people who just might hold your future in their hands, is tough. But if you write to the same people via e-mail, the prospect seems less threatening. You can be more philosophical if they don't respond; the rejection isn't as direct or personal.

Keeping Tabs on Publishers

You'll want to put together a list of all the best, most active publishers, and the Internet is the ideal place to start. Once you compile your list of names from the web, your immediate priority will be to separate the ones who only promote full catalogues they've already acquired, such as a catalogue by Rodgers and Hammerstein or The Beatles, from those who are eager to take on new material and new songwriters. Recordcontacts.com supplies an extensive list of publishers, in addition to managers and producers.

Hirschhorn's Hints

When I'm not working, I'm usually online reading about other writers and identifying with their dreams and aspirations. The Internet makes me feel I'm part of a huge, artistic fraternity, and when I pull up stories about other people in the music field, it stimulates my own creativity, gives me new ideas, and gets me writing.

Expand Your Horizons Online

Listening is just one way to internalize music. Carefully read as many websites as you can that give musical background and history about the giants in each musical genre. Learn what drove them to excel in their chosen areas and what their music means to them. From blues legend Taj Mahal to Jimmy Webb, Savage Garden to Sisqo, biographies of fellow composers and lyricists always prove to be an inspiration. Read about Jewish music, Irish music, jazz, blues, pop, Latin, heavy metal, R&B, hip-hop, and rap. Search for stories, interviews, and historical information.

Look no further than the web when you want to know what appeals to others and to understand the relative merits of what's being done. Whether it's general music criticism (rec.music.reviews, alt.cd-rom.reviews) or extensive *Billboard* coverage, the Internet fills you in on contemporary music culture.

The Least You Need to Know

◆ You can use the web to promote songs.

◆ Creating your own website is a way to raise your profile as a writer or artist.

◆ You can find publishers, producers, and potential partners on the Internet.

◆ The web has hundreds of music-oriented sites that offer songwriting tips; information on conferences, expos, and festivals; legal advice; and performing arts organizations.

Chapter 25

What's Happening Today

In This Chapter

- ◆ The best examples of current music
- ◆ The freelance writer's heroine
- ◆ Analysis of hit songs
- ◆ Common denominators of hit songs
- ◆ Hit self-hypnosis

When history books refer to the golden age of songwriting, they usually mean the period before 1950. Few will doubt that Richard Rodgers, Larry Hart, George Gershwin, Cole Porter, E. Y. (Yip) Harburg, Harold Arlen, Oscar Hammerstein, and Jerome Kern wrote immortal melodies.

But golden ages take different forms. If diversity is the definition of a creatively rich time, the twenty-first century is a golden age that offers new, unprecedented opportunities for songwriters.

When I first started out as a Brill Building composer, the avenues for songwriters were sharply divided. Pop writers didn't go to Nashville, and if they did, they were looked upon with suspicion. R&B writers rarely crossed onto the pop charts. Country writers stayed on the country charts; a crossover to the Hot 100 was almost impossible unless the tune was redone with a pop star. Today there are no hard-and-fast lines separating songs, artists, or types of material.

An Overview of Grammy Categories

A study of various nominees in 2004 Grammy categories shows how many areas a songwriter can venture into. For a broad overview of the whole of music, listen to all my choices on the following lists. By the time you're done, you'll have a wide understanding of the market and what stimulates enthusiastic response from record buyers around the world.

Hirschhorn's Hints

You'll find several sites that provide full lyrics for your study and enjoyment. Check out alt.music.lyrics. Print lyrics out and go over them line by line.

Nominees for 2004 Song of the Year

- ◆ "Dance with My Father" by Richard Marx and Luther Vandross (Luther Vandross)

- ◆ "Keep Me in Your Heart" by Jorge Calderon and Warren Zevon (Warren Zevon)

- ◆ "Beautiful" by Linda Perry (Christina Aguilera)

Nominees for 2004 Rock Song of the Year

- ◆ "Seven Nation Army" by Jack White (The White Stripes)

- ◆ "Bring Me to Life" by David Hodges, Amy Lee, and Ben Moore (Evanescence featuring Paul McCoy)

- ◆ "Someday" by Chad Kroeger, Mike Kroeger, and Irving Moorson (Nickelback)

Nominees for 2004 R&B Song of the Year

- ◆ "Crazy in Love" by Shawn Carter, Rich Harrison, Beyoncé Knowles, Eugene Record (Beyoncé featuring Jay-Z)

- ◆ "Danger" by Erykah Badu, J. Poyser, B. R. Smith, and R. C. Williams (Erykah Badu)

- ◆ "Comin' from Where I'm From" by Mark Batson and Anthony Hamilton (Anthony Hamilton)

Nominees for 2004 Country Song of the Year

- "Celebrity" by Brad Paisley (Brad Paisley)

- "Beer for My Horses" by Scotty Emerick and Toby Keith (Willie Nelson and Toby Keith)

- "Forever and For Always" by Robert John "Mutt" Lange and Shania Twain (Shania Twain)

Hirschhorn's Hints

When writing a lyric, make sure your protagonist is in the grip of a powerful emotion. As Diane Warren put it, "I'm always attracted to strong characters."

The MTV Music Video Awards

Every year MTV awards top music videos in various categories. Watching these musical mini-movies offers songwriters a visual and aural knowledge of the current musical culture. Videos particularly worthy checking out are:

- Best Male Video   "Cry Me a River" (Justin Timberlake)

- Best Female Video   "Crazy In Love" (Beyoncé)

- Best Group Video   "The Scientist" (Coldplay)

- Best Rap Video   "In Da Club" (50 Cent)

- Best Rock Video   "Somewhere I Belong" (Linkin Park)

- Best Hip-Hop Video   "Work It" (Missy "Misdemeanor" Elliott)

Billboard Favorites

Whereas MTV Music Video Awards and other award ceremonies base their decisions on a blend of artistic value and commercial success, *Billboard*'s awards are based only on actual record sales. Pay attention to these from 2003 to get a realistic picture of what audiences actually buy.

- **Hot 100 Female Artist of the Year**

    Ashanti

    Christina Aguilera

    Aaliyah

    Beyoncé

◆ **Hot 100 Male Artist of the Year**

50 Cent

R. Kelly

Sean Paul

Justin Timberlake

◆ **Best-selling Single of the Year**

American Idol Finalists, "God Bless the U.S.A."

Clay Aiken, "This Is the Night"/"Bridge Over Troubled Water"

◆ **Country Artist of the Year**

Dixie Chicks

Toby Keith

Tim McGraw

Shania Twain

◆ **Rock Artist of the Year**

50 Cent

Chingy

Fabolous

Sean Paul

◆ **R&B/Hip-Hop Artist of the Year**

50 Cent

Aaliyah

Jay-Z

R. Kelly

 Trouble Clef _____

Don't let yourself get boxed into certain categories. Just because you feel you're a specialist in one area doesn't mean you shouldn't attempt different styles and genres. That's the way to grow as a composer and lyricist. Bruce Springsteen isn't known as a country composer, yet he wrote "If I Should Fall Behind," which was placed in the Grammy country category. My own eclectic career ranges from blues (Taj Mahal) to country (Charlie Rich) to rock (Elvis Presley).

The Freelance Writer's Heroine

Diane Warren pulls off miracles, and most of the time she does it without co-writers. Billboard estimates her number of hits at 84, a number certain to escalate, and she has been inducted into the Songwriter's Hall of Fame. Warren has an uncanny, instinctive grasp of what record buyers need to hear. In 2001, 15 of her songs were in contention for Grammys. Among them:

- ◆ "After Tonight" (with David Foster and Mariah Carey)
- ◆ "Could I Have This Kiss Forever?"
- ◆ "I'll Be"
- ◆ "Need to Be Next to You"
- ◆ "Painted on My Heart"

Standing the Test of Time

Certain writers never go out of style, and it's more important to study them than to concentrate only on the latest flashes in the pan. Their songs are today, because the material always returns in updated forms. Witness "Bridge Over Troubled Water," a triumph again in *American Idol* Clay Aiken's 2003 version of the Simon and Garfunkel number-one hit from 1970. Or the return of "Candle in the Wind," by Elton John and Bernie Taupin, which reached number six in 1988 and topped the charts in 1997 after Princess Diana's death.

These writers possess a mastery of songwriting craft that all writers should analyze: newcomers, so they can learn the basics, and professionals, for a refresher course. Their genius lies in versatility, handling any groove or subject.

Study the artists on the following list of all-time hitmakers, compiled by *Billboard*'s Joel Whitburn, which details pop music top hitmakers. Some of them, like McCartney, Jagger, Joel, and Simon, wrote for themselves. Others, like Carole King, wrote for other artists as well as themselves.

- ◆ Paul McCartney (169)
- ◆ Burt Bacharach (130)
- ◆ Smokey Robinson (123)
- ◆ Carole King (118)
- ◆ Curtis Mayfield (94)

- James Brown (90)

- Diane Warren (84)

- Bob Crewe (75)

- Mick Jagger (70)

- Elton John (65)

- Paul Simon (49)

- Chuck Berry (48)

- Billy Joel (40)

The Many Moods of 2003

The following songs are an exciting and varied cross-section of contemporary hit music, expressing modern attitudes and rhythms. It's a good idea to study them carefully, and apply the same analytical eye to the rhythms, chords, and lyrical content of as many songs as possible—new releases as well as classics. Write out the chords and rhythms, and study the lines carefully:

- **"Miss Independent"** (by Aguilera, Clarkson, Lawrence, and Morris; performed by Kelly Clarkson). Kelly Clarkson's hit song opens with one of the best current examples of a recurring instrumental figure. The beat has a punchy, in-your-face quality that matches the mood of the lines.

  Although it features a modern-day, independent woman as a protagonist, the heroine decides not to miss out on true love. Tough but tender, the lyric and music blend together seamlessly.

  The hook is soft and melodically insinuating, then bursts forth emotionally as Clarkson discovers what she really wants and needs.

- **"Fighter"** (by Aguilera and Storch; performed by Christine Aguilera). Equaling the drive of "Miss Independent," Christine Aguilera's "Fighter" portrays the kind of powerful woman popular in the rock world today. The protagonist is betrayed by her boyfriend, but she doesn't play the victim. Instead of falling apart (as female song characters of the '50s generally did), she thanks her errant boyfriend for making her work harder, and for making her a fighter.

- **"This Is the Night"** (by Nova, Burr, and Braide; performed by Clay Aiken). Clay Aiken's exposure on *American Idol* and his powerful vocal are only part of the reason this song was such a smash. When the hook explodes, "Lift me *up*," it's a brilliant demonstration of prosody, a lifting of melody to accentuate the emotional words. There's plenty of repetition, but the tune is so memorable that you don't get bored; instead, you want to hear it over and over again.

"This Is the Night" also adheres to a pop formula that rarely fails—one in which the lover is worshipful and adoring. Aiken tells his love that he's been waiting forever, and guarantees her that after tonight, they'll never be lonely again. It's a message fans never grow tired of.

♦ **"Snake"** (written and performed by R. Kelly). R. Kelly's "Snake" has a dynamite line, urging his partner to move her body like a snake, and the distinction of this track is its snakelike movement. The production mixes animal noises with snake-charmer, gypsy flavoring. Drums give way to brass and throughout, the rhythm makes it impossible for anyone listening to stand still.

♦ **"Flying Without Wings"** (by Mac and Hector; performed by Ruben Studdard). The richly melodic "Flying Without Wings" builds musically from start to finish. In addition, the lyrics cover a huge amount of ground, using the imaginative title to define love—love for children, for friends, for every dream. The words are a strong demonstration to all writers how words can be honestly, unashamedly sentimental without ever getting corny.

It's a song of hope, because every line tells us that love can be found in the strangest places, places we never would have expected.

♦ **"Why Don't You and I"** (by C. Kroeger; performed by Santana with Alex Band of The Calling). A definitive example of Latin pop, with Santana and the hungry, urgent vocal of Alex Band of The Calling. The syncopations are clipped and edgy and when Band arrives at the hook and pleads his cause, "Why don't you and I get together?" you're bouncing along with him "from cloud to cloud," buoyed up with a feeling that you're never coming down.

When you're not being captivated by the tune and vocal, your ear can fasten on instrumental figures that show why thinking in riffs is so important.

♦ **"Addicted"** (by Lanni, Comeau, Stinco, and Bouvier; performed by Simple Plan). "Addicted" is a word that never goes out of style, and Simple Plan belts it out in a funky power ballad. It's a masterful mix of sexual hunger and masochism, served up with a crushing backbeat and an electric guitar figure that spins round and round. The vocalist repeats "heartbreaker," twice to slam across the point.

The infectious melody and desperate lyrics make this one of the top rock ballads to appear in a long time.

◆ **"Cry Me a River"** (by Timberlake, Mosley, Storch; performed by Justin Timberlake). A simple five note figure played against the sounds of rain opens "Cry Me a River." The song is a subtle mixture of love and revenge. The chords are appropriately minor, and the syncopations have an unusual, fragmented quality that sounds like natural speech.

◆ **"Dance with My Father"** (by Vandross and Marx; performed by Luther Vandross). Finding a fresh point of view is one of the toughest challenges facing a songwriter, and "Dance with My Father" shows how a simple family story can be expressed in distinctive, unexpected terms.

Enhanced by a tasty downward progression and soulful R&B tune, the lyric tells of a little boy whose dad would lift him high in the air, then dance with him and his mother. In a particularly moving part, Vandross says, "I'd love, love, love" to dance with my father again.

Beautiful imagery ("he left a dollar under my sheet") and sensitive storytelling make this a sample of superb R&B writing and a song worthy of line-by-line, note-by-note study.

Common Denominators

The exciting array of alternatives is enough to make a songwriter dizzy, but as varied as these alternatives are, they still demand the same rules of craftsmanship:

◆ An unforgettable hook

◆ A memorable title

◆ A dynamite idea

◆ Powerful visual imagery

◆ A vivid beat

◆ An interesting chord progression

Hirschhorn's Hints

Success is as much about the song as it is the singer. I've had superstars sing my songs and they've languished at Number 50 (or lower), but I've also seen my other tunes reach Number One with newcomers.

The future promises more and more technological innovations, such as thousands of new sounds and additional tracks (the mind boggles at how many tracks studios will eventually offer). But remember: state-of-the-art isn't the same as art.

You can have all the technology at your fingertips, but it means little if you can't come up with an infectious tune and a lyric that connects emotionally with your listener.

You can have the biggest star in the country sing your song, but it won't be successful unless the song has most of the hit ingredients on the preceding lists.

Hit Yourself over the Head (Repeatedly)

When you think of the word hit, think of the following words:

H = Hook

I = Idea

T = Title

Say the word "hit" over and over again, and then keep telling yourself what the letters H-I-T stand for. Go to sleep repeating, "Hook, Idea, Title" followed by "hit." The silent songwriter within you will burst forth within two weeks. Within four weeks, you'll shock yourself by how ingrained the key hit-making ingredients are in your psyche.

Funkadelic's George Clinton once proclaimed, "Funk is the future." Then rock critic Jon Landau told the world, "I've seen the future of rock and roll, and his name is Bruce Springsteen." But the future isn't any one thing. It's a constant flow of evolution and change. There will always be some new, unexpected future, and that future could be you.

The Least You Need to Know

◆ Study every successful song—not just the ones that you like to write and perform.

◆ To be a complete songwriter, study songs that have stood the test of time.

◆ MTV, VH1, and other music channels turn songs into visual movies, and offer an ideal way to study visual writing.

◆ Adopt this as your mantra: H-I-T means Hook-Idea-Title.

Glossary

a cappella   Singing without instrumental accompaniment.

A&R (artists and repertoire) director   Record company executive who signs new artists and chooses songs for them.

acoustic instrument   An instrument that is neither amplified nor electronic.

administration   In the music industry, administration involves the handling of financial and contractual matters of the music business.

advance   Money paid up front to writers and later deducted from their royalties.

AFM (American Federation of Musicians)   Union for musicians and arrangers.

AFTRA   American Federation of Television and Radio Artists. A union representing announcers, narrators, and vocalists.

alliteration   Group of words in which the first letter is the same.

alternative music   Music that goes against the mainstream, including grunge, techno, and punk.

analog recording   Recording medium in which the sound is made up of physical or magnetic particles.

arrhythmic   Music without rhythm or rhythmic change.

ASCAP (American Society of Authors, Composers, and Publishers)   One of three societies responsible for collecting royalties from airplay.

atonality   Music without a key or tonal center.

augmented   Raising the tone half a step.

bitonality   Music composed in two separate keys that are played simultaneously, which often produces a dissonant, jarring effect.

blue notes   Flatted thirds, fifths, sixths, or sevenths that project a distinctive blues sound.

BMI (Broadcast Music, Inc.)   One of three societies responsible for collecting royalties for airplay.

bridge   Mid-section of the song that follows the hook, and is different—sometimes musically, sometimes rhythmically—from the rest of the tune. Also known as the release.

chord   Three tones or more struck at the same time.

chorus   Repeated section of a song.

CHR   Contemporary hit radio.

chromatic scale   A scale built totally on half steps.

compressor   Device that limits sound and keeps it more consistent and even.

co-publish   Ownership of publishing rights to a song by two or more individuals.

copyist   Individual who copies and often transposes a musical score. This work is also known as music preparation.

copyright   A means of protecting works by establishing ownership of them and protecting them from being stolen by registering them with the U.S. Copyright Office.

counterpoint   Note against note. The simultaneous sound of two or more notes or melodies that weave together musically and rhythmically.

cover record   The release of a re-recorded song.

crossover   Airplay garnered for a record in two or more markets.

cue   Musical segment written by a composer or orchestrator to back action or dialogue sequences in film, television, or videos.

DAT   Digital audio tape.

digital recording   Recording medium in which the sound source is turned into a numerical value. CDs are digital recordings.

dummy line   A musical line used by writers to get started in the songwriting process, to give him or her a sense of rhythmic or musical pattern. These words are throwaways and rarely, if ever, make it to the final draft.

engineer   Person skilled at operating studio equipment for record or film sessions.

enharmonic   Two same-sounding notes with different names, for example, F-sharp and G-flat.

fader   Control used to alter sound levels.

figure   A melodic fragment repeated through the song, often serving as an extra hook.

flat   Lowering of a note by a half step. Perfect intervals (4th, 5th, octave) or any major interval (maj 2nd, 3rd, 6th, 7th) reduced by a half step are called diminished notes.

Harry Fox Agency   Organization that specializes in collecting mechanical royalties.

hip-hop   A musical genre that blends R&B, disco, and rap.

hold   In the music business, a period of time requested by the producer to consider a song, with the understanding that it will not be shown to anybody else during that period.

hook   A catchy, repetitive section of a song, which is generally required if the song is to become a hit.

house   Dance music incorporating samples from other tunes.

interval   Distance between two tones.

lead sheet   A composer's self-written sheet music that includes the tune, lyrics, and chords.

leader   Blank sections of recording separating one song from another.

leitmotif   A musical theme that recurs throughout a show to refer to a specific event, idea, or character.

limiter   Device that minimizes peaks of sound.

manager   Person who supervises the development of a performer's career.

master   Completed and produced song converted into a CD and ready for release.

mechanical royalties   Earnings from CD and cassette sales.

minimalist harmonies   Nondissonant, repetitive harmonies that rarely modulate and focus on simple scales and triads.

mixing   Balancing and combining separate tracks and choosing which tracks and parts (instrumental, vocal, and so on) to highlight for dramatic effect.

modulation   Changing from one key to another.

MP3   Small file format designed to store audio files on a computer.

music library   A library of canned music, available to film, television, radio, and commercial producers for use in their shows.

music publisher   Individual or company that specializes in acquiring commercial songs and placing them with artists or on film and television. The publisher collects royalties generated by its catalogue of songs.

NARAS   National Academy of Recording Arts and Sciences. An organization promoting the interests of the recording industry.

new country music   Country with strong rock influences.

octave   Interval between the first and eighth note of the diatonic scale.

overdub   Recording of vocal or instrumental parts onto a basic multi-track recording.

package deal   A situation in which a company hires someone to handle all elements of a recording: composing, scoring, conducting, studio costs, mixing, and delivering the master tape. The person hired is responsible for accomplishing everything without exceeding that overall payment.

pitch   Presenting your material to a publisher, a producer, or an artist.

polyrhythm   Two rhythmic patterns played at the same time.

producer   Individual who helps the artist find material and supervises the recording and mixing of the final product.

professional manager   In the songwriting business, a staff member of a publishing firm who evaluates and acquires material and then promotes it to producers, artists, and film and television companies.

program director   In the radio business, the person who decides which records will be added to a radio station's playlist.

prosody   The proper, seamless blending of words and music.

public domain Works that are not copyrighted or whose copyrights have lapsed.

residuals Compensation to singers and musicians for their participation in a television show or a commercial.

rate Agreed-upon royalty percentage.

recitative singing A talking style of singing.

RIAA Recording Industry Association of America. A nonprofit organization dedicated to promoting the interests of record labels.

riff A short, rhythmic pattern repeated with no melodic variation (called *ostinato*, in musical language).

sample The reuse (in all or in part) of an already successful track to serve as the foundation for a rap vocal.

scale Minimum union wage.

self-contained artist A singer-songwriter who writes his or her own songs, rather than having them written by other composers.

SESAC (Society of European Stage Authors and Composers) Like BMI and ASCAP, a performing rights organization that collects airplay royalties for writers and publishers.

SFX Sound effects.

SGA Songwriter's Guild of America. This organization protects songwriters in their dealings with publishers and makes available a fair, up-to-date contract.

sharp Raising of a note by a half step.

SOCAN (Society of Composers, Authors, and Music Publishers of Canada) Performing rights organization that collects Canadian airplay royalties.

soundtrack Audio portion of a motion picture or videotape that includes narration and music.

split publishing Division of publishing that can encompass two, three, or more publishers.

spotting The process of watching a film and deciding where music should be placed.

storyboard Sketches illustrating scenes for film, television, or video.

synchronization Timing procedure of a musical soundtrack to action on video or film.

synesthesia   The process by which a certain color or colors provokes the hearing of certain sounds.

synthesizer   Electronic instrument that can emulate any orchestral sound and that contains unusual sounds of its own.

temp track   Musical examples cut and dubbed into the film prior to scoring.

through-sung   In a musical, a song that's sung in its entirety, without dialogue.

tonic   The first note of a scale.

trade magazines   Publications that deal with the music industry, such as *Billboard*, *Music Connection*, and *Rolling Stone*.

transpose   To take a key and change it to another one: to take a song written in the key of C, for example, and write or play it in D.

underscoring   Background music that is meant to support screen action. The purpose of it is to heighten dramatic and comedic sequences.

up-front payment   Money given before a job is completed.

urban music   Dance, rap, and R&B.

verse   First portion of a song, prior to the hook.

Appendix **B**

Resources

Music Publications of Special Interest

American Songwriter
1009 17th Avenue South
Nashville, TN 37212-2201
615-321-6096
www.americansongwriter.com

Billboard
5505 Wilshire Boulevard
Los Angeles, CA 90036
323-525-2300
www.billboard.com

Music Connection
4731 Laurel Canyon Boulevard
North Hollywood, CA 91607
818-755-0101
www.musicconnection.com

R & R (Radio & Records)
10100 Santa Monica Boulevard
Los Angeles, CA 90067
310-553-4330

Rolling Stone
5750 Wilshire Boulevard
Los Angeles, CA 90036
323-930-3300
www.Rollingstone.com

Songwriter's Market
F&W Publications
1507 Dana Avenue
Cincinnati, OH 45207
1-800-289-0963

Motion Picture Publications

Daily Variety (New York)
245 West 17th Street
New York, NY 10011
212-337-7001
www.variety.com

Daily Variety (Los Angeles)
5700 Wilshire Boulevard, Suite 120
Los Angeles, CA 90036
323-857-6600
www.variety.com

The Hollywood Reporter
5055 Wilshire Boulevard
Los Angeles, CA 90036-4396
323-525-2000
www.hollywoodreporter.com

The Hollywood Reporter Blu-Book Directory
5055 Wilshire Boulevard
Los Angeles, CA 90036
323-525-2150
www.hollywoodreporter.com/thr/thrblu/letter.jsp

Organizations

Academy of Country Music
4100 West Alameda Avenue, Suite 208
Burbank, CA 91505-4151
818-842-8400
www.acmcountry.com

This organization promotes country music, and its membership includes songwriters, producers, recording artists, and other participants in the music industry.

American Federation of Musicians (AFM)
7080 Hollywood Boulevard, Suite 1020
Los Angeles, CA 90028
323-461-3441
www.afm.org

This union protects musicians by establishing fair wage scales and working conditions.

American Federation of Television and Radio Artists (AFTRA)
261 Madison Avenue .
New York, NY 10016-0800
212-532-0800
www.aftra.com

West Coast Office of AFTRA
5757 Wilshire Boulevard
Los Angeles, CA 90036
323-634-8100

This union was established to protect announcers, narrators, and vocalists.

American Society of Composers, Authors, and Publishers (ASCAP)
www.ascap.com

Los Angeles Office
7920 West Sunset Boulevard, Third Floor
Los Angeles, CA 90046
323-883-1000

New York Office
1 Lincoln Plaza
New York, NY 10023
212-621-6000

Nashville Office
2 Music Square West
Nashville, TN 37203
615-742-5000

London Office
8 Cork Street
London W1X1PB
England
011-44-207-439-0909

Miami Office
420 Lincoln Road, Suite 385
Miami Beach, FL 33139
305-673-3446

Chicago Office
4042 North Pulaski
Chicago, IL 60641
773-545-5744

Puerto Rico Office
510 Royal Bank Center
355 Ponce de Leon Avenue
Hato Rey, Puerto Rico 00197
787-281-0782

Broadcast Music, Inc. (BMI)
www.bmi.com

Los Angeles Office
8730 Sunset Boulevard, Third Floor West
West Hollywood, CA 90069-2211
310-659-9109

Nashville Office
10 Music Square East
Nashville, TN 37203-4399
615-401-2707

New York Office
320 West 57th Street
New York, NY 10019-3790
212-586-2000

Miami Office
5201 Blue Lagoon Drive, Suite 310
Miami, FL 33126
305-266-3636

Atlanta Office
PO Box 19199
Atlanta, GA 31126
404-261-5151

Puerto Rico Office
255 Ponce de Leon, East Wing, Suite A-262
BankTrust Plaza
Hato Rey, Puerto Rico 00917
787-754-6490

London Office
84 Harley House
Marylebone Road
London NW1 5HN
England
011-44-171-486-2036

Broadway on Sunset
10800 Hesby, Suite 9
North Hollywood, CA 91601
818-508-9270
http://rrnewmedia.com/bos

This organization offers composers the opportunity to test their musical theater material in front of audiences. Workshops, lectures, interviews with successful writers, and consultation services are included.

The Dramatists Guild, Inc.
1501 Broadway, Suite 701
New York, NY 10036
212-398-9366
www.dramaguild.com

This organization protects composers, lyricists, and playwrights.

Gospel Music Association (GMA)
1205 Division Street
Nashville, TN 37203
615-242-0303
www.gospelmusic.org

This organization is for gospel publishers, writers, and recording or performing artists.

The Harry Fox Agency, Inc.
711 3rd Avenue, 8th Floor
New York, NY 10017
212-834-0100
www.harryfox.com

This agency protects publishers by collecting mechanical royalties and auditing record labels.

Library of Congress Copyright Office
101 Independence Ave. S.E.
Washington, DC 20559-6000
202-707-3000
www.copyright.gov

Government agency that handles all copyright registration in the United States.

Nashville Songwriters Association, International (NSAI)
1701 West End Avenue, 3rd Floor
Nashville, TN 37203
615-256-3354
www.nashvillesongwriters.com

This organization promotes songwriters worldwide.

National Academy of Popular Music (NAPM)
330 West 58th Street, Suite 411
New York, NY 10019-1827
212-957-9230
www.songwritershalloffame.org

This organization includes songwriters, producers, publishers, and record executives.

National Academy of Recording Arts and Sciences (NARAS)
3402 Pico Boulevard
Santa Monica, CA 90405
310-392-3777
www.thanksforthemusic.com

Everyone involved in making records, including songwriters, producers, singers, musicians, and recording engineers, belongs to this organization.

National Association of Composers/USA
PO Box 49652
Los Angeles, CA 90049
310-541-8213
www.music-usa.org/nacusa

This society promotes and publicizes songwriters.

National Association of Music Merchants (NAMM)
5790 Armada Drive
Carlsbad, CA 92008
760-438-8001
www.namm.com

This organization promotes the music products industry.

National Association of Recording Merchandisers (NARM)
9 Eves Drive, Suite 120
Marlton, NJ 08053
609-596-2221
www.narm.com

This organization specializes in the interests of distributors, software suppliers, and retailers.

National Music Publishers Association (NMPA)
475 Park Avenue South, 29th Floor
New York, NY 10016
212-370-5330
www.nmpa.org

Recording Industry Association of America
www.riaa.com

Trade group representing the U.S. recording industry.

SESAC (Society of European Stage Authors and Composers)
55 Music Square East
Nashville, TN 37203
615-329-9627
www.sesac.com

One of three organizations (along with BMI and ASCAP) that log airplay internationally for writers and publishers.

Songwriter's Guild of America (SGA)
1560 Broadway, Suite 1306
New York, NY 10036
212-768-7902
www.songwriters.org

This organization protects songwriters in their dealings with publishers and offers a fair, up-to-date contract.

Toronto Musicians' Association
101 Thorncliffe Park Drive
Toronto, Ontario M4H 1M2
Canada
416-421-1020
www.Torontomusicians.org

You must be a Canadian citizen or show proof of immigrant status to join this organization.

Music Publishers

Almo Music Corp.
360 North La Cienega Boulevard
Los Angeles, CA 90048
310-289-3080
www.radiomoi.com

BMG Music Publishing
8750 Wilshire Boulevard
Beverly Hills, CA 90211
310-358-4700
www.BMG.com

Chrysalis Music
8500 Melrose Avenue, Suite 207
Los Angeles, CA 90069
310-652-0066
www.radiomoi.com

Disney Music Publishing
500 South Buena Vista Street
Burbank, CA 91521-6182
818-569-3251
www.disney.go.com/music/today/index.html

DreamWorks SKG Music Publishing
9268 West 3rd Street
Beverly Hills, CA 90210
310-288-7700
www.dreamworkspublishing.com

EMI Music Publishing
1290 Avenue of the Americas, 42nd Floor
New York, NY 10104
212-830-2000
www.emimusicpub.com

Fricon Music Company
11 Music Square East, Suite 301
Nashville, TN 37203
615-826-2288

Sony Music Publishing
550 Madison Avenue, 18th Floor
New York, NY 10022
212-833-8000
www.sonyatv.com

Warner/Chappell Music, Inc.
10585 Santa Monica Boulevard, 3rd Floor
Los Angeles, CA 90025-4950
310-441-8600
www.warnerchappell.com

Zomba Music Publishing
137-139 West 25th Street
New York, NY 10001
212-824-1744
www.radiomoi.com

Selected Record Labels' Websites

A&M Records
www.amrecords.com

Arista Records
www.arista.com

Atlantic Records
www.atlantic-records.com

Capitol Records
www.hollywoodandvine.com

Columbia Records
www.columbiarecords.com

Curb Records
www.curb.com

Elektra Records
www.elektra.com

Geffen Records
www.geffen.com

J Records
www.jrecords.com

MCA Records
www.mcarecords.com

Motown Records
www.motown.com

RCA Records
www.rcarecords.com

Warner Brothers Records
www.wbr.com

Online Resources

ASN (All Songwriter's Network)
www.craftofsongwriting.com

Billboard On Line
www.billboard.com

Harmony Central
www.harmony-central.com

Jeff Mallett's Songwriter Site
www.lyricist.com

Jeff Jackson Songwriting and Music Business Page
www.mindspring.com/~hitmeister

Lyrical Line
www.lyricalline.com

Online Thesaurus
www.thesaurus.com

Seattle Songwriting Workshop
www.knab.com

Steve Schalchlin's Survival Site
www.bonusround.com

Words in over 400 dictionaries
www.onelook.com

Appendix

Contests and Competitions

Entering contests seems like a long shot, but writers are often surprised and delighted to find that they've won money, prizes, as well as recognition. The following are contests that offer both.

American Songwriter Magazine Lyric Contest
American Songwriter Magazine
50 Music Square East, Suite 604
Nashville, TN 37212
615-321-6096
www.americansongwriter.com

This lyrics-only contest is held six times per year. Winners of the bi-monthly contests receive a Sigma DR-1ST guitar from Martin Guitars and compete for a trip to Nashville to produce a master demo of their song; plus, the annual winner plus four runners-up have their lyrics published in *American Songwriter Magazine*.

Entry fee: $10 per song; you may submit up to three songs.

Billboard Song Contest
PO Box 470306
Tulsa, OK 74147-0306
www.billboard.com/billboard/songcontest/index.jsp

Dozens of winners in several categories receive prizes plus placement of their songs on the *Billboard* Song Contest winners CD. A bonus: All songs receive a personalized judging report that gives tips on structure and content. To be eligible to enter, you must have received less than $5,000 per year total royalties earned from music since 1999.

Entry fee: $30 per song; no limit on the number of songs you submit.

Contemporary Christian Songwriting Contest
www.ccmni.mmgi.org

An annual contest offering prizes for top Christian songs.

Entry fee: Contact the Contemporary Christian Music Network for details.

European International Competition for Composers
226 East 2nd Street, Suite 5D
New York, NY 10009
212-387-0111
www.ibla.org/comp.composer.engl.html

Annual contest open to pianists, singers, instrumentalists, and composers from all over the world.

Entry fee: $120; limited to one entry.

Great American Song Contest
PMB 135
6327-C SW Capitol Hill Highway
Portland, OR 97201-1937
503-515-9025
http://greatamericansong.com

Categories in this annual contest include pop, rock/alt, country, contemporary acoustic/folk, Christian/gospel, instrumental, R&B/hip-hop/rap, and lyrics only. All submissions receive a written critique; winners are awarded cash and prizes.

Entry fee: $20 per song for first two songs; $15 per song for all songs thereafter. You may enter as many songs as you like.

International Songwriting Competition
211 Seventh Avenue North
Suite LL-20
Nashville, TN 37219
615-251-4441
www.songwritingcompetition.com

Amateur and professional songwriters have a chance to share in $100,000 in cash and prizes for songs in 13 categories, including pop/top 40, country, jazz, and gospel/Christian.

Entry fee: $30 for the first song; additional entries are $20 extra. You may enter as many songs as you like.

The John Lennon Songwriting Contest
459 Columbus Avenue, Box 120
New York, NY 10024
Fax: 212-579-4320
www.jlsc.com

This international annual contest is open to amateur and professional songwriters who submit entries in any one of 12 musical categories. Some winners will receive EMI publishing contracts, plus recording equipment and other prizes. One entry will be named "Song of the Year" and that winner will receive an additional $20,000 in cash. Overall, 120 winners will split more than $225,000 in cash and prizes.

Entry fee: $30 per song; no limit on the number of songs you may submit.

LadySixString Lyrics Writing Competition
Attn: Lyric Writing Contest
Box 10414
Russellville, AR 72812-0414
www.ladysixstring.com/lyricwritingcontest

Females only need apply to this annual lyric writing contest, the winner of which receives a new guitar. The contest is open to all genres, including pop, rock, urban, R&B, alternative, country, gospel/inspirational, instrumental.

Entry fee: $10 per song; no limit on the number of entries.

LadySixString Songwriting Competition
Attn: Songwriting Contest
Box 10414
Russellville, AR 72812-0414
www.ladysixstring.com/songwritingcontest

Females only need apply to this annual songwriting contest, the winner of which receives a new guitar. The contest is open to all genres, including pop, rock, urban, R&B, alternative, country, gospel/inspirational, instrumental.

Entry fee: $10 per song; no limit on the number of entries.

Pulitzer Prize in Music
709 Journalism
Columbia University
New York, NY 10027
212-854-3841
www.Pulitzer.org

According to the official website, "For distinguished musical composition of significant dimension by an American that has had its first performance in the United States during the year." Cash prizes and certificates are awarded.

Entry fee: $50; see website for details.

SongoftheMonth.com Contest
1848 Grey Ridge Road
Maryville, TN 37801
www.songofthemonth.com

Cash and prizes are awarded monthly for top songs at the online songwriting competition.

Entry fee: $10 per song; enter as many songs as you like.

Songs Inspired by Literature Project
Artists for Literacy
2601 Mariposa Street
San Francisco, CA 94110-1426
www.siblproject.org/competition.html

Write a "groove-oriented" song inspired by one of 10 books chosen by the Artists for Literacy organization. Up to 10 winners will receive promotional prizes and will have their songs included on a CD/DVD promoting literacy.

Entry fee: No entry fee for songs inspired by one of the 10 books listed on the website and submitted online; $20 fee for songs inspired by other literature or for any entries submitted via the mail. No limit on the number of entries.

USA Songwriting Competition
Dept. AW98, Box 15711
Boston, MA 02215
781-397-0256
www.songwriting.net

Songwriters from around the world may compete in 15 categories for cash prizes and merchandize.

Entry fee: $30 per song; no limit on the number of submissions.

Woody Guthrie Folk Festival Songwriting Competition
PO Box 6298
Moore, OK 73153
www.oksongwriters.org/members/WGSW.html

Lucky winners receive cash prizes plus the chance to perform their songs live at the Woody Guthrie Folk Festival. All submissions "should represent the spirit of Woody Guthrie's music."

Entry fee: $20 for the first song; $10 for each additional song. No limit on the number of submissions.

Index

M

A Little Knowledge Goes a Long Way ...

Check Out These
Best-Selling
COMPLETE IDIOT'S GUIDES®

Understanding Catholicism
SECOND EDITION

1-59257-085-2
$18.95

Learning Spanish
THIRD EDITION

0-02-864451-4
$18.95

The Bible
SECOND EDITION

0-02-864382-8
$18.95

Grammar and Style
SECOND EDITION

1-59257-115-8
$16.95

Playing the Guitar
SECOND EDITION

0-02-864244-9
$21.95 w/CD

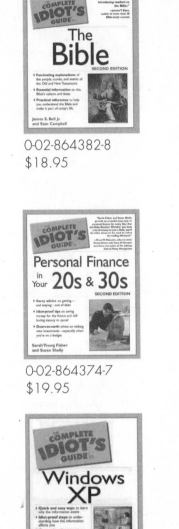

Personal Finance in Your 20s & 30s
SECOND EDITION

0-02-864374-7
$19.95

The Perfect Resume
THIRD EDITION

0-02-864440-9
$14.95

Buying and Selling a Home
FOURTH EDITION

1-59257-120-4
$18.95

Windows XP

0-02-864232-5
$19.95

More than *400 titles* in *30 different categories*
Available at booksellers everywhere

ALPHA